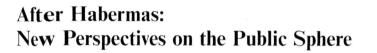
After Habermas:
New Perspectives on the Public Sphere

A selection of previous *Sociological Review* Monographs

Gender and Bureaucracy*
eds Mike Savage and Anne Witz
The Sociology of Death: theory, culture, practice*
ed. David Clark
The Cultures of Computing
ed. Susan Leigh Star
Theorizing Museums*
ed. Sharon Macdonald and Gordon Fyfe
Consumption Matters*
eds Stephen Edgell, Kevin Hetherington and Alan Warde
Ideas of Difference*
eds Kevin Hetherington and Rolland Munro
The Laws of the Markets*
ed. Michael Callon
Actor Network Theory and After*
eds John Law and John Hassard
Whose Europe? The turn towards democracy*
eds Dennis Smith and Sue Wright
Renewing Class Analysis*
eds Rosemary Cromptom, Fiona Devine, Mike Savage and John Scott
Reading Bourdieu on Society and Culture*
ed. Bridget Fowler
The Consumption of Mass*
ed. Nick Lee and Rolland Munro
The Age of Anxiety: Conspiracy Theory and the Human Sciences*
eds Jane Parish and Martin Parker
Utopia and Organization*
ed. Martin Parker
Emotions and Sociology*
ed. Jack Barbalet
Masculinity and Men's Lifestyle Magazines
ed. Bethan Benwell
Nature Performed: Environment, Culture and Performance
eds Bronislaw Szerszynski, Wallace Heim and Claire Waterton

*Available from Marston Book Services, PO Box 270, Abingdon, Oxon OX14 4YW.

The Sociological Review Monographs

Since 1958 *The Sociological Review* has established a tradition of publishing Monographs on issues of general sociological interest. The Monograph is an edited book length collection of research papers which is published and distributed in association with Blackwell Publishing. We are keen to receive innovative collections of work in sociology and related disciplines with a particular emphasis on exploring empirical materials and theoretical frameworks which are currently under-developed. If you wish to discuss ideas for a Monograph then please contact the Monographs Editor, Rolland Munro, at *The Sociological Review*, Keele University, Newcastle-under-Lyme, North Staffordshire, ST5 5BG.

After Habermas:
New Perspectives on the Public Sphere

Edited by Nick Crossley and John Michael Roberts

Blackwell Publishing/The Sociological Review

Blackwell Publishing
9600 Garsington Road, Oxford OX4 2DQ, UK

and

350 Main Street, Malden, MA 02148-5018, USA

First published 2004 by Blackwell Publishing Ltd

Transferred to digital print 2006

Library of Congress Cataloging-in-Publication Data

ISBN 1-4051-2365-6

A catalogue record for this title is available from the British Library.

Printed and bound in Great Britain by Marston Book Services Limited, Oxford

For further information on Blackwell Publishing, visit our website:
http://www.blackwellpublishing.com

Contents

Introduction

John Michael Roberts and Nick Crossley

The concepts of the 'public sphere', 'public opinion' and the 'public use of reason' have a long and complex genealogy. Jurgen Habermas' (1989) early study, *The Structural Transformation of the Public Sphere*, traces much of that genealogy, revealing the shifting meanings that have attached to these concepts and the various struggles and socio-historical changes which have occasioned them. In recent years, however, it has been Habermas' own work on the public sphere, both in *Structural Transformation* and later studies, which has set the agenda for much of the debate on these issues. Habermas has been criticized, extensively and perhaps sometimes unfairly. But even when his work has been strongly criticized it has remained central. seminal text

This book has been compiled with the aim of deepening and extending the Habermasian project by way of both an engagement with Habermas and, more particularly, a consideration of other theories and frameworks which afford us different ways of problematizing and exploring the public sphere. Although we cannot speak for our contributors, we, as editors, believe that it is important to begin to consider other possible frameworks for understanding the public sphere than those presented by Habermas. Or rather, since this process has already begun (see below), to provide a central reference point where some of the main alternatives can be brought together. This book is therefore 'after Habermas' in two senses. It *follows* him to a point but then seeks also to break new ground *beyond* his work.

We will offer a brief overview of the alternatives considered in the book in the latter part of this introduction. First, however, it is necessary briefly to reiterate the main points of Habermas' own position and some of the key criticisms that have been levelled against him. It is only against this yardstick that it will be possible to gauge whether the various attempts to move beyond Habermas, as spelled out in the main chapters of the book, really do constitute useful alternatives or additions.

The Habermasian public sphere

Habermas' first key intellectual engagement with the idea of the public sphere was in the context of the above-mentioned study, *The Structural Transformation*

of the Public Sphere (Habermas, 1989). This was published in English translation in 1989, after many of the important studies for which Habermas had
become well-known in the English speaking world. It was originally published
in Germany in 1962, however, long before those studies. The lateness of the
translation undoubtedly posed obstacles to the understanding of Habermas'
work in the anglophone context. It was not untimely, however. *Structural Transformation* has increased rather than decreased in relevance. Furthermore, it
anticipates and thus, for the late reader, rejoins many of the key themes explored
by the later Habermas. It could have been written much more recently. And it
is important from the point of view of Habermas exegesis because it fills in
important sociological gaps in his *oeuvre*, affording a much more concrete feel
to his conception of society. In contrast to many of Habermas' works, which
tend to operate on the plane of 'pure theory' or philosophy, at a high level of
abstraction, *Structural Transformation* weaves philosophical and empirical (historical and sociological) detail together in a tight and coherent texture.

The book makes two central claims. The first is that a variety of social
changes during the late eighteenth and nineteenth centuries in Germany, France
and Britain, gave rise for a short period to an effective bourgeois public sphere.
That is to say, over a relatively brief period social conditions provoked and facilitated a situation in which large numbers of middle class men, *qua* private individuals, came together to engage in reasoned argument over key issues of mutual
interest and concern, creating a space in which both new ideas and the practices
and discipline of rational public debate were cultivated. Furthermore, the emergence of this new public space, which effectively formed a zone of mediation
between the state and the private individual, shaped and was shaped by the
emergence of a philosophical concept and consciousness of 'publics' and their
importance. This is reflected in the work of many key philosophers of the day,
including Tocqueville, Mill, Kant, Hegel and Marx, each of whom Habermas
briefly discusses. The second key claim of the book is that conditions effectively
served to undermine this public space almost the moment it had come into
being, such that the public space of the twentieth century—now we might add
the twenty-first—is riven with contradictions and conflicting tendencies and
characteristics. The ideals and theorization (in political theory and philosophy)
of publics remain intact but the reality is a pale imitation of these ideals. From
Habermas' point of view this leaves a gap ripe for imminent critique. Modern
democracies fall short of adequacy even when measured against the yardstick
of their own ideals and values.

The dates and precise details of the 'rise and fall' of the public sphere differ
between the three national contexts studied by Habermas. The general picture,
however, is the same in each case. One of the key historical changes facilitating
the rise of the public sphere was the increasing differentiation of society and
particularly a separation of political authority from the sphere of everyday and
domestic life. This was constituted, in part, through the centralization of political power in the national state, a process which made effective power remote,
and also by the separation of church and state and the differentiation of public

norms (eg law) and private moral belief consequent upon this separation. The state was progressively 'decoupled', as Habermas (1987) would later put it, from the intersubjective fabric of everyday life, and from the normative texture of that fabric. Significantly this separation occurred at the same time that increased military activities were driving up the tax burden imposed upon individuals by the state. The simultaneity of these trends inevitably generated a collective demand for accountability. Agents formed themselves as publics in an effort to control a state which was at once more remote and more demanding.

The forming of publics, as a process of collectivization, could only take place against the background of a new form of privatization, however; that of self and subjectivity. Public spheres mediate between the state and private individuals, for Habermas, and as such they presuppose a private sphere and private subjectivity, such as was beginning to emerge within the bourgeoisie during the eighteenth century. At one level Habermas conceives of both home and work as belonging to the private realm, since ownership and control of the means of production were at this time still usually fused in the person of a named and known (male) individual who entered into private contracts with his workers—a legal arrangement which was itself new. At another level, however, the separation of home from work also set the scene, particularly amongst the rising bourgeoisie, for an increasing privatization of the home and of the family. The home, now separated from the workplace, became a private retreat from the 'outside world' and, even within the home, architecture increasingly separated out private from public elements, generating a space in which privatized individuals and subjectivities could take shape and, indeed, wherein the bourgeoisie were increasingly devoting themselves to the project of self-cultivation. It was only against the backdrop of this new concept and experience of individuality and privacy that the notion of a public made sense. The public issues discussed in public spheres were constituted as such through a filtering out of what were now perceived as private issues and the very idea of a public sphere itself involved the coming together of private individuals.

Projects of self-cultivation were important to the constitution of the public sphere in another way too, however. The self-cultivation of the bourgeoisie was pursued in a significant way through art and literature. On one level this involved the private consumption of artistic and literary works, a process which, in the case of literature, contributed to the privatization of subjectivity in Habermas' view. Novels and memoirs, in particular, given their exploration of the 'internal life' of individuals and characters, offered new templates of 'interior' subjective life. At the same time, however, art and literature became a focus of public discussion and debate. The famous coffee houses and salons, which sprung up in considerable numbers in key urban centres through the course of the eighteenth century, were the central locus of these debates. These spaces of literary debate effectively constituted the infrastructure of what became political publics according to Habermas, as topics of debate shifted from art and literature to politics and economics. And literary debate played a considerable role in generating the cultural resources necessary for critical and rational political debate.

Literary 'jousts' spawned and sharpened tools of argument which would later be set to work on more political materials. They generated the convention of meeting to discuss and also the rhetorical competence, discipline and 'rules of the game' constitutive of public reason. They were a rationalizing force:

> Public debate was supposed to transform *voluntas* into a *ratio* that in the public competition of private arguments came into being as the consensus about what was practically necessary in the interests of all. (Habermas, 1989: 83, his emphasis)

The salons were an important social form for the emerging public sphere but equally important were improvements in printing technologies and the emergence of popular newsletters and journals. Newsletters and journals were an important source of information about the world which participants in public debate could take as a basis for their arguments and critiques. The prototypes for these journals, Habermas notes, were prompted by the expansion of trade. As trade expanded over greater distances, the need for information grew. Traders needed speedy access to the far-flung corners of their various markets and the newsletter emerged to fill this gap. Soon, however, the remit of these newsletters was expanded to include opinions and argument. Along with pamphlets of various sorts, they became the medium through which individuals could express their views and spell out their arguments and critiques. Initially the content of these newsletters was strictly censored by the state. In response to mounting pressure, however, censorship was relaxed and the newsletters became relatively open spaces of debate.

The importance of these developments, for Habermas, is twofold. Firstly, the bourgeois public fostered a critical rationality. They constituted a space in which the chief operative force was that of the better argument. Secondly, they were important because they were relatively powerful. They created a pressure and a force for change, approximating an ideal to which Habermas appears to have subscribed in much of his later work; namely, a situation in which the critical reasoning of the public constitutes an effective steering force in both society and polity.

The nineteenth century bourgeois public sphere, however, was only ever an approximation. By the time it had become 'political' it was a predominantly male domain. It was also predominantly middle class. And even in this imperfect form it was not destined to last. race ?

As when he discusses the emergence of the public sphere, Habermas outlines a range of conditions, too numerous to cover comprehensively here, which have conspired to compromise the public sphere. And as with his account of the emergence of the public sphere, he acknowledges both general trends and regional differences between France, Germany and Britain. For our purposes it will suffice to note four critical factors.

In the first instance, Habermas argues that the sharp delineation of state and society, which formed an essential pre-requisite of the public sphere, qua intermediary between the two, has, if not collapsed, at least become very blurred.

The state, as a welfare state, now increasingly intervenes in people's lives, assuming their private concerns and interests as its own. And at the same time, as interest groups have come to occupy an ever greater role within the structure of the state, the state has been infiltrated by a range of private interests. These transformations have various effects, some good but many negative in Habermas' view. Perhaps most important, however, as he would reiterate in *The Theory of Communicative Action*, the relationship of the individual to the state has increasingly become one of client or consumer of services, rather than citizen. Individuals have become increasingly dependent upon the state, losing the independence that is central to the citizen role. And by the same route, political debate has increasingly lost its political edge by degenerating into utilitarian wrangling over the distribution of resources and private (domestic) interests. In the place of public debate between private citizens regarding public/political issues (ie, a public sphere) we find interest groups, representing sectional interests from within the state's clientele, competing and negotiating for a greater slice of the public purse.

This blurring of state and society has been amplified by a second change. Much of the argument and activity constitutive of the public sphere, having once taken place in society between private individuals, now takes place within the confines of the state between professionalized politicians. More to the point, although this may maintain something of the appearance of a public debate, argumentation and debate are now subordinated to the logic of the competition for power between parties. The effect of party based organization, Habermas argues, is that views tend to be stuck to or strategically manipulated rather than genuinely argued over. Furthermore, the function of argument at the interface between politicians and their voters is to win votes rather than engaging the thoughts of voters and, by this means, educating and cultivating them—as the earlier publics had done for their participants. Politics becomes a stage show. This is compounded by the constitution of the electorate. Those who know most about politics, Habermas argues, tend also to know who they will vote for and are inclined to stick with them through thick and thin. The floating voters, who waver and are undecided, also tend to be those least knowledgeable and least interested in politics. And yet these floating voters are precisely the voters whom the politicians are seeking to attract. Consequently, debates shift further from the issues and more towards whatever tricks and treats attract the largely disinterested body of floating voters. To use contemporary language, there is a dynamic of 'dumbing down'. Not that tricks and treats work as a means of seducing the politically apathetic. Even in the 1960s there was a noticeable decline in public interest in politics, indicated by, amongst other things, declining electoral turnouts. This fuels the degenerate trend in public political life, for Habermas, but it is also a consequence of it. Although some social groups, particularly those active in civil associations of various kinds, retain an interest in politics, the stage show makes politics less meaningful for many and drives them away from it.

These changes are accompanied, Habermas notes, by a shift in the meaning of public opinion which has been effected, in large part, by the efforts of professional social scientists. 'Public opinion' is increasingly synonymous with the results of polling surveys (and now 'focus group' research), which politicians use and seek to manipulate for their own ends. There are many problems with these surveys in Habermas' view. Firstly, they are artificial because they solicit 'votes' for pre-determined categories of opinion which may not reflect the categories that those polled would use themselves and often induce individuals to select opinions on issues they would not otherwise, and will not subsequently, give thought to. Secondly, they call for an expression of views, seeking out the loudest voice, rather than, as in the public sphere, facilitating a process of discourse in which the 'best argument' can win. Finally, they treat the loudest voice as a technical variable, rather than engaging it as a moral voice. Public opinion is no longer the ultimate authority, as democratic theory demands. It is an object and target for intervention strategies designed to manipulate and control it in a variety of ways. Here Habermas echoes his forebears, Adorno, Horkheimer and Marcuse, in lamenting the manner in which the 'value neutrality' of positivist social science allows it to become a technical tool in an overly administered society.

Finally, Habermas notes that, and how, media markets generate problematic dynamics and tendencies within public space. As the mass media began to establish itself as a viable economic market, he argues, it was both hijacked for the purpose of selling goods, via advertising, and became a considerable saleable commodity in its own right. This has meant that public communication, by this means at least, has been moderated by the demands of big business and it has led to a regressive 'dumbing down' of the level of public debate as editors, pursuing new and larger markets, have been inclined to play to the lowest common denominator. Where the early public sphere, as a domain of self-education and cultivation, tended to 'level up', the modern media, in its pursuit of the widest audience, is inclined to 'level down'.

To some degree the thesis of *Structural Transformation* reiterates the pessimism of Habermas' Frankfurt School mentors and subscribes to their negative view of modern society and subjects—dominated and dumbed down. However, anticipating his own later reflections on the twin currents of modernity, positive and negative, critical and emasculated, his final word is of a world of public life pulled in different directions. The forces of professionalized PR politics and scientized public opinion may have the upper hand in the contemporary world, for Habermas, but they have not completely undermined the forces of rational deliberation and critical argument. This, moreover, is what makes critical theory possible and what makes the presentation of its theses a worthwhile endeavour. The hope behind the project, at a very general level, is that the critical potential of public argument will achieve a wider audience and stimulate the processes of transformation that it calls for; that it will reclaim and reinvigorate the public sphere, as a first step in a wider process of emancipatory social change.

Later Habermas

Much that Habermas has written since *Structural Transformation* has reiterated, elaborated and added to this basic account. For the most part the additions have been philosophical. In particular Habermas' 'discourse ethics' has served to bolster the normative dimension of his critique by making a strong case to suggest that publicly binding norms can only make a legitimate claim to rationality, and thus a claim to rational legitimacy, insofar as they emerge out of open discourse and free argument between all parties affected by them; that is, insofar as they emerge out of contexts corresponding in all crucial respects to a public sphere (Habermas, 1992, 1993). Downplaying the dialogical and communicative emphasis he had identified with Kant in *Structural Transformation*, Habermas criticizes the latter for entrusting the philosopher or legislator to make monological assessments of what 'any reasonable person' would agree in respect of normative matters—the view of the reasonable person being the ultimate arbiter of what is reasonable and right. Claims as to what 'any reasonable person' would accept as right can only be justified, Habermas argues, by putting them to the test (ibid.). Normative claims must be subject to rational public scrutiny and public spheres or publics thereby assume a crucial role. Integral to this line of argument, moreover, is a strong rebuttal of positivist and related claims to the effect that moral statements do not admit of truth or falsity. They do, Habermas argues, though only in the context of a communicatively rational discourse (ibid.).

A crucial bridge between this discourse ethics and *Structural Transformation* is provided in *The Theory of Communicative Action* and a number of works leading up to it, including *Legitimation Crisis* and *Communication and the Evolution of Society*. These works, anticipating the work on discourse ethics, considerably bolster the normative grounding of Habermas' position by developing a communicative conception of rationality, focused upon dialogue, argument and the exchange of reasons. This positive conception of reason allows Habermas, contra both post-structuralism and 'early' critical theory, to make a claim for the emancipatory potential of reason. He is able to disentangle 'reason', in its communicative form, as a positive force, from rational domination, as a negative social condition. Moreover, he thus casts the Enlightenment and the process of rationalization in a more nuanced light, as a process which has potentiated both a more enlightened/democratic way of living and a 'totally administered society'. The latter tendency may have won out for the present, Habermas concedes, but we should note that the victory is not complete and reflects dynamics in the economic and political systems rather than issuing from any inherent tendencies within rationality towards domination (see below).

At the same time, however, he offers a historically rooted account of the decoupling of the economic and political systems from the normatively rooted and communicatively rational sphere of everyday life, the lifeworld, thereby indicating that and how the emancipatory potential of reason is routinely sidelined in the modern world. The economic and political systems increasingly work in

7

a delinguistified way, he argues: that is to say, they are increasingly steered by the flow of money and political power and are thereby decreasingly responsive to the force of rational, moral argument. They both facilitate and demand that agents act strategically, on the basis of utilitarian rather than communicatively rational deliberations.

In the case of the political system this has involved labour movements abandoning the broad ethical and life-political concerns that animated their pioneers, in the pursuit of more narrow material gains. The movement has become a party which plays the political game. Moreover, mirroring this, at a broader level, the decoupling of the state has effected a situation wherein citizens forgo their 'right' to effective political participation in return for the rewards offered by the welfare state:

> The expression 'social welfare state-mass democracy' mentions two properties of the political system which are effective for legitimation. On the one hand it tells us that the opposition to the system which emerged in the labour movement has been defused by regulated competition between political parties. Among other things, this has institutionalized oppositional roles, formalized and rendered permanent the process of legitimation, periodized variations in legitimation and canalized the withdrawal of legitimation in the form of changes of regime, and finally it has involved everyone in the legitimation process as voting citizens.
>
> On the other hand, threats to legitimacy can be averted only if the state can credibly present itself as a social welfare state which intercepts dysfunctional side effects of the economic process and renders them harmless for the individual (Habermas, 1987b: 194).

Rational dialogue between citizens, and between citizens and the state, is replaced by systemic and strategic exchanges of power. Citizens offer the state legitimacy (in the form of votes for parties and basic compliance with laws) in return for the benefits of the welfare state, whilst the state 'spends' its power in the form of the laws and policies it imposes upon citizens; always mindful of the need to win votes.

This is compounded by the sheer complexity of modern societies and the degree of specialization and differentiation. There is no need for a dominant ideology in contemporary societies, Habermas argues, since the division of the social world into ever more 'specialisms', each with its form of expertise, defies the possibility of a coherent overview or narrative. In truth nobody can conceptualize the totality. Citizens are 'culturally impoverished'.

The potential legitimation problems these trends pose are offset, Habermas continues, only insofar as 'citizens' remain relatively disinterested in political life and manifest a preference for the pursuit of private pleasures. In *Legitimation Crisis*, building upon the empirical findings of a number of sociological studies, he argues that this is largely the case and coins the phrase 'civil privatism' to denote this disposition. However, he also identifies the social conditions necessary to sustain civil privatism, as a prevailing disposition, suggesting that these conditions are far from being secure. And he picks up this same issue again in the final chapters of *The Theory of Communicative Action*, where he offers an account of 'the colonization of the lifeworld' and 'new social movements' (Habermas 1987b). The thesis of the colonization of the lifeworld posits that the economic and political systems, having been decoupled from the lifeworld, are now expanding back into it in a manner which is corrosive of it. Ever more areas of social life are either bureaucratized or commodified, such that the potential for communicative engagement and reasoning within them is undermined and open dialogue is replaced by bureaucratic procedures and economic transactions. Habermas identifies a range of pathological consequences, social and psychological, which follow from this, but he also believes that colonization constitutes a crucial fault line of society, which in turn has given rise to a range of oppositional 'new social movements' who have taken up the mantle, dropped by the labour movement, of pursuing both a rational-ethical reconstruction of society and a broader project of emancipation, thereby revitalizing the public sphere.

Colonization is linked to the rise of new social movements in at least three ways. Firstly, and most obviously, it has generated a range of problems and strains which, if not sufficient, have at least constituted necessary causes of mobilization (on the problems of strain based theories of social movements see Crossley 2002a). Secondly, by disturbing traditional forms of life and the taken-for-granted or habitual legitimations they presuppose, colonization has served to bring many previously unquestioned aspects of society into question. More to the point, insofar as we are referring to colonization by the state, in the form of the welfare state, this process of bringing the unquestioned into question has occurred in a political context and has therefore simultaneously served to politicize everyday life:

> At every level administrative planning produces unintended unsettling and publicizing effects. These effects weaken the justification potential of traditions that have been flushed out of their nature-like course of development. Once their unquestionable character has been destroyed, the stabilization of validity claims can occur only through discourse. The stirring up of cultural affairs that are taken for granted thus furthers the politicization of areas of life previously assigned to the private sphere. But this development signifies danger for the civil privatism that is secured informally through the structures of the public realm. (Habermas, 1988:72)

The politicization of everyday life doesn't begin with the new social movements, for Habermas, even if, in an ideal world, it might end with them. It begins with the political colonization of everyday life by the state. The state politicizes the lifeworld and new social movements respond (politically) to this. Finally, however, colonization, *qua* both bureaucratization and commodification, contributes to the shrinking of the public sphere. Having stirred up a hornets' nest it reduces the formal opportunity for issues to be discussed, thereby prompting interested parties to set up their own discussion forums (and protests) outside of the formal political channels. New social movements form new, critical publics. By means of communicatively rational engagement they call the system into question and set the agenda for a normative revitalization of it. As in *Struc-*

tural Transformation then, Habermas concludes *The Theory of Communicative Action* with a mixed prognosis. Expansion in and colonization by the economic and political systems is suffocating society and yet it has also contributed to the rise of new social movements who, embodying the promise and potential of rationalization in its positive sense, are seeking to regenerate both the private and the public spheres of society.

Habermas' concern with the public sphere has, of course, continued in the work completed after *The Theory of Communicative Action*, most notably in his major intervention in legal theory, *Between Facts and Norms*. This latter text, in many respects, illustrates and advances the theoretical framework which reached its fullest expression in *The Theory*. And it begins to iron out some of the problems. One of the key theoretical criticisms of *The Theory* had been its tendency to posit rigid typologies and conceptual dichotomies which, though useful to the argument Habermas himself was making, often prove problematic to those seeking to apply and develop his work. *Between Facts* is important, from this point of view, because Habermas uses his categories here in a much more relaxed and fluid manner. Furthermore, after the abstraction of *The Theory* we find Habermas returning to a slightly more concrete context of the various *fora* of public debate and discussion which make up the public sphere.

Problems and critiques

Reading *Structural Transformation* one has to constantly remind oneself that it was written in the 1960s. It could so easily have been written in and for the present day. Contemporary debates about 'dumbing down' and 'spin', which echo many of Habermas' concerns, suggest that his arguments are as relevant as they ever were. Furthermore, the recent emergence of an enormous anti-corporate movement (Crossley, 2002b, 2003; Hertz, 2001; Klein, 2000; Kingsnorth, 2003; Neale, 2002), many of whose spokespeople use a language akin to that of 'colonization' (Crossley, 2003), whilst it may call for some revision to the Habermasian position, nevertheless resonates very strongly with his account of new social movements and their efforts to reclaim the lifeworld (ibid, see also Edwards in this volume). Habermasian themes and issues echo very real debates and issues which are being fought out beyond the boundaries of the academy. An *oeuvre* of such breadth and ambition, however, inevitably has flaws and attracts critics keen to identify them. It would be impossible to contemplate a comprehensive review of these flaws and critiques here but a brief overview is necessary. We begin with what we call the practical criticisms of Habermas' account.

Practical criticisms of Habermas

Practical criticisms start from the common basis of suggesting that Habermas engages in a one-sided analysis. Habermas, so the argument goes, seems too satisfied with a narrow perspective through which to explore the public sphere, namely that of the bourgeoisie. Specifically critics detect three main practical problems with Habermas's argument on this issue. First, Habermas implies that the bourgeois public sphere was founded upon free and equal access and upon willing consent between participants. By taking this as his starting point, he tends to overlook the more coercive and power-driven attributes of the bourgeois public sphere. Second, the colonization thesis simplifies complex media practices. Third, the bourgeois public sphere disparages the emancipatory potential of 'counterpublic spheres'. We will take each of these points in turn.

Discussion between the eighteenth-century bourgeoisie was, for Habermas, motivated by rational-purposive action framed within an autonomous public sphere. Keane (1984) makes an astute observation on this point:

> To live a genuinely public life, according to this latter inference, consists in deciding everything exclusively through good-natured argument and deliberation orientated to reaching an understanding. Not the skill and cunning of strategic and instrumental action, but words and persuasion, are the distinguishing mark of public life (Keane, 1984: 184–5).

In other words Habermas is accused of idealizing rational discussion as it relates to the public, ignoring 'the extent to which its institutions were founded on sectionalism, exclusiveness and repression' (Eley, 1992: 321). Rational communication is not merely an *end* product as Habermas is apt to suggest. The *means* to achieve this are highly significant. Modern communication techniques are not simply a medium of thought and argument but also a potential source for power, domination and oppression (Holub, 1991; Negt and Kluge, 1993; McLaughlin, 1993; Fraser, 1992). Some contemporary theorists go as far as to say that the bourgeois public sphere arose as a response to the ambivalent, expressive and effectual practices of the Other; practices which the bourgeois public sphere sought to contain (Hetherington, 1997; Peters, 1993). At the very least this implies that Habermas' sense of wonderment at rational consensus belies a less than pleasant conclusion. Any consensus reached is accomplished through an evolving process of coercion and exclusion.

Moving to the second practical criticism, Habermas' anxiety over dumbing down and colonization of the public sphere, encompassing as it does the invocation of a 'golden age' of media production (Hallin, 1994: 6), stands accused of both elitism and cultural snobbery (Dahlgren, 1995; Hartley, 1996; McGuigan, 1996; Thompson, 1995). Habermas's view is deemed misplaced for three main reasons. First, media practices have always been inscribed with a manipulated bias. We need only to look at reportage of such events as the French Revolution to see this (Hartley, 1996: 87). Secondly, conceptions of 'mass communication' and 'mass media' are unhelpful in trying to understand how people and social groups actively use and manipulate the media for their own interests in contemporary settings. People never passively consume images but actively and consistently debate and discuss everyday dilemmas, however small, within their day-to-day lives (Billig, 1991). Indeed a plausible argument exists to suggest that the mass media in fact shifts power away from political apparatus plural such as the state by reinvesting power back to a local level. The media can dictate to rather than be dictated by politicians (Garnham, 1986: 50). What is required if we are to escape either a condemnation or celebration of the media, it seems, is to gain an understanding of the socially constructed 'symbolic packages' through which social issues are fought out by social groups and the media (Eder, 1996: 206). Thirdly, although perhaps more controversially, it is argued that the infiltration of the market into the media need not sound the death knell of public debate. Indeed, some positive insights can be salvaged. The market can curtail to some degree the amount of state interference in the provision of funding and appointments in large media corporations. Also the market can encourage the cultural and ideological diversity of the public to be mirrored in the media. The trick is to combine market imperatives with collectivist approaches (Curran, 1991: 48).

A third practical criticism of Habermas' notion of the public sphere, often posed in the literature, concerns his neglect of public spheres other than the male bourgeois public sphere. It is a neglect that has profound consequences, not only for historical and social investigation but also for theoretical speculation. For example, equating 'male' with 'public' establishes all sorts of false and misleading dichotomies. Not only is such a representation empirically false (men bring to the public domain 'private' issues and not all private issues need be deemed apolitical, eg, personal matters such as definitions of 'the family' are often deeply political) but it actually impedes a thorough theoretical investigation of the public sphere by refusing to examine the exclusion of many social groups from public issues (Siltanen and Stanworth, 1984).

Theoretical criticisms of Habermas

Problems evident in Habermas's account have prompted some to ditch the public sphere concept for alternative though similar ideas (eg, Lii, 1998). The majority, however, have sought to overcome these problems by keeping the public sphere concept but thinking about it from a different theoretical level. By moving in this direction, the complex social practices involved in public discussion and debate through a variety of practices and media can be readily highlighted and theorized. In recent years at least three broad schools have emerged to construct a theoretical base from which we might be able to understand more fully the complexities associated with the public sphere. These schools are not exhaustive and, indeed, a prime object of this book is to document new and emerging theoretical schools associated with prominent theorists like Mikhail Bakhtin and Pierre Bourdieu. Our purpose in focusing upon three particular schools of thought is merely to indicate the growing plurality of approaches on public sphere theory.

The late-modern school

The first school, which can be categorized as 'late-modern', stresses the Habermasian prerequisites of general accessibility to information, the eradication of privilege, the quest for 'truth' and the quest for general norms along with their rational legitimization (Garnham, 1986; Jones, 1998; Weintraub, 1997). What makes this public sphere 'late-modern' is its acceptance of normative foundations for public debate and discussion whilst recognizing that in contemporary societies these normative foundations are not the exclusive property of the white male bourgeoisie (Blaug, 1999; Taylor, 1997). Perhaps the most forthright defence of the late-modern public sphere can be found in the work of Cohen and Arato (1988, 1992), who stress that the public sphere is a definable and coherent institution within late-modernity.

Cohen and Arato build upon the later work of Habermas (eg, Habermas, 1987b, 1991a). In this sense they provide an innovative conceptualization of the public sphere insofar that they use Habermas' later work in order to critique his early work. They begin by following the later Habermas (1984, 1989) in dividing the modern world into 'system' and 'lifeworld'. It is through the lifeworld, they argue, that people communicate with one another in a non-instrumentalist but intersubjective manner. The lifeworld, situated within civil society, has two distinct levels: i.) the level of implicitly known traditions and background assumptions embedded in language and culture, which are drawn upon by individuals in everyday life; ii.) the level of three distinct structural components, namely culture, society and personality. Both aspects of the lifeworld are reproduced through the communicative processes of cultural transmission, social integration and socialization.

> But this is the main point for us—the structural differentiation of the life-world (an aspect of the modernization process) occurs through the emergence of institutions specialized in the reproduction of traditions, solidarities and identities. It is this institutional dimension of the lifeworld that best corresponds to our concept of civil society (Cohen and Arato, 1988: 42).

Civil society under this definition defines the processes of social integration for co-ordinating action within the communicative boundaries of institutional and associational forms. In other words, civil society is regarded as the institutionalized lifeworld. The normal three-part model of state, economy and civil society 'becomes articulated as a four-part model understood in terms of the redoubling not only of the public sphere . . . but of the private sphere as well' (Cohen and Arato, 1992: 429). This insight allows Cohen and Arato to suggest that both system and lifeworld have a public and private dimension. The public sphere of the system relates to the political subsystem whilst its private sphere relates to the economic subsystem. The public sphere of the lifeworld relates to institutionalized public communication wherein individuals can campaign for juridical rights whilst its private sphere relates to an intimate space of personal relationships.

Three advantages emerge from Cohen and Arato's model. The first relates to its ability to theorise about the increasingly complex input-output relations and the increasing autonomy and differentiation of the four social spaces. The second advantage relates to the idea that the penetration of the state into the economy should not necessarily be conflated with state penetration of the private sphere any more than economic liberalization must imply the erosion of public and private spheres. Thirdly, Cohen and Arato go beyond Habermas' negative conception of the public sphere as marked by the penetration of the system. According to Cohen and Arato, social movements can positively construct voluntary associations in order to promote their interests. And such associations are encouraged by the very nature of the institutions which go to make up civil society. Cohen and Arato attempt to bridge the divide between lifeworld and system and thereby overcome Habermas' difficulties.

The postmodern school

The second school can be characterized as postmodern. This school of thought suggests that in the contemporary climate, public discussion is structured around 'cults and cliques' ordered by different kinds of 'knowingness' (Tolson, 1991: 196). Thus it is not at all clear how discussion can be founded upon any noramtive foundations of 'Truth'. It does not follow that there is no longer any sense of 'publicness'. But it is to concede that the popular public sphere always oscillated between entertainment and information. The implosion of both into one another, however, undermines the notion of a 'general public' (Hartley, 1996, 1997, 1998).

Politics, so the post-modern argument goes, encapsulates all of society, making untenable the idea of 'closed totality' through which rigid social categories such as 'class' are discoverable. Each social location is 'overdetermined' by a multitude of social processes. Only 'chains' of political activity stretching across society, binding different spheres and domains together, can achieve any success in articulating hegemonic projects (Laclau and Mouffe, 1985). This being the case, some have sought to stress less the negotiated and reflexive nature of the modern public sphere and opt instead for a view which underlines the inherently conflictual and contested nature of public communication. In essence these theorists wish to argue for a public sphere with 'open' boundaries. Discursive contestation implies, at a minimum, that common interests can no longer be decided in advance but must be actively sought through dialogue (Fraser, 1992:129). Neither an epistemologically driven, unified consensus-based public realm nor an ontologically driven common public space are possible or desirable in a postmodern world inhabited by a 'micro-physics' of power and contestation (Villa, 1992).

Fraser (1992, 1995) is the most vocal spokesperson for a post-modern conception of the public sphere. She argues for a position which recognizes the legitimate discursive claims of those residing in alternative public spheres. Fraser terms these alternative public spheres, 'subaltern counterpublics'. These refer to 'parallel discursive arenas where members of subordinated social groups invent and circulate counterdiscourses. Subaltern counterpublics permit them to formulate oppositional interpretations of their identities, interests and needs' (Fraser, 1995:291).

Subaltern counterpublics demonstrate well the inadequacies of the liberal concept of the public sphere. For instance, liberal theory argues that public discussion must be structured around a common interest. Subaltern dialogue suggests that fixed boundaries on topics of public interest do not exist. These can only be established through discourse itself whereby minority voices have the opportunity to convince others of the just nature of their argument. Similarly subaltern dialogue demonstrates the fallacy in the liberal idea that inequalities between participants can be bracketed during discursive deliberation. Such bracketing merely *informally* conceals real inequalities which in turn have drastic consequences for the outcome of debate and discussion, such as access to resources.

For Fraser, therefore, a postmodern and post-liberal conception of the public sphere must incorporate at least three characteristics. Fraser provides a concise summary of these characteristics. We therefore quote her at length.

> (1) a postmodern conception of the public sphere must acknowledge that participatory parity requires not merely the bracketing, but rather the elimination, of systematic social inequalities;
> (2) where such inequality persists, however, a postmodern multiplicity of mutually contestatory publics is preferable to a single modern public sphere oriented solely to deliberation;
> (3) a postmodern conception of the public sphere must countenance not the exclusion, but the inclusion, of interests and issues that bourgeois masculinist ideology labels 'private' and treats as inadmissible (Fraser, 1995: 295).

The postmodern response to Habermas also usefully focuses our attention on the historical *limits* of publicness. For the very attempt by a social group to establish their own 'norm' by which to publicly judge everyday reality actually begins to enable the social group in question publicly to think about the normalizing procedures which establish the norm in the first place (cf. Ewald, 1990). The main thrust of this critical observation is to suggest, *contra* Habermas' attempt at universalism, that there is a need to be alert to the historical processes that construct the boundaries and limits of that which is defined as 'normative'.

Obviously by speaking about 'normalization' in this manner is to stray close to a Foucaultian reading of 'public reason'. On this account norms refer to those procedures that establish rules of judgements. These procedures then lead to ways and means of producing those very same rules. By making us vigilant of the social and historical processes involved in selecting out rules and procedures with which to regulate social life, Foucault (1984) encourages us to reflect upon the limits of modern reason itself. Of particular importance for Foucault is the necessity to reflect upon practical systems which constitute modes of subjectivity and which, in turn, establish ways of reflecting and acting upon ourselves and our environment. Public reason, under this framework, is directed to the dissection of these practical systems, to the critical reflection and historical understanding of their disciplining effects, to the problematizing of the experience of modes of subjectivity and to the public questioning of the contingent nature of their limits (Foucault, 1984; cf. Dean, 1999; Ingram, 1994; Owen, 1999; Rose, 1999). By making visible the heterogeneous properties which go to construct a space, the 'normal' everyday meaning peculiar to the context in question can become disrupted. Such dis/ordering exposes the ideological limits and historical contingency of the context in question so that a gap opens up through which an alternative rationality can be constructed (Foucault, 1984; see also Simons, 1995).

Viewing public reason in this way means that we can break reason down in a myriad of practical and habitual modes of regulating public dialogue. On this estimation, as Wittgenstein (1953: 98–100) insists, 'normative' justification for one's action through dialogue is not as discontinuous with everyday life as Habermas implies that it is (cf. Tully, 1989). To think otherwise, to erect a sharp distinction between pre-ideological understanding and habitual understanding, is to misapprehend the qualitative and multiple ways of engaging in critical reflection and public dialogue (although for a defence of Habermas against the postmodern critique see Jones, 1998).

The relational and institutional school

Based largely in the United States, the relational and institutional school consciously seeks to embed the public sphere both within an historical milieu and within wider social relations. Those working within this school suggest that the public sphere is a particular institution and a particular relational setting. Institutions are defined as 'organizational and symbolic practices that operate within networks of rules, structural ties, public narratives, and binding relationships that are embedded in time and space' (Somers, 1993: 595). A relational setting is defined as 'a patterned matrix of institutional relationships among cultural, economic, social and political practices' (Somers, 1993: 595). The public sphere, on this estimation, is one such institutional and relational arena.

It is in this line of thinking that Somers (1993) defines the public sphere as

a contested participatory site in which actors with overlapping identities as legal subjects, citizens, economic actors, and family and community members, form a public body and emerge in negotiations and contestations over political and social life (Somers, 1993: 589; cf. Somers, 1994; 1995a; 1995b).

Similarly Emirbayer and Sheller (1998) argue that the public sphere represents

open-ended flows of communication that enable socially distant interlocutors to bridge social-network positions, formulate collective orientations, and generate psychical 'working alliances', in pursuit of influence over issues of common concern. Publics are not simply 'spaces' or 'worlds' where politics is discussed . . . but, rather, interstitial *networks* of individuals and groups acting as citizens. States, economies, and civil societies may all be relatively 'bounded' and stable complexes of institutions, but publicity is emergent (Emirbayer and Sheller, 1998: 738).

On both definitions, the public sphere and, more generally, political culture, is a special space for the articulation of symbolic codes, values and representations which help to formulate individual and political orientations. In this regard political culture is firmly rooted in a Parsonian heritage. This is because the relational and institutional school stress social-structural, cultural as well as social-psychological factors. However, the relational and institutional school refuse to embrace the underlying theoretical assumptions of Parsonsion sociology, namely the heavy reliance upon the state and civil society model or the underlying assumptions of functionalism and/or systems theory.

In order to avoid this blind alley, the relational and institutional school seeks to underline both the qualitative difference of discrete social spheres as well as their various linkages. In the case of political culture, for example, they wish to move beyond an approach which places culture on one side of an analytic divide and society on the other. The most crucial distinction to make is that between *analytic* autonomy and *concrete/empirical* autonomy. The distinction implies that it is important to treat cultural structures as analytically distinct from other material forces by exploring their internal logic and history apart from other forms of life. Yet in concrete instances the two domains are intertwined. Precisely how they are intertwined is an empirical question which cannot be answered in advance (Somers, 1995a: 130).

Recently, some within the relational and institutional school have combined their insights with contemporary metaphors associated with 'flows', 'fluidity', 'mobilities' and 'networks'. For example, it is said that globalization 'de-differentiates' public and private domains. On this account 'globalization can be seen in terms of global fluids constituted of waves of people, information, objects, money, images, risks and networks moving across regions in heterogeneous, uneven, unpredictable and often unplanned shapes' (Sheller and Urry, 2003: 117). The fluidity associated with globalization is thus a de-territorialized movement that moves across the world at different speeds, from the local processing of information by people in their daily lives, to the global turnover of financial capital that runs into billions of dollars. Sheller and Urry (2003) note that these changes at the global level have altered the meaning of the public sphere in four ways. First, new forms of leisure and consumption patterns can be detected associated with global events like the World Cup and MTV. Second, global economic public spheres have emerged that revolve around organizations like the World Bank and IMF. Third, global political publics exist that act as 'states', examples being the EU, UN and UNESCO, and global political publics exist in the form of NGOs such as Amnesty International, along with global social movements. Fourth, globalization has reconstituted what is meant by the term, 'general public'. People increasingly know about global events and global organizations and this knowledge helps them construct a fluid cosmopolitan identity in small but significant ways. People know of other cultures and open themselves up to mobile opportunities presented by the idea that 'cultures travel' and that prospects arise in relationship to a publicly visible global 'other' (Sheller and Urry, 2003: 117–18).

This volume

The work of Habermas' critics prompts many questions and raises many problems of its own. There are issues pertaining to the adequacy of the various interpretations made of Habermas and indeed also of the alternatives proposed. The debate goes on. And true to the principles of his discourse ethics, Habermas himself has been a constant party to these debates, engaging and revising. Significantly his involvement in these debates has persuaded him to take on board a number of criticisms, particularly pertaining to the plurality of publics in contemporary society.

> the modern public sphere now comprises several arenas in which, through printed materials dealing with matters of culture, information, and entertainment, a conflict of opinions is fought out more or less discursively. This conflict does not merely involve a competition among various parties of loosely associated private people; from the beginning a dominant bourgeois public collides with a plebeian one (Habermas, 1992b: 430).

In this same spirit of dialogue, the contributions in this volume seek to bring fresh perspectives and ideas to bear on the public sphere.

In the first three chapters, Michael Gardiner, Ken Hirschkop and John Michael Roberts each respectively use the work of the Bakhtin Circle to outline an alternative theory of the public sphere to that provided by Habermas. The Bakhtin Circle emerged shortly after the Bolsheviks took power in Russia, principally in the west Russian city of Nevel in 1918. Centred around Mikhail Bakhtin, the circle included such Soviet luminaries as the linguist V. N. Voloshinov, the philologist L. Pumpianskij, M. V. Judina, who later became a celebrated Russian pianist, and I. I. Sollertinskij, a future artistic director of the Leningrad Philharmonic. When Bakhtin moved to the near city of Vitebsk in 1920, the influential literary theorist P. N. Medvedev joined the group (Holquist, 1996). The Bakhtin Circle debated and discussed about a wide range of subject areas that included philosophy, ethics, discourse and literature. Their innovative insights have proved immensely influential in the social sciences and humanities. In many respects this wide-ranging appeal is not difficult to understand for many reasons. The much heralded 'linguistic turn' in the humanities and social sciences has obvious affinities with the Bakhtin Circle's enormous output on language, semiotics, discourse and utterances. An important aspect of the linguistic turn has been a post-structuralist sensibility towards the democratic value of diverse voices being heard in the public sphere. Again, this post-structuralist viewpoint chimes well with the Bakhtin Circle's emphasis upon the 'multiaccentual' and 'double-voiced' dialogue of everyday speech. The Bakhtin Circle also wrote on a number of issues which have an obvious charm with those who identify themselves with leftist causes. In particular Mikhail Bakhtin's wonderful study of the sixteenth century French novelist François Rabelais has helped to popularise the notion of 'the carnivalesque'—the idea that spaces and times exist in society in which power relations can be inverted through popular, 'earthly', 'grotesque' and wildly funny culture.

In Chapter Two, Michael Gardiner, drawing primarily upon the work of Bakhtin, addresses some of these carnivalesque dimensions to dialogue in order to criticize Habermas's overly serious and rationalistic discourse perspective. Like other theorists already noted in this introduction, Gardiner observes that Habermas works with a number of dualisms—that between public and private, state and public sphere, reason and non-reason, and ethics and aesthetics. This precise demarcation is reinforced, according to Gardiner, by Habermas' proclivity for thinking in terms of formal unities. The advantage that Bakhtin has over this way of looking at the world is to suggest that everyday dialogue—the sort of dialogue that is really meaningful to 'ordinary' people in their daily lives—is in fact fluid, permeable and always contested. Thus, far from speaking about abstract formal unities or abstract and formal rules of argumentation, people implicitly think and talk about the complexities and multiplicities that they face in real living social contexts. This is a much more realistic picture of dialogue, suggests Gardiner, because it directly engages with the level of the 'everyday' and thereby tries to construct theoretical concepts that seek to understand the ambiguous and complex nature of dialogue in concrete situations.

Gardiner formulates his argument through three areas of enquiry: ethics and intersubjectivity; language; and the life world and the everyday. As regards ethics and intersubjectivity, Gardiner argues that Habermas' fascination in delegating morality to an abstract and transcendental realm means that he brackets empirical motives from what might constitute the 'good society'. By recourse to Bakhtin, Gardiner suggests that this moves Habermas to construct a social theory that denigrates the importance of personal and embodied ethical concerns. From the standpoint of Bakhtin, ethical concerns of people are performed through daily 'events' by which they confront the ethical concerns of others. This means that one's ethical standpoint must simultaneously answer the ethical standpoint of others through everyday dialogue. In respect to language, Gardiner argues that Habermas privileges clarity of utterances in discourse in terms of the intentions of participants and in terms of the semantic content of signs. Gardiner quite rightly points out that in everyday life clarity of discursive intent is sometimes the last thing on people's minds. Everyday life is full of contradictions, it's messy, and this messiness is evident in concrete utterances. Thus, for Bakhtin, everyday dialogue, living and real utterances, is structured by diverse intentions, different evaluations and a number of polemical qualities. There is no neutral discourse, as Habermas insinuates, but rather only utterances mediated by different social positions and locations. As regards the lifeworld and the everyday, Gardiner believes that Habermas concentrates upon abstract moral forms of discourse at the expense of prereflexive, taken for granted utterances situated within common sense perceptions of the world. This leads Gardiner to agree with Bakhtin when the latter suggests that creative dialogic reflection upon the world is located in 'mundane' and 'ordinary' speech. In this dialogic realm, people experience a 'festive', 'carnivalesque'

19

view of the world exactly because it is based within the sensuous materiality of incarnate human existence.

In Chapter Three, Ken Hirshkop takes a somewhat different approach in examining the relationship between Habermas and Bakhtin. Hirshkop begins by noting a shift in Habermas' position on the public sphere. In *The Structural Transformation of the Public Sphere*, suggests Hirschkop, Habermas was concerned with demarcating the public sphere in two dimensions: empirical and normative. In the first instance Habermas described the emergence of a specific institutionalized form of written and interactive communication. In the second instance Habermas abstracted a normative component to the public sphere, namely that it was based upon the formation of political public opinion through a type of open argumentation. Hirshkop observes that in later works such as *Between Facts and Norms*, Habermas drops the normative component to the public sphere in favour of a more 'fluid' and 'mobile' conception of debate and discussion. The complexity of contemporary societies has, according to Habermas, produced a 'linguistification' of the public sphere. What this means in practice is that far from being one normative political public sphere, contemporary societies have witnessed a proliferation of public spheres, each catering for a diverse range of identities evident in civil society. The rise of identity politics from the 1960s onwards has thus given rise to a more mobile organizational spontaneity for public discussion than is the case for more established institutions, like those associated with the labour movement. This proliferation, or multiplicity, of spontaneity has relieved the public sphere of having to act as a national institution for discussing public policy for society as a whole. Today the public sphere can act as a noninstitutionalized forum for public debate based upon a wide variety of expressive concerns.

It is at this point that Hirshkop brings in Bakhtin. If Habermas now equates the public sphere with expressive spontaneity, then Bakhtin is a natural theorist to turn to in order to flesh out in more detail about how we might go about theorizing this latest transformation in the public sphere. What Hirshkop takes from Bakhtin is the latter's interest in understanding everyday dialogue at some distance from institutionalized forms like the state. Hirshkop addresses this issue by looking at Bakhtin's insights into novelestic dialogue. In the modern novel, according to Bakhtin, we see that language is presented to the reader in a particular style. Modern novels dramatize language, set it within a context and provide a narrative frame. Indeed, Bakhtin argues that narrators of modern novels are also framed by the narratives they use, thus ensuring that the modern novel is structured by a 'double-voiceness'. A modern novel is based upon the expressive intentions of an author, or narrator, and by the narrative frame in which it is set. This is important for Bakhtin, continues Hirschkop, because it prompts an author to take note of a second-person narrative between themselves and another person whilst, simultaneously, forcing an author to be reflexive about the overarching third-person narrative frame that binds dialogue together. Effectively Bakhtin reminds us that we must develop a double-form of reflexivity between our selves and others, and between ourselves and wider dialogic structures that frame everyday dialogic encounters. But once we pursue this double-form of reflexivity then the possibility presents itself of breaking down different framing mechanisms into a multiplicity of different languages. That is to say, the modern novel demonstrates how language creates what Hirshkop terms as a 'narrative scaffolding' and shows, in the process, how the sort of expressive spontaneity that Habermas now advocates might come about. For Hirshkop, a novelistic public sphere can make connections between everyday suffering experienced by people in liberal capitalist societies and the narratives that determines suffering in the first place. In practice this means what Hirshkop suggests is 'a different *style* of discourse, in which the narrative of our social history emerges out of the various languages we use rather than serving as their mute, but all powerful background'. Quite rightly, Hirshkop says that such a reimagining of our present depends upon our, first, using institutionalized resources at hand to, second, renarrate our past in a manner that does justice to the suffering people experience today. Although Hirshkop does not provide specific examples as to how this might come about, it's not difficult to imagine such examples. In the UK history is still usually narrated to schoolchildren as being created by 'great leaders', such as members of the British royal family or military leaders or British politicians. What such a narrative leaves out is the creation of British history by populist and leftist democratic movements like the Diggers and Levellers of the seventeenth-century, radical artisans of the early nineteenth-century, Chartists of the mid-nineteenth century, the Reform League, the International Working Men's Association and the establishment of radical trades unions of the late-nineteenth century, the various strands of the Suffragette movement of the early twentieth century, and so on.

In Chapter Four, John Michael Roberts charts some of these alternative narratives on the public sphere when he focuses upon the work of John Stuart Mill. Mill is often regarded as one of the modern founders of a theory of free speech. In *On Liberty* Mill sets out what he considers to be the necessary prerequisites for individuals to enjoy 'the liberty of thought and discussion'. In particular Mill outlines four 'grounds' through which the 'liberty of thought and discussion' might flourish. These are: (i) the recognition that an opinion could be fallible; (ii) the necessity for the collision of different opinions to establish truth; (iii) that prejudice should be eliminated; and (iv) that dogma should also be eliminated. Roberts demonstrates, however, that Mill constructs not so much a rationale for free speech as a defence of the liberal form of the bourgeois public sphere. This defence is predicated upon a peculiar aesthetic of cultivated intelligence that is itself based upon what Mill terms the pursuit of 'higher pleasures'. Through the dialogic theory of the Bakhtin Circle, Roberts argues that, *in reality*, such a standpoint is highly restrictive. This is because, dialogically speaking, the very nature of the utterance, 'higher pleasures', suggests that there are some in society who are satisfied to pursue 'lower pleasures'. According to Roberts, Mill equates 'lower pleasures' with those who seek have their rights heard in proletarian public spheres. Thus the liberty of thought and discussion acts a device to silence the public utterances of the majority of individuals by suggesting proletarian public spheres only ever really sanction 'uncultivated' forms of discussion. But more than this, Roberts also argues that this restrictive viewpoint legitimates a novel form of regulating the proletarian public sphere because it complements and justifies a particular ideological form of the capitalist state, namely the *liberal* form of the state. Thus those public spheres which do not practise higher pleasures can expect their utterances to be regulated through the coercive body of the liberal state. Roberts illustrates his points by showing how Mill constructs his theory of the liberty of thought and discussion through an implicit dialogue with Chartist public spheres. Chartism is an interesting case study because Chartists enjoyed enormous success in constructing a set of public spheres that challenged the limits of the capitalist state form. By highlighting the success that Chartist public spheres enjoyed, Roberts places Mill's theory within an historical framework and highlights how his ideas sought to reconstitute liberal theory through the challenge posed by the heteroglossic utterances of nineteenth century socialist utterances. Thus while Roberts does not directly engage with Habermas (although see Roberts, 2003, 2004), he does nevertheless show how the work of the Bakhtin Circle can be extended to explore critically one of the most important theorists in the liberal tradition.

In Chapter Five, Nick Crossley considers another possible theoretical source for extending and deepening our critique of the public sphere: the work of Pierre Bourdieu. Bourdieu, he argues, shares many of Habermas' concerns about the shrinking of the public sphere in contemporary society. In Crossley's view, however, Bourdieu provides us with a set of conceptual tools for exploring contemporary publics which are both more robust and more sensitive than those offered by Habermas. Whilst the conceptual dichotomies posited in Habermas' work are useful for building and defending a normative model of publics, that is, a model of how publics ought to be, he argues, they often obscure the possibility for a clear understanding of the ways in which actually existing publics depart from these ideals and the reasons for this departure. Bourdieu allows us to overcome this limitation without substantively departing from the normative ideal upheld by Habermas. More centrally, Bourdieu realizes the project of critical theory outlined in Habermas' early work (*Knowledge and Human Interests*). He develops a programme of work focused around the issue of 'systematically distorted communication' and develops a set of 'socio-analytic' concepts which effect and operationalize a critical epistemology for social analysis which mirrors many aspects of psychoanalytic epistemology but transposes them onto the social plane. Furthermore, Bourdieu develops this approach in relation to a critical investigation of a variety of forms of public. In this respect he achieves what the early work of Habermas promised but failed to deliver. More importantly, this achievement bears great fruit in Crossley's view. It affords a critique of publics which is at once powerful and pragmatic; which 'deconstructs' but in a way which points to positive possibilities for change and reform.

In contrast to the earlier chapters in the book, the final three deal less with theories competing against that of Habermas and more with aspects of contemporary society which pose obstacles and raise questions for our understanding of contemporary publics. In her chapter, Gemma Edwards reflects both upon the growth of anti-corporatism as a social movement and a recent case of industrial unrest in the UK (the fire-fighters' dispute) which might, *prima facie*, be taken as an archetypal example of an 'old social movement' struggle. Both of these instances of political activity challenge the concept of 'new social movements' which is central to Habermas' conception of the public sphere in *The Theory*, she argues, and they call for a more complex understanding of the process of 'colonization' around which these movements are said to mobilize. Given this more complex rendering, however, Habermas' framework proves perhaps even more fruitful than one might first imagine. The seam between system and lifeworld, Edwards argues, turns out to be a crucial site for the production of a range of social movements (old, new and 'even newer') and Habermas' theory of new social movements thereby turns out to be a special case of what might be a much broader approach. Interestingly, Edwards' attempt to broaden the horizons of Habermas' approach draws both from the critical theory which preceded him (Marcuse) and that of those who succeed him (Honneth). In this respect, more than any other contributor to the book, Edwards seeks to address the problems of Frankfurt critical theory by recourse to Frankfurt theory.

In Chapter Seven of the book, James Bohman tackles the thorny issue of the internet and its significance for contemporary publics and their future prospects. Moreover, in doing so he seeks, as an integral aspect of this analysis, to push the issue of publics beyond the national arena towards global society. Central to both of these concerns, he argues, is the notion of a 'public of publics'; that is, the idea of a global public sphere formed through the intersection of various more localized publics. The internet can provide the basis for a new and effective form of public sphere, he claims, but this is necessarily a different form of public, and we are thus required to rethink what we mean by the terms 'public' and 'public sphere'. To the extent that we continue to think about publics along the lines of the printing press or *a fortiori* the salons and coffee shops, we miss the significance of the internet as a specific mode of communication. Not that determinate effects can be read off from the internet *qua* technology. On the contrary, Bohman is clear in rejecting any form of technological determinism and the central plank of his argument is that the 'hardware' of the internet is largely indeterminate and must be given shape by 'software', a term which he interprets broadly to include human uses of the technology and its organization. In this respect his chapter, whilst ostensibly about technologies of communication, turns very centrally upon issues of organization and institution. Only if we get these issues right will the internet turn out to be a positive contribution to the public sphere of global society.

In 'Feminism and the Political Economy of Transnational Public Space', the final chapter of the book, Lisa McLaughlin addresses the question of the contemporary relevance of Habermas' notion of the public sphere, arguing that this largely national arrangement was changing its identity at the very moment that critics were preparing their responses to the English translation of his book *The Structural Transformation of the Public Sphere* (1989). Critics of Habermas, she argues, have tended to focus on parochial concerns, and, as a result, have not sufficiently addressed a context in which the public sphere has come under stress through the ascendance of a neoliberal economic orthodoxy prioritizing a policy framework based in deregulation, liberalization, and privatization. She focuses on the work of feminist scholars, who have written discerning analyses of the exclusionary mechanisms that characterized the liberal-bourgeois public sphere, but who have followed Habermas' recent lead in treating as relatively unproblematic the question of gaining access to channels of communication for the expression of women's needs and interests. McLaughlin explores the ways in which neoliberal market policies promoting commercialization and concentration in media ownership threaten the prospects for the emergence of a transnational feminist public sphere. But she also argues that public sphere theory has become a threat to its own aspirations to forge a productive engagement with issues related to transnational public spaces. Public sphere theory, she maintains, has burdened itself with too many rigidly distinguished analytical categories— rise/demise, lifeworld/system, civil society/state/economy, culture/economy, and, lastly, globalization from below/globalization from above. McLaughlin suggests that if feminist public sphere theory is to confront the political-economic complexities of the development of transnational public space, it will have to move beyond the nation-centred and West-centric assumptions that inform most of its current contributions and recognize the contributions that 'Third World feminist' approaches to transnational feminism have made to considerations of the public sphere, even though most transnational feminist scholars have not often used the language arising from public sphere theory and debates.

Bibliography

Billig, M. (1991) *Ideology and Opinions: Studies in Rhetorical Psychology*. London: Sage Publications.

Blaug, R. (1999) Democracy, Real and Ideal: Discourse Ethics and Radical Politics. New York: SUNY Press.

Calhoun, C. (1992) 'Introduction: Habermas and the Public Sphere', in C. Calhoun (ed.), *Habermas and the Public Sphere*. Massachusetts: The MIT Press.

Calhoun, C. (1993) 'Civil Society and the Public Sphere', *Public Culture* 5(2): 267–280.

Cohen, J. and Arato, A. (1988) 'Civil Society and Social Theory', *Thesis Eleven*, 21: 40–64.

Cohen, J. and Arato, A. (1992) *Civil Society and Political Theory*. Cambridge, Massachusetts: The MIT Press.

Crossley, N. (2002a) *Making Sense of Social Movements*. Buckingham, Open University Press.

Crossley, N. (2002b) 'Global Anti-Corporate Struggle: A Preliminary Analysis', *British Journal of Sociology* 53(4), 667–91.

Crossley, N. (2003) 'Even Newer Social Movements', *Organisation* 10(4), 287–305.

Curran, J. (1991) 'Rethinking the Media as a Public Sphere', in P. Dahlgren and C. Sparks (eds) *Communication and Citizenship: Journalism and the Public Sphere in the New Media Age*. London: Routledge.

Dahlgren, P. (1991) 'Introduction', in P. Dahlgren and C. Sparks (eds) *Communication and Citizenship: Journalism and the Public Sphere in the New Media Age*. London: Routledge.

Dahlgren, P. (1995) *Television and the Public Sphere: Citizenship, Democracy and the Media*. London: Sage.

Dean, M. (1999) 'Normalising Democracy: Foucault and Habermas on Democracy, Liberalism and Law', in S. Ashenden and D. Owen (eds) *Foucault Contra Habermas*. London: Sage.

Delanty, G. (1999) *Social Theory in a Changing World: Conceptions of Modernity*, Cambridge: Polity Press.

Eder, K. (1996) 'The Institutionalisation of Environmentalism: Ecological Discourse and the Second Transformation of the Public Sphere', in S. Lash, B. Szerszynski and B. Wynne (eds) *Risk, Environment and Modernity: Towards a New Ecology*. London: Sage.

Eley, G. (1996) 'Nations, Publics, and Political Cultures: Placing Habermas in the Nineteenth Century', in C. Calhoun (ed.) *Habermas and the Public Sphere*. Massachusetts: The MIT Press.

Emirbayer, M. and Sheller, M. (1998) 'Publics in History', *Theory and Society* 27(6): 727–79.

Eward, F. (1990) 'Norms, Discipline and the Law', *Representations*, 30: 138–61.

Fiske, J. (1996) *Media Matters: Race and Gender in U.S. Politics*. Minnesota: University of Minnesota Press.

Foucault, M. (1975/1991) *Discipline and Punish: The Birth of the Prison*, trans. by Alan Sheridan. London: Penguin.

Foucault, M. (1984) 'What is Enlightenment?' in *The Foucault Reader* edited by Paul Rabinow. London: Penguin.

Fraser, N. (1995) 'Politics, Culture, and the Public Sphere: Toward a Postmodern Conception', in L. Nicholson and S. Seidman (eds) *Social Postmodernism: Beyond Identity Politics*. Cambridge: Cambridge University Press.

Fraser, N. (1992) 'Rethinking the Public Sphere: A Contribution to the Critique of Actually Existing Democracy', in C. Calhoun (ed.) *Habermas and the Public Sphere*. Massachusetts: The MIT Press.

Garnham, N. (1986) 'The Media and the Public Sphere', in P. Golding, G. Murdock and P. Sclesinger (eds) *Communicating Politics: Mass Communications and the Political Process*, Leicester: Leicester University Press.

Habermas, J. (1987b) *The Theory of Communicative Action vol. II*, Cambridge: Polity.

Habermas, J. (1988) *Legitimation Crisis*. Cambridge: Polity.

Habermas, J. (1989) *Structural Transformation of the Public Sphere*. Cambridge: Polity.

Habermas, J. (1991a) *The Theory of Communicative Action: Reason and the Rationalisation of Society* (Vol 1). Cambridge: Polity.

Habermas, J. (1991b) *Communication and the Evolution of Society*. Cambridge: Polity.

Habermas, J. (1992) *Moral Consciousness and Communicative Action*. Cambridge: Polity.

Habermas, J. (1993) *Justification and Application*. Cambridge: Polity.

Hallin, D. C. (1994) *We Keep America on Top of the World: Television Journalism and the Public Sphere*. London: Routledge.

Hartley, J. (1996) *Popular Reality: Journalism, Modernity and Popular Culture*. London: Arnold.

Hartley, J. (1997) 'An Aboriginal Public Sphere in an Era of Media Citizenship', *Culture and Policy* 8(2): 43–63.

Hartley, J. (1998) 'That Way Habermadness Lies'. *Media International Australia: Culture and Policy* no. 89 November: 125–35.

Hertz, N. (2001) *The Silent Takeover*. London: Heinemann.

Hetherington, K. (1997) *The Badlands of Modernity: Heterotopia and Social Ordering*. London: Routledge.

Holub, R. C. (1991) *Jürgen Habermas: Critic in the Public Sphere*. London: Routledge.

Hoynes, W. (1994) *Public Television for Sale: Media, the Market and the Public Sphere*. Oxford: Westview Press.

Ingram, D. (1994) 'Foucault and Habermas On the Subject of Reason' in G. Cutting (ed.) *The Cambridge Campion to Foucault*. Cambridge: Cambridge University Press.

James, M. R. (1999) 'Tribal Sovereignty and the Intercultural Public Sphere', *Philosophy and Social Criticism* 25(5): 57–86.

Jones, P. (1998) 'Between Cultural Studies and Critical Sociology', *Media International Australia: Culture and Policy* no. 88 August: 121–33.

Keane, J. (1984) *Public Life and Late Capitalism: Toward a Socialist Theory of Democracy*. Cambridge: Cambridge University Press.

Kingsnorth, P. (2003) *One No, Many Yeses*. London: Free Press.

Klein, N. (2000) *No Logo*. London: HarperCollins.

Laclau, E. and Mouffe, C. (1985) Hegemony and Socialist Strategy. London: Verso.

Lichterman, P. (1999) 'Talking Identity in the Public Sphere: Broad Visions and Small Spaces in Sexual Identity Politics', *Theory and Society* 28(1) February: 101–41.

Lii, D-T. (1998) 'Social Spheres and Public Life', *Theory, Culture and Society* 15(2): 115–35.

McGuigan, J. (1996) *Culture and the Public Sphere*, London: Routledge.

McLaughlin, L. (1993) 'Feminism, the Public Sphere, Media and Democracy', *Media Culture and Society* 15: 599–620.

Neale, J. (2002) *You are G8, We are 6 Billion*. London: Vision.

Negt, O. and Kluge, A. (1993) *Public Sphere and Experience: Toward an Analysis of the Bourgeois and Proletarian Public Sphere* foreword by M. Hansen, translated by P. Labanyi, J. O. Daniel and A. Oksiloff. Minneapolis: University of Minnesota Press.

Owen, D. (1999) 'Orientation and Enlightenment: An Essay on Critique and Genealogy', in S. Ashenden and D. Owen (eds) *Foucault Contra Habermas*. London: Sage.

Peters, J. D. (1993) 'Distrust of Representation: Habermas on the Public Sphere'. *Media, Culture and Society* 15: 541–71.

Roberts, J. M. (2003) *The Aesthetics of Free Speech: Rethinking the Public Sphere*. London: Palgrave.

Roberts, J. M. (2004) 'The Stylistics of Competent Speaking: A Bakhtinian Exploration of some Habermasian Themes', *Theory, Culture and Society*, forthcoming.

Rose, N. (1999) *Powers of Freedom*. Cambridge: Cambridge University Press.

Sheller, M. and Urry, J. (2003) 'Mobile Transformations of 'Public' and 'Private' Life', *Theory, Culture and Society* 20(3): 107–25.

Siltanen, J. and Stanworth, M. (1984) 'The Politics of Private Woman and Public Man', in J. Siltanen and M. Stanworth (eds) *Women and the Public Sphere: A Critique of Sociology and Politics*. London: Hutchinson.

Simons, J. (1995) *Foucault and the Political*. London: Routledge.

Somers, M. R. (1993) 'Citizenship and the Place of the Public Sphere: Law, Community, and Political Culture in the Transition to Democracy', *American Sociological Review* 58 October: 587–620.

Somers, M. R. (1994) 'Rights, Relationality and Membership: Rethinking the Making and Meaning of Citizenship', *Law and Social Inquiry* 19(1): 63–112.

Somers, M. R. (1995a) 'Narrating and Naturalizing Civil Society and Citizenship Theory: The Place of Political Culture and the Public Sphere', *Sociological Theory* 13(3): 229–74.

Somers, M. R. (1995b) 'What's Political or Cultural About Political Culture and the Public Sphere? Toward an Historical Sociology of Concept Formation', *Sociological Theory* 13(2): 113–44.

Taylor, C. (1995) 'Liberal Politics and the Public Sphere' in *Philosophical Arguments*. Cambridge, Massachusetts: Harvard University Press.

Thompson, J. B. (1995) *The Media and Modernity: A Social Theory of the Media*. Cambridge: Polity Press.

Tolson, A. (1991) 'Televised Chat and the Synthetic Personality', in P. Scannell (ed.) *Broadcast Talk*. London: Sage Publications.

Tully, J. (1989) 'Wittgenstein and Political Philosophy: Understanding Practices of Critical Reflection', *Political Theory* 17(2): 172–204.

Villa, D. (1992) 'Postmodernism and the Public Sphere', *American Political Science Review*, 86 (September): 712–21.

Weintraub, J. (1997) 'The Theory and Politics of the Public/Private Distinction', in J. Weintraub and K. Kumar (eds) *Public and Private in Thought and Practice: Perspectives on a Grand Dichotomy.* Chicago: University of Chicago Press.

Wittgenstein, L. (1953) *Philosophical Investigations* trans. by G.E.M Anscombe. Oxford: Basil Blackwell.

Wild publics and grotesque symposiums: Habermas and Bakhtin on dialogue, everyday life and the public sphere

Michael E Gardiner

Introduction

The publication of Jürgen Habermas' *The Structural Transformation of the Public Sphere* in 1962 is widely acknowledged to be the primary impetus for post-war research on the public sphere in Western societies (Asen and Brouwer, 2001: 3). The central thesis of this study can be summarized fairly succinctly: in the eighteenth and nineteenth centuries, a distinct forum for rational public debate emerged in most Western European countries. It constituted an area of social life, separate from the state apparatus, in which citizens gathered to converse about the issues of the day in a free and unrestricted fashion, either literally, as in the town square, or in the pages of diverse journals and periodicals. Debate proceeded according to universal standards of critical reason and argumentative structure that all could recognize and assent to; appeals to traditional dogmas, or to arbitrary subjective prejudices, were ruled inadmissible. Thus, it was in the public sphere that 'discursive will formation' was actualized in a manner that represented the *general* social interest, as opposed to a class or sectional one. Of course, Habermas is sanguine enough to realize that this generalized commitment to collective and rational self-determination was never fully realized. The bourgeois ideal of unhindered free speech was always some distance from reality, and this gap widened as the capitalist economy became more centralized and concentrated. Under these conditions, the public sphere was significantly reduced in scope and influence, and decision-making became an increasingly technocratic prerogative. Indeed, the very concept of public opinion, according to Habermas, becomes transformed into public relations, the manipulation of mass consciousness through the culture industries *à la* Adorno and Horkheimer. Habermas further acknowledges that very nearly all participants in the classical public sphere were individuals of well-educated bourgeois stock and, needless to say, male. Yet he remains adamant that this sphere was characterized by an 'element of truth that raised bourgeois ideology above ideology itself, most fundamentally in that area where the experience of "humanity" originates' (Habermas, 1989: 48). By transcending the sociohistorical limitations of the actual public sphere, the principle of open and rational public debate remains to this day an immanent possibility. Notwithstanding his narrative of decline from the 'golden age of communicative reason' (Arantes and Arantas, 2001: 48) to the technocratic present, tempered somewhat by his keen (though not uncritical) interest in the upsurge of such new social movements as feminism or environmentalism, what is noteworthy is that the main ideas originally expounded in *The Structural Transformation* have been defended by Habermas with only minor modifications ever since it first appeared (see Habermas, 1992a). Despite its uncharacteristically sociological and historical style of exposition, the major theme of this study is hardly an anomalous one: on the contrary, as William Outhwaite has suggested, 'the ideal of rational, informed discussion of public policy is one which runs like a red thread through the whole of his later work' (1994: 8). Habermas' firm belief that ideological factors and competing material interests could be effectively set aside in the pursuit of genuine consensus through interpersonal dialogue in the public sphere represents the core notion that informed such later theoretical innovations as the ideal speech situation, universal pragmatics, and discourse ethics.

Yet Habermas' reflections on dialogical democracy and the public sphere have certainly not been without their detractors. These include such postmodernists and poststructuralists as Foucault (1996) or Lyotard (1984), who reject Habermas' wish to fulfill the promise of a 'radicalized modernity' through the medium of communicative reason, mainly because this goal masks a pervasive 'will to power' and threatens the irreducible value pluralism that marks the postmodern age. Habermas' arguments have also been scrutinized critically by feminist theoreticians like Seyla Benhabib (1992, 1995) and Nancy Fraser (1992) who, whilst working broadly within the tradition of critical theory, nonetheless chastise Habermas for such disabling blind-spots as a lack of sensitivity about gender issues, his devaluing of an 'ethics of care', or failure to comprehend the limitations of formal rationality and representative democracy. More recently, another wrinkle has been added to the debate: many argue for a virtual abandonment of Habermasian-inspired notions of the public sphere in favour of a theory of 'counterpublics'. This call is meant to underscore the heterodox and pluralistic nature of such spheres, which are often in opposition to the procedures of the dominant public sphere, as well as to sensitize us to the wide variety of normative ideals that regulate interaction in different areas of sociocultural life. Habermas' stress on a relatively monolithic, overarching public sphere characterized by specific regulative mechanisms for rational debate and consensus-building, according to this view, actively 'suppresses sociocultural diversity in constituting an arena inimical to difference' (Asen, 2000: 425).

These developments are certainly interesting and important, and I will return to some of them in the final section. But what I propose here is to reflect on some of the core elements of Habermas' thoughts on the public sphere, ethics, and rational dialogue by contrasting these with the work of the Russian philosopher Mikhail M. Bakhtin (1895–1975).[1] Despite some similarities in their respective projects, the differences are much more salient. Whereas Habermas seeks to delineate sharply between particular realms of social activity and forms of discourse—between, for instance, public and private, state and public sphere, reason and non-reason, ethics and aesthetics—Bakhtin problematizes such demarcations, sees them as fluid, permeable and always contested, and alerts us to the power relations that are involved in any such exercise of boundary-maintenance. Similarly, whilst Habermas likes to think in terms of formal unities, Bakhtin prefers to meditate on the irreducible complexities that inhere in particular lived contexts, and to think with (and through) the implications of multiplicity and alterity *vis-à-vis* concrete phenomena. Less abstractly, perhaps the central theme of this chapter can be stated as follows: that despite his ostensive stress on pragmatics and frequent evocation of the concept of the 'lifeworld' in *Theory of Communicative Action* and other writings, Habermas fails to grasp adequately the significance of the embodied, situational and dialogical elements of everyday human life, mainly because his desire to supercede the constraints of a 'subject-centred reason' leads him to embrace an account of intersubjectivity that remains overly abstract and formalistic. In many respects, Habermas is an archetypally modernist thinker, one who strives to achieve a high degree of rational 'purity' and conceptual order. By contrast, if not the 'proto-postmodernist' some have made him out to be, Bakhtin is more critical of modernity and the Enlightenment, and tends to privilege complexity and ambiguity over clarity—which is not to say he is deliberately obscurantist, or for that matter a straightforwardly anti-modernist thinker. That I prefer Bakhtin's approach to many of these issues should be evident from the ensuing discussion, but my goal is hopefully more constructive: to tease out some of the more obvious *lacunae* to be found in Habermasian notions of dialogical democracy and ethics, and to provide an impetus to revise these concepts along more Bakhtinian lines. In what follows, I will focus on the following three areas of inquiry: i) ethics and intersubjectivity; ii) language; and iii) the lifeworld and the everyday. This will be followed by some brief concluding remarks.

Ethics and intersubjectivity

Habermas' concept of communicative reason is essentially about establishing formal criteria, which are simultaneously inclusive and universal, of what constitutes (relatively) ideology-free dialogue oriented towards genuine consensus with respect to issues of public concern. Behind this conception of moral reasoning and discursive democracy is a wish to dispense with the 'philosophy of consciousness' that has bedevilled earlier theories, so as to embrace an intersubjective model. But in seeking to grasp the generic and universal features of human communicative action, and to incorporate these elements into a comprehensive social theory, a significant problem emerges. Habermas' thoughts on rational dialogue and the public sphere do not in a substantive way concern themselves with, much less address, the embodied experiences and activities of actual people in the context of their everyday lives. As Ted Stoltz observes, because Habermas focuses almost entirely on the legal-juridical principles that 'regulate the flow of discursive will-formation,' his theories are effectively 'subjectless' (2000: 150). This is somewhat overstated: perhaps it would be more accurate to say that there is a Habermasian subject, but it is a rather insubstantial entity, one marked by an interchangeable, 'minimalist' body (mainly having to do with the human capacity for labour), subtended by a rational mind that engages in purposive dialogue and moral reflection. Such a Habermasian body does not seem to be marked by difference, of a gendered nature or otherwise, and nor does it evince the kind of dense, material 'fleshiness' that thinkers like Merleau-Ponty have striven to comprehend, via what Hwa Jol Jung (1990) has usefully termed a 'carnal hermeneutics'. It can be argued (albeit not without qualification) that there is something of a *de facto* mind/body dualism operating within Habermas' theories, one that has received relatively little attention in the critical literature to date.[2] An important exception is Joan Alway's article 'No Body There: Habermas and Feminism'. Although preoccupied mainly with the limitations of Habermas with respect to feminist criticism and politics, Alway makes several valuable points germane to our discussion:

> [Habermas espouses] a universalism that depends on a communicatively competent, but disembodied subject. Such a subject leaves us unable to acknowledge the important bodily dimensions of autonomy and self-realization; such a subject limits our ability to understand the ways in which domination and resistance have materialized in and around the bodies of women and members of other oppressed groups; and such a subject inhibits analysis of the concrete, lived and different experiences of embodied actors in their everyday/everynight worlds. (1999: 138)

The recourse to such dualisms in Habermas' work helps to explain his overly schematic and underdeveloped account of the nature and significance of everyday life. For purposes of illustration, let us focus briefly on one such dichotomy: the universal versus the particular. This is a distinction that bears directly on the connection between ethics and communicative action, which is especially noteworthy given that everyday life is to a significant degree about the experience of particularity and contingency. As Habermas writes in *Moral Consciousness and Communicative Action*, ethical reasoning 'comes about when the social world is moralized from the hypothetical attitude of a participant in argumentation and split off from the world of life. [Moral] questions are thereby dissociated from their contexts and moral answers are dissociated from empirical motives' (1990: 180). Accordingly, evaluative questions—about relatively abstract issues pertaining to the nature of the 'good society', or more specific concerns about everyday ethical decisions—are considered by Habermas to be entirely separate from considerations of justice. Issues of care or affective regard for others are viewed by him as personal concerns that must be separated from the realm of morality *per se*, whereas all quasi-utopian talk about what a good society might look like involves the ends of dialogic democracy, but not the procedures through which such dialogues are to be carried out, and hence are not relevant to his communicative paradigm.

But others have argued that such evaluative or contextualizing judgements, which are rooted by and large in the circumstances of everyday life, cannot be easily separated from moral reflection. There are, that is to say, coherent alternatives that do not jettison the promise of rational dialogue by embracing some sort of spurious postmodernist relativism, yet do not subscribe to the Habermasian image of a disembodied and idealized public sphere. The work of Mikhail Bakhtin stands as a useful example of just such an approach. In his early writings (*circa* 1919–24), Bakhtin develops what could be termed an 'ethics of personalism', which turns on an unequivocal acknowledgment of the value of otherness in the context of everyday sociality. His thoughts on such a personalistic ethics are developed through a critique of Kant's moral philosophy. Kant, as is well-known, asserted that people's moral decisions had to be premised on the belief that they had universal applicability. This is what he famously called the categorical imperative, which expressed the binding 'universality of the ought'. However, Bakhtin feels that Kantianism is too abstract and prescriptive, and its use of transcendental *a prioris* renders it unable to address ethical problems as they emerge within everyday life. Kant's moral philosophy is an example of what Bakhtin calls 'theoretism': in maintaining a disjuncture between immediate experience and 'extra-local' symbolic representations, and by privileging the latter, such approaches subsume the open-ended and 'messy' qualities of real-life communicative and social acts into an all-encompassing explanatory system. For Bakhtin, this suppresses the 'eventness' of the everyday social world, its sensuous particularity. It can only be combatted by a repudiation of theoretical abstraction pursued as an end to itself, so as to grasp the concrete deed as the axiological centre around which our existence revolves. We must remain aware of the fact that the terrain of daily life constitutes the paramount reality in which 'we create, cognize, contemplate, live our lives and die—the world in which the acts of our activity are objectified and the world in which these acts actually proceed and are actually accomplished once and only once' (Bakhtin, 1993: 2).

What Bakhtin is striving to outline here is a phenomenology of 'practical doing', one that focuses on our incarnated activities within the lifeworld. Only if we think and act in a 'participative' fashion, in tune with the rhythms and textures of everyday life, can we be wholly answerable for our actions, in the sense that we are conscious of and can actively respond to their existential and ethical implications. Being-as-event must therefore be lived through, and not passively contemplated from afar. And a crucial aspect of answerability involves an unconditional recognition of otherness, because for Bakhtin no genuinely moral philosophy can be formulated outside the 'contraposition' of self and other. Any attempt to answer the solicitation of the world must be aware of the fact that self and other commingle in the ongoing event of Being, yet remain distinctively incarnated. This co-participation in the everyday lifeworld, which is constitutive of selfhood and evinces affective, value-laden and ethical qualities, cannot occur solely through the medium of 'cognitive-discursive thought'. A fully participative life requires an engaged and embodied—in a word, *dialogical*—relation to the other, and to the world at large, mainly because the architectonic value of my embodied self can only be affirmed in and through my relation to a concrete other: 'the body is not something self-sufficient, it needs the *other*, needs his [*sic*, and *passim*] recognition and form-giving activity' (Bakhtin, 1990: 51). Our capacity for abstract cognition and representational thinking is, on its own terms, incapable of grasping the incarnate linkage between different subjects within the fabric of daily life, cannot comprehend their 'organic wovenness' in overlapping (but non-merging) contexts.

What conclusions can be drawn from the above discussion *vis-à-vis* Habermas' account of rationality and ethics—and, by extension, his perspective on everyday life? First, it raises important questions about precisely how, and in what manner, Habermas is committed to a theory of intersubjectivity. On the surface, admittedly, Habermas does appear to reject the notion of the solitary monological subject by suggesting normative reason must be grounded in communicative exchanges. But in positing a realm of rarified ethico-political debate that conforms to universalistic principles abstracted from real subjects and their daily lives, the result is that Habermas 'constructs total systems that seek to engulf the alterity of things in the unity of thought. [D]eontological reason expresses this logic of identity by eliminating otherness in at least two ways, the irreducible specificity of situations and the difference among moral subjects' (Young, 1987: 61). In retaining a sharp distinction between impartial reason on the one hand and the embodied and 'non-rational' features of human existence on the other, that is to say, Habermas effectively smuggles a Cartesian mind/body dichotomy in through the back door. Bakhtin provides a useful point of departure here, because for him it is precisely such an attunement to the vicissitudes and rhythms of daily life that is the hallmark of genuine dialogue and the ethical moment. The upshot is that moral reason does not, *contra* Habermas, have to be impartial and 'extra-local', as in deontological ethics, mainly because authentic answerability is not about fidelity to abstract notions of duty or obligation. Rather, it involves continual communication with, and responsibility to, real situations and concrete others. Bakhtin writes that each individual should understand the 'ought of his performed act [not as an] abstract law[,] but the actual, concrete ought conditioned by his unique place in the given context of the ongoing event' (1993: 30). Certainly, he would agree with Habermas that a large part of the onus of Being is that we must be 'answerably rational' creatures. But for Bakhtin this is a *practical* rationality, rooted in the actualities of the everyday and not detachable from specific conditions and projected as some sort of speciously universalistic and decontextualized 'Truth'. Whereas Bakhtin argues that we must always put our personal signature, an 'emotional-volitional tone', upon any act we perform, Habermas says that it is precisely this personal tone that must be expunged in rational dialogue. To Bakhtin's way of thinking, this sort of abstract moral reasoning would be to remain at the level of 'cognitive-discursive thought'—or, to use his famous phrase, to find an 'alibi' in Being. In attempting to ground moral theory and ideological criticism in the universal norms that he believes regulate speech-acts, Habermas arguably replaces the incarnate and differentiated moral subject with a generic, hyper-rational being. What is lost in such a transcription is our 'compellent, ought-to-be relationship to the world[,] the actuality of the world[, resulting in an] indifferent Being not rooted in anything' (Bakhtin, 1993: 47, 43). Or, as Agnes Heller cogently observes, the Habermasian subject lacks 'the sensuous experiences of hope and despair, of venture and humiliation. The creature-like aspects of human beings are missing'. It is a subject with 'no body, no feelings, the "structure of personality" is identified with cognition, language and interaction. [One] gets the impression the "good life" [for Habermas] consists solely of rational communication and needs that can be argued for without being felt' (Heller, 1982: 21, 22).

Bakhtin is obviously very suspicious of reductive and totalizing theories that dissolve concrete particularities into a system of abstract concepts and relations. But it should not be implied that he fetishizes lived experience or espouses a phenomenology of the immediate. Nor does he always reject the value of abstract theorizing and the use of more generalizing categories and explanations. Although Bakhtin is adamant that abstract contemplation cannot in and of itself gain entry to the terrain of everyday life, because the latter requires 'actual communion' with the concrete actions that I perform through my living corporeality, at the same time the answerable deed is not inextricably mired in the mundane and the particular. Rather, the 'answerability performed act' constitutes an architectonic activity that brings together the 'sense and the fact, the universal and the individual, the real and the ideal'. By bridging the gap that separates our 'small scrap of space and time' and the 'large spatial and temporal whole', the answerable deed brings the sphere of intimate personal life and the more public realm of politics and culture into closer alignment, but without negating the specificity of each (Bakhtin, 1993: 29, 51). In striving to understand such connections and the wider historical and sociocultural developments that condition them, more abstract forms of theorizing certainly have their place in Bakhtin's work (see Gardiner, 2003; Hirschkop, 1999). It also means that he is not as vulnerable to charges of contextual relativism as might be supposed. Bakhtin consistently argues, for instance, that our access to the world is mediated by our body, and our embeddedness in concrete time/space makes each of our perceptual openings onto the world unique and non-interchangeable. But this does not conform to a Nietzschean perspectivalism that, in much contemporary theorizing, slides all too easily into a postmodernist solipsism. This is because self and other continue to inhabit the same world: we are *co-participants* in a universe that ultimately transcends any particularistic viewpoint. Such an emphasis on intercorporeal 'blending', through which we participate *collectively* in a complexly structured and shared environment, implies that although our placement in the world is not shared identically by any other person, this is no barrier to dialogic exchanges in which the differences between interacting elements are not sublated into an overarching conceptual unity. Hence, in the

Bakhtinian view, a given phenomenon should not be thought of as an 'innate one-and-only, but as a dialogic *concordance* of unmerged twos or multiples' (Bakhtin, 1984a: 289).

'Ideal speech' versus the 'grotesque symposium'

This brings us to the issue of language. For Habermas, language-use is oriented towards reaching mutual understanding and rational consensus through the raising and vindication of four major validity-claims (truth, appropriateness, sincerity, and comprehensiveness) that are intrinsic to the speech-act (Habermas, 1979). As is well-known, Habermas regards other forms of language-use (including humour, irony, or parody) as secondary and 'parasitic', presumably because they compromise the lucidity and openness that ideally marks the communicative process, or introduce elements of strategic action. T. Gregory Garvey (2000) points out that the key watchword here is transparency, and, *inter alia*, the 'purity' of the ideal speech situation. More specifically, for rational communication to function properly in the Habermasian model, transparency must be evident at two levels: that of the individual (because autonomous action is premised on subjects knowing their intentions through rational reflection), as well as the social (interlocutors must know the motivations of other speakers via rational discussion in a shared vernacular, because any motive apart from a desire to participate fully in the collective search for truth is ruled out of court. Normative legitimations that are not thoroughly understood by all interlocutors and premised entirely on the force of the better argument are *prima facie* invalid.) As Habermas himself puts it, 'The experience of reflection articulates itself substantially in the concept of the self-formative process. Methodically it leads to a standpoint from which the *identity of reason with the will freely arises*' (1978: 197; italics added). So both the self and socially binding norms are rationalized through a process of 'self-revelation', whereby private needs are brought to consciousness and adjudicated through rational dialogue, and which effects a convergence of individual and collective interests. Ideal speech must bracket off potentially distorting material forces and inequities of power and vouchsafe the transparent nature of communicative action, thereby preventing the 'forms of economic and administrative rationality' intrinsic to system from 'colonizing' the lifeworld, which would result in the 'one-sided rationalization or reification of everyday communicative practice' (Habermas, 1987: 330). Only when speech-acts are brought into the public arena and subjected to collective scrutiny can the rational promise of intersubjective dialogue be brought to fruition.

There are certainly parallels between Bakhtin and Habermas concerning their respective treatments of language. But on many fundamental issues, especially the role of transparency in language, they are sharply divided. Habermas privileges clarity, in terms of both the intentions of speaking subjects and the semantic content of signs, and the conduct of rational dialogue rests on the ability of any competent speaker to 'express his intentions in such a way that the linguistic expression accurately renders what is said [and thereby] transparently represen[ts] one's own subjectivity' (McCarthy, 1981: 280–1). This situation is possible, to a large extent, because Habermas assumes a relatively straightforward referential system that, through the agency of a communicatively competent subject, connects given utterances to a world of objects, motives or norms (see Young, 1987: 70–1). But this formulation is strikingly at odds with the dialogical model of language-use. For Bakhtin, a particular utterance is only part of a potentially endless chain of signification, one that stretches in the distant past and anticipates responses in an unknowable future—what he calls 'great time'. As such, the meanings that utterances evoke are only provisionally stable because linked to shifting contexts and situations. Moreover, utterances are inherently value-laden; they are 'always-always' inscribed with a wide range of moral, cognitive, aesthetic and affective qualities, designed to provoke active responses and express broader perspectives and world-views. 'Languages are philosophies,' writes Bakhtin, 'not abstract but concrete, social philosophies, penetrated by a system of values inseparable from living practice and class struggle' (1984b: 471). Our utterances necessarily reflect systemic social contradictions, the social location of particular speakers, and the forms of material and rhetorical power that regulate the relevant speech genres. This explains why Bakhtin continually stresses that the word is the terrain of 'an intense ideological struggle', and that all linguistic expressions are subject to a continuous process of dialogical 're-accentuation'. Speakers are simply not in full control of the semantic resonance of the words they use: 'Quests for my own word are in fact quests for a word that is not my own, a word that is more than myself' (Bakhtin, 1986: 149). Or, to be more precise, utterances do not belong to any particular person or group, but neither, for that matter, do they belong to 'no one'. There are no 'voiceless words' not least because utterances are, in an important sense, 'made flesh' or materialized in and through the performances of embodied speaking subjects. In dialogue, Bakhtin says, 'a person participates wholly and throughout his whole life, with his eyes, lips, hands, soul, spirit, with his whole body and deeds' (1984a: 293).

Bakhtin's position here can be summarized as follows: in contradistinction to Habermas' ideal speech, we cannot have a clear, unmediated understanding of either our own or others' intentions whilst engaging in communicative acts. Living discourse (as opposed to an hypostasized ideal language) is necessarily charged with polemical qualities, myriad evaluative and stylistic markers, and populated by diverse intentions. To participate in dialogue is to immerse ourselves in a plethora of alien words and discourses, which 'inevitably leads to an awareness of the *disassociation* between language and intention, language and thought, language and expression' (Bakhtin, 1981: 368–9; italics added). There is no simple homology between the intentions and motives of speakers and the meaning of the utterances they generate—no Habermasian 'identity of reason with the will'. Of course, individuals can impart their own 'emotional-volitional tone' to the word through various techniques (the use of irony, selective paraphrase, parody, and so forth) but they cannot unilaterally determine its meaning, which is constituted through the struggle between polyphonic voices and never subject to closure. This insight prompts Bakhtin to develop a series of overlapping terms to conceptualize this phenomenon, including 'double-voicedness', 'indirect speech', 'multi-accentedness', or 'words with a sideways glance'. But all express the same basic idea: that utterances are fundamentally 'impure' or hybridized constructions, complex amalgams of different points of view, residues of past uses and anticipations of future responses, diverse idiomatic expressions, and the like. They always evince a multiplicity of actual and potential meanings, like a 'loophole left open', which 'accompanies the word like a shadow' (Bakhtin, 1984a: 233).

Bakhtin's position here further implies that the desire to achieve such communicative transparence indicates an interest in regulating language-use, especially by ranking different social languages according to perceived differences in value and legitimacy, which generally benefits powerful groups in a disproportionate manner *vis-à-vis* the disadvantaged. Bakhtin says as much when he suggests the belief a given discourse can or should have a 'direct, objectivized meaning', with the goal of securing a '*maximum* of mutual understanding', has historically been complicit in a process of sociocultural and political centralization (1981: 271). So whereas Habermas understands transparency as ideologically neutral, a mere facilitator of non-distorted communication and normative consensus, Bakhtin regards the aspiration to 'know' the other's motives and the meaning of their utterances in some sort of clear and unmediated fashion as something that cannot be disentangled from the social position of given speakers and their divergent material interests. The assertion that there is an immanent *telos* in speech oriented towards 'mutual understanding' can therefore have a darker and more pernicious side than Habermas seems willing to countenance. For Bakhtin, the impulse to secure 'direct unconditional intentionality' through any privileged discursive form is 'authoritarian, dogmatic and conservative' (1981: 286–7). Thus, it can be argued that Habermas' wish to clarify meaning and open up the individual's motives to public scrutiny is, despite his undoubted intentions to the contrary, complicit with this pervasive desire to control the power to mean, to limit the semantic flux of the sign. And insofar as Bakhtin regards opacity as an intrinsic feature of concrete language-use—at one point he suggests the word is best understood as a 'mask' that obfuscates, rather than a 'face' that reveals—his view would be that semantic clarity can only be 'forced on the sign by arbitrary social power' (Garvey, 2000: 380). Habermas wants no 'hidden agendas' in dialogue, but the relatively powerless would be at a considerable disadvantage if they accepted without reservation the kind of transparency he thinks is necessary for legitimate dialogical outcomes. In situations of ingrained asymmetries of power, whether relatively informal or more highly structured and institutionalized, the dispossessed often need such agendas, to rely on what Michel de Certeau (1984) calls the 'weapons of the weak'. Accordingly, for Bakhtin freedom and autonomy are not premised on the acquisition of communicative competence *vis-à-vis* a *particular* version of rational dialogue but, rather, on the ability to effectively 'dialogize' any given discourse that claims the mantle of truth or rationality, to relate to the 'alien word' in a manner that allows us to assess it critically and invest it with novel meanings and associations. Speakers need to become more cognizant of the multiplicity of different discourses at play, to realize that the power of any one language to signify is always a relative and contested one, and to strive to live on the 'borderline' between myriad languages, styles of expression, and world-views. Whilst unitary discourses habitually project themselves as universalistic ' "languages of truth",' we need to understand that in reality they represent the restricted point of view of certain 'social groups, professions and other cross-sections of everyday life' (Bakhtin, 1981: 367).

It should come as no surprise that Bakhtin's work evinces a distinct prefer-ence for a 'grotesque symposium' that breaks down fixed and hierarchical dis-tinctions, as opposed to something resembling Habermas' ideal speech, mainly because the latter bears too much of the mark of the 'authoritative word' for Bakhtin's comfort. And indeed, one of the most consistent features of Bakhtin's project is his deep suspicion of a purified or formalized language. He soundly rejects the image of an 'extrahistorical language, a language far removed from the petty rounds of everyday life,' advocating instead a 'prosaic' outlook that retains a 'deliberate feeling for the historical and social concreteness of living discourse, as well as its relativity, a feeling for its participation in historical becoming and in social struggle' (Bakhtin, 1981: 331). This is why he would regard with a considerable degree of skepticism Habermas' belief in formalized speech-acts as the vehicle of rational consensus that anticipate the supersession of social antagonisms. For Bakhtin, it is crucial that a primordial heteroglossia 'wash over a culture's awareness of itself and its language, penetrate it to the core, relativize the primary language system underlying [the] ideology [of a unified language] and *deprive it of its naive absence of conflict*' (1981: 368; italics added).

It is worth noting that for Bakhtin the public sphere in European history never did conform to the realm of sober and virtuous debate of the sort that Habermas claims to have identified in *The Structural Transformation*. The mar-ketplace and public square in early modern times were witness to a tumultuous intermingling of diverse social groups and widely divergent styles and idioms of language, ranging from the serious to the ironic and the playful. Such a 'free and familiar' mode of interaction undermined the pretence on the part of any one language to monological authority. In such contested spaces—or what Young calls the 'wild public' (1987: 64)—existing social hierarchies were often questioned and subverted through carnivalesque strategies of remarkable variety and invention, including the use of parodic and satirical language, grotesque humour, and symbolic degradations and inversions. There never was a 'golden age of the communicative utopia': the *real* public sphere was always marked by a pluralistic and conflictual heteroglossia. As such, the utopian appeal to a world of ideal speech and pristine rationality without reference to concrete forms of life, one that does not explicitly seek to recognize and preserve 'radical difference', merely reconciles the existing contradictions and antimonies of modern society at the level of discourse alone and projects an image of what Theodor Adorno called a 'spurious harmony'.[3] So precisely what Habermas regards as 'parasitic' or derivative in language-use—namely, irony, humour, or paradox, as well as the rhythms, cadences and inexhaustible metaphorical richness of living speech—are not only what Bakhtin would consider to be the most interesting and important features of human communication. They also constitute a crucial resource through which the popular masses can retain a degree of autonomy from the forces of sociocultural homogenization and centralization.

At the same time, the preceding discussion should not be taken to imply that Bakhtin regards some sort of provisional consensus over specific pragmatic issues to be impossible; again, he is not espousing an absolute linguistic incommensurability *à la* Lyotard. For whilst Bakhtin does stress the agonistic qualities of concrete language-use, he also notes that 'agreement' is a very significant feature of dialogue. This notion receives its most sustained attention in his study of Dostoevsky, where he discusses at some length how the dialogic tradition in Western society, at least since the time of Socrates, provides us with an exemplar of an unstructured, non-teleological approach to the 'testing' of various ideas and viewpoints through the auspices of free and open debate. Such a position bears a passing resemblance to Habermas' ideal speech situation, which gains more credibility if we take into account two additional Bakhtinian concepts, the 'superaddressee' and the 'confession'.[4] But there are telling and crucial differences. In Bakhtin's view, the dialogical tradition provides a vital counterweight to an abstract Enlightenment version of truth, which 'knows only a single mode of cognitive interaction among consciousnesses' (Bakhtin, 1984a: 81). Such an impersonal and monolithic conception of truth is one that transcends the existential situation of individual speakers and actual communities, and negates the integrity of 'independent and autonomous speech and semantic centers' (Bakhtin, 1984a: 204). Dogmatism in any form (which would include various species of rationalism) makes genuine dialogue impossible, in that the process by which truth is revealed is foreordained. But Bakhtin equally rejects relativism, because it assumes *a priori* the mutual incomprehension of views and renders authentic dialogue superfluous. Indeed, Bakhtin asserts that a 'unified truth' can only be properly expressed through a plurality of perspectives and should not be 'subordinated to the verbal and semantic dictatorship of a monologic, unified style and a unified tone' (Ibid.). Dialogue should therefore be regarded as an end in itself, and not something that evinces any particular 'purpose' or is oriented to specific outcomes. As Seyla Benhabib contends, discourse ethics should concern itself not so much with the question of whether the result of a given dialogical exchange is rationally vindicated or justified but with how we can sustain an ongoing moral conversation, understood as a 'form of life' based on an unequivocal respect of otherness. 'It is not the *result* of the process of moral judgment alone [ie, a Habermasian normative consensus] that counts but the *process* for the attainment of such judgment which plays a role in its validity, and I would say, moral worth' (Benhabib, 1992: 37–8). This shift from outcome to process accords entirely with a dialogical perspective, not least because Bakhtin feels there can only be penultimate words in communicative exchanges. The clash of utterances in the dialogic encounter, even if motivated by the highest consensual aspirations, can never be completely reconciled: 'even *agreement* retains its *dialogic* character, that is, it never leads to a *merging* of voices and truths in a single *impersonal* truth, as occurs in the monologic world' (Bakhtin, 1984a: 95). Bakhtin's position on this score has been cogently described by William H. Thornton (1994: 92) as a 'politics of impurity—one without final solutions or "finalizable" (positivistic or "poetic") representation'. If so, the ideal speech situation as Habermas interprets it would seem to be indicative of a 'politics of purity', one that, in the words of Iris Marion Young,

> expels and devalues difference, the concreteness of the body, the affective aspects of speech, the musical and figurative aspects of all utterances, which all contribute to the formation and understanding of their meaning. [. . .] Habermas's model of discourse abstracts from the specifically bodily aspects of speech—gesture, facial expression, tone of voice, rhythm. One can add to this that it also abstracts from the material aspects of written language, such as punctuation, sentence construction and so on. This model of communication also abstracts from the rhetorical dimensions of communication, that is, the evocative terms, metaphors, dramatic elements of the speaking, by which a speaker addresses himself or herself to this particular audience. [In] the model of ideal discourse that Habermas holds, moreover, there appears to be no role for metaphor, jokes, irony and other forms of communication that use surprise and duplicity. [. . .] Implicitly this model of communication supposes a purity of the meaning of utterances by separating them from their expressive and metaphorical aspects. (Young, 1987: 71)

The everyday and the lifeworld

Habermas' account of the relationship between language, ethics and rationality is echoed by—and to a certain extent grounded in—his theory of everyday life, which is developed primarily through his system/lifeworld distinction. In the second volume of *Theory of Communicative Action*, Habermas identifies system as the realm of formal-bureaucratic structures, institutions and processes that utilize the media of money and power, whereas the lifeworld is described as a 'linguistically organized stock of interpretive patterns' (Habermas, 1987: 124), which are largely implicit but necessary for the conduct of practical social interaction and communication. Such background assumptions and stock knowledges, which are rooted in usually unquestioned cultural traditions, constitute something of a backdrop for the operation of more specialized knowledges and formal institutions. The everyday lifeworld is therefore not only epistemologically and ontologically 'prior' to official society; it is temporally prior as well, in the sense that it is linked, though traditions and cultural memories, to a 'primordial' or pre-modern form of sociality. Steve Crook (1998) points out, however, that this characterization leads to a curious tension in Habermas' social theory. Habermas says that human morality is based on the practical, reciprocal interactions and speech-acts oriented towards mutual understanding that constitute the elemental fabric of the lifeworld. Yet because the lifeworld consists of sedimented and largely unreflexive meanings, values and orientations— not unlike Gramsci's 'common sense'—it is not itself amenable to overt rationalization, and must be transcended in the pursuit of 'higher' forms of moral dialogue and reflection (see Habermas, 1992b: 110). In part, this is due to Habermas' adherence to Kohlberg's theory of moral development, which supposes that in engaging in post-conventional moral reasoning, the individual rises above the naively pragmatic and inward-looking character of daily existence and ethical considerations can be effectively decoupled from the unexamined 'cultural givens' that characterize the lifeworld.

According to Crook (1998: 527), one major problem with this formulation is that although Habermas sets out to distinguish conceptually between the everyday lifeworld and communicative/moral reason, in practice he continually elides the two. But the everyday cannot simultaneously be a realm of unquestioned prejudices (opacity) and the terrain of rational dialogue oriented towards mutual understanding (transparency). It could be argued that this difficulty arises because of Habermas' desire to see the everyday lifeworld as a distinct and relatively undifferentiated realm of sub-institutional social life, what Crook describes as a 'homogeneous soup of taken-for-grantedness' (1998: 528). Similarly, as Bakhtin reminds us, 'Pure everyday life is fiction, a product of the intellect' (1986: 154). Rather than purify the 'messy' and heterodox character of everyday life, the alternative would be to eschew defining it by any specific quality (for example, routinization or taken-for-grantedness), or construing it as a specific, delimited sector of the social world (as ontologically distinct from system, in Habermas' formulation), but instead to see it as riven with numerous contradictions, marked by a considerable degree of heterogeneity, and exhibiting manifold connections to all areas of social life (see Gardiner, 2000). Although everyday life can certainly display routinized, static and unreflexive characteristics, it is also capable of a surprising dynamism and moments of penetrating insight and boundless creativity. The everyday is, as Michel Maffesoli (1989) puts it, 'polydimensional': fluid, ambivalent and labile. So whilst Habermas regards the lifeworld as the realm of the mundane and the ordinary—and one that is curiously bereft of life, as Alway (2000) rightly points out—it can also be understood as a complex of knowledges and practices is that is vitally alive and (at least potentially) *extra*ordinary. The ordinary can become extraordinary not by eclipsing the everyday, or imagining that we can arbitrarily leap beyond it to some 'higher' level of moral reflection or action, but by fully appropriating and activating the possibilities that lie hidden, and typically repressed, within it. 'The everyday has its experience and wisdom, its sophistication, its forecasting,' writes Karel Kosík in *Dialectics of the Concrete*. 'It has its replicability but also its special occasions, its routine but also its festivity. The everyday is thus not meant as a contrast to the unusual, the festive, the special, or to

History: hypostatizing the everyday as a routine over History, as the exceptional, is itself the *result of* a certain mystification' (1976: 43).

This passage by Kosík neatly encapsulates Bakhtin's approach to the everyday, which is a demonstrably more dynamic and nuanced conception than that maintained by Habermas. Unarguably, Bakhtin adheres to what Morson and Emerson (1990) have termed a 'prosaic' outlook, in the sense that he is clearly suspicious of the more extravagant and aggrandizing claims of many modern philosophical traditions. Bakhtin continually emphasizes the presence of what Roland Barthes once called the 'grain of the voice', the trace of the flesh-and-blood personality that lies behind every utterance or deed. His acute sense of the dense particularity of lived experience leads him to decry the reification of language and the attendant hypostatization of concrete human activities and relationships effected by formalist and rationalist approaches. This explains why some of Bakhtin sharpest critical barbs were reserved for the arid abstractions of philosophical idealism, as exemplified by the 'agelasts', the humourless and pedantic scholars that are so often the butt of Rabelais' comic jests. For Bakhtin, dialogism must come to grips with the ambivalent, sensuous materiality of incarnate (and intercorporeal) human existence, and also with the pragmatic moral demands that are continually thrust upon us in the course of our daily lives. But this preoccupation with the everyday and its manifold valences is palpably not insulated from his interest in the carnivalesque, because Bakhtin feels we must understand the transgressive, utopian and festive qualities of human societies as well. Put differently, carnival and prosaics are not antithetical notions, as is sometimes implied in the literature (see Gardiner, 2002). Bakhtin's evocation of the carnivalesque is best understood as indicative of his desire to draw our attention to the underlying sociocultural forces that continually subvert our received commonsensical notions and habitualized viewpoints, and to encourage a renewed awareness of the hidden and all-too-often suppressed potentialities that lie within 'the dregs of an everyday gross reality' (Bakhtin, 1981: 385).

Conclusion: wild publics

In this concluding section, I would like tentatively to link up some of the key points discussed above to the debate around publics and counterpublics touched on briefly in my introductory remarks. In attempting to overcome the subjectivist tendencies of earlier monological accounts of moral reasoning, Habermas envisages a form of ethical dialogue that unfolds in an inclusive public sphere and is governed by transparent, universalistic principles. Such a sphere evinces a form of communicative rationality that acknowledges only the force of the better argument; other manifestations of power or strategic action are ruled out of court. The public sphere is ideally insulated from wider systemic conflicts over the distribution of power and resources in society, as well as the prejudices of private life (or else the latter must be translated into a shared vernacular).

Habermas therefore posits the public sphere as a realm of 'general interest', which all members of society can participate in and have a stake in preserving. Many critics, however, charge that Habermas' quest for a 'universal collective subject' (one that is constituted through rational discourse) is vulnerable to a host of objections. Firstly, it is argued that Habermas' position is idealist in both the philosophical and everyday senses of the word, because it supposes that material conflicts of a socio-economic nature can be effectively transcended or at least effectively sublimated into a rational discourse that can suspend ingrained power differentials. The key objection here is that domination is not simply a matter of the intrusion of ideas or media that reflect particular (rather than universal) interests, or ideological distortions of ideal speech of the sort that can be resolved through rational dialogue. Instead, power is largely a material phenomenon: as Foucault (1980) has frequently argued, the operation of power crucially involves the application of disciplinary pressures on the individual and collective body, and the internalization of these forces by particular subjects, which further means that domination must be resisted first and foremost by bodies. Warren Montag suggests, for instance, that there can be no genuinely neutral or impersonal dialogue between powerful and marginalized groups, namely because 'between ideas there are relations of force, in that they are embodied in the broader relationship of forces in a society characterized by a perpetual, if latent, civil war that renders some dominant and others subordinate, usually in inverse proportion to their validity or truth and certainly in inverse proportion to the degree of their "criticality".' Critical theory, as such, must ultimately be premised on 'critical practice, upon struggles that diminish the effects of coercion and discipline in workplaces and communities' (Montag, 2000: 142). A second and related line of criticism focuses on Habermas' position that the public sphere can be a relatively open and inclusive arena. By promoting an ideal of impartial reason operating in an abstract space disconnected from experiential, embodied and affective human qualities, Habermas' vision of dialogic democracy has 'not simply been dogged by, but is constituted on the basis of domination and exclusion' (Hill and Montag, 2000: 10). Several prominent feminists have developed this position most extensively, suggesting that Habermas' approach is implicitly masculinist and thereby devalues women's experiences, concerns and styles of expression. Others have elaborated on this basic insight, asserting that Habermas has failed to recognize the innumerable axes of difference beyond gender *per se* that is the distinguishing feature of late modern (or postmodern) societies. It is not sufficient to simply add more 'subaltern' public spheres (of a class or ethnic nature, for example) to the mix, as Habermas appears to suggest in response to his critics, because this still maintains the ideal of a generalized public sphere (or spheres) that functions to erase the differences between particular groups.[5] Given this irreducible value pluralism, approaches that are informed by an alternative concept of counterpublics strive to abandon the misguidedly utopian goal of a 'universalizing ideal of a single public and [attend] instead to the actual multiplicity of distinct and overlapping public discourses, public spheres, and scenes of evaluation that already exist, but that the usual idealizations have screened from view' (Robbins, 1993: xii).

Part of this shift in thinking involves locating culture and its role in the formation of identities centre-stage, rather than to view them as 'pure and corrupting epiphenomenon imposed on a pristine realm of rational openness in which citizens once communicated transparently' (Polan, cited in Robbins, 1993: xix–xx). It also means that many key Habermasian distinctions, such as between public and private, communicative and corporeal action, or rationality and non-rationality, have to be thoroughly revised. There are, for example, many forms of sociocultural criticism (including aesthetic gestures, street demonstrations, and the like) that are entirely legitimate on their own terms, but which do not conform to Habermas' model of rational dialogue oriented towards mutual understanding. As Alberto Melucci has argued, excluded or underprivileged groups are often motivated to pursue quite different strategies of action and representation than their more privileged counterparts. These subaltern discourses and strategies, which are rooted in the particularistic concerns of everyday life, are formulated at some distance from the official public sphere and aim to celebrate difference through diverse expressions of identity and community. In Melucci's view, new social movements are not simply 'defensive', designed to protect the lifeworld from the intrusion of system. Rather, they are much more dynamic than Habermas suggests, in that they seek actively to modify the social order 'by means of changes in language, sexual customs, affective relationships, dress and eating habits' (Melucci, 1988: 249). For many commentators, then, public spheres (or counterpublics) are as much sites of impassioned and embodied contestation as arenas of impartial, reasoned debate—and, moreover, such conflicts are not anomalous but constitutive of these spaces (see Asen, 2000). This position underscores why many of the current debates in our society are focussed on the very question of what is and is not political, and what the legitimate boundaries of the *polis* might be. New social movements often express the idea that so-called 'private' and everyday concerns surrounding health, sexuality, ecology or personal morality, of a sort that Habermas would likely regard as inadmissible unless subject to a process of rationalization, are deserving of public recognition and expression. As Anthony Giddens (1991) suggests, we might well be witnessing a movement away from the heroic and Promethean 'emancipatory politics' of earlier phases of modernity towards the more existential and everyday concerns of what he calls 'life politics' (see also Featherstone, 1992; Gouldner, 1975).

In favouring the notion of multiple counterpublics endowed with diverse rationalities and modes of interaction and expression over a singular public sphere regulated by a narrowly circumscribed form of rational argumentation, the essential point is that we need to 'foster a conception of public which in principle excludes no persons, aspects of persons' lives, or topic of discussion and which encourages aesthetic as well as discursive expression. In such a public, consensus and sharing may not always be the goal, but the recognition and appreciation of differences, in the context of confrontation with power' (Young,

1987: 76). It is my belief that such arguments, which are in many respects persuasive, find considerable (though perhaps unexpected) support in the writings of Mikhail Bakhtin. Bakhtin consistently strives to protect multiplicity (discursive and otherwise) against the forces of unification, prioritizes the phenomenon of alterity over the isolated, self-sufficient monad, and champions 'radical difference' in opposition to an enforced homogeneity. As a post-Cartesian thinker, he strives to grasp the experiential and affective qualities of human embodiment within diverse lived contexts, and is sensitive to full range of inter-human (and human-nature) relations that are not simply cognitive or narrowly 'rational'. And although Bakhtin has often been criticized for subscribing to an underdeveloped theory of power, I would suggest that his work often evinces a more subtle and realistic account of power, domination and resistance than does Habermas, especially *vis-à-vis* Bakhtin's thoughts on carnivalesque subversions of officialdom and the nature of ideological and linguistic hegemony. In rethinking the public sphere and theories of ethics and dialogic democracy, therefore, Bakhtin's ideas might well prove to be a fecund source of inspiration.

Notes

1 For other comparisons of Bakhtin and Habermas, see Gardiner (1992); Garvey (2000); Hirschkop (2000); and Nielsen (1995, 2002).

2 In an important article entitled 'Corporeality and Communicative Action' (1996), Nick Crossley discusses in some detail the theme of embodiment *vis-à-vis* the work of Habermas. Crossley asserts that Habermas does not subscribe to a mind/body dualism, insofar as Habermas's theories are premised on the idea that human communication involves interacting agents with bodies who can acquire broad competencies and engage in meaningful dialogue through various media (speech, writing, etc.). Furthermore, Habermas assumes the existence of bodies when he makes a labour/interaction distinction, identifying the former with instrumental action oriented towards modifying nature for the satisfaction of human needs. But in many respects Crossley's article is an exercise in theoretical reconstruction that tries to imagine what a Habermasian critical theory might look like if it properly incorporated a plausible account of embodiment. This explains why Crossley turns to Merleau-Ponty's concepts of intercorporeality and perception to augment Habermas. But because Habermas leaves embodiment largely assumed (or at least woefully undertheorized), for a variety of reasons Crossley astutely dissects, and because Habermas adheres to a mainly cognitivist theory of communication, one can still argue that he is not a post-Cartesian thinker, or at least in the manner in which, for example, Merleau-Ponty and Bakhtin are.

3 This is not to imply that Bakhtin is hostile to all utopian thinking; far from it. But it does mean he embraces, for lack of a better term, an 'anti-utopian utopianism' (see Gardiner, 1993).

4 In his discussion of the 'superaddressee'—a kind of hypothetical interlocutor—Bakhtin advances a notion of undistorted communication that, like Habermas' ideal speech, is relatively free of the pressure of divergent material interests or ideology. In one passage, Bakhtin writes that 'Every utterance makes a claim to justice, sincerity, beauty, and truthfulness (a model utterance), and so on' (1986, 123), which leads Garvey (2000: 384–5) to claim the superaddressee is remarkably similar to Habermas' idea of validity claims. To the idea of the superaddressee we could add Bakhtin's comments on the confession in his study of Dostoevsky, where he argues that a sincere confession cannot be solicited through any form of coercion or violence; it is a form of self-revelation that, unlike most utterances, lacks apparent loopholes or 'false ultimate words' (see Bakhtin, 1984a: 292). For more on Bakhtin's account of the confession, see Gardiner (1996).

5 Some, including Outhwaite (1994: 13) and Warner (2002: 55–6), have disputed the suggestion that Habermas posits a monolithic public sphere, arguing that there is no contradiction between his conception and the possibility of multiple publics. This assertion is problematic, however, because to be legitimate, such multiple spheres (whether in the pages of a bourgeois periodical or the proletarian tavern) still have to be informed by a vision of rational dialogue that effectively dissolves power imbalances. Arguably, what is monological in Habermas is the discursive form he expects ideal speech to take, not the content or social location of any speech-act.

Bibliography

Alway, J. (2000) 'No Body There: Habermas and Feminism,' *Current Perspectives in Social Theory*, 19, 117–41.

Arantes, O. B. F. and Arantas, P. E. (2001) 'The Neo-Enlightenment Aesthetics of Jürgen Habermas,' *Cultural Critique* 49, 43–57.

Asen, R. (2000) 'Seeking the "Counter" in Counterpublics,' *Communication Theory* 10, 4, Nov., 424–446.

Asen, R. and Brouwer, D. C. (2001) 'Introduction: Reconfigurations of the Public Sphere,' in R. Asen and D. C. Brouwer (eds), *Counterpublics and the State*. Albany, State University of New York Press, 1–32.

Bakhtin, M. (1981) *The Dialogic Imagination: Four Essays by M. M. Bakhtin*, M. Holquist (ed.). Austin: Texas University Press.

Bakhtin, M. (1990) *Art and Answerability: Early Philosophical Essays by M. M. Bakhtin*, M. Holquist and V. Liapunov (eds). Austin: Texas University Press.

Bakhtin, M. (1984a) *Problems of Dostoevsky's Poetics*, C. Emerson (ed.). Manchester: Manchester University Press.

Bakhtin, M. (1984b) *Rabelais and His World*. Cambridge (Mass.): The MIT Press.

Bakhtin, M. (1986) *Speech Genres and Other Late Essays*, C. Emerson and M. Holquist (eds), Austin: Texas University Press.

Bakhtin, M. (1993) *Toward a Philosophy of the Act*. Austin: Texas University Press.

Benhabib, S. (1992) *Situating the Self: Gender, Community and Postmodernism in Contemporary Ethics*. London and New York: Routledge.

Benhabib, S. (1995) 'The Debate Over Women and Moral Theory Revisited,' in J. Meehan (ed.), *Feminists Read Habermas*. London and New York: Routledge, 181–204.

Certeau, M. de. (1984) *The Practice of Everyday Life*. Berkeley: The University of California Press.

Crook, S. (1998) 'Minotaurs and Other Monsters: "Everyday Life" in Recent Social Theory,' *Sociology* 32, 3, 523–40.

Crossley, N. (1996) 'Corporeality and Communicative Action: Embodying the Renewal of Critical Theory,' *Body and Society* 3, 1, 17–46.

Featherstone, M. (1992) 'The Heroic Life and Everyday Life,' *Theory, Culture and Society* 9, 159–82.

Foucault, M. (1980) *Power/Knowledge: Selected Interviews and Writings 1972–77*, C. Gordon (ed.). New York: Pantheon Books.

Foucault, M. (1996) *Foucault Live: Interviews 1961–1984*, Sylvère Lotinger (ed.). New York: Semiotext(e).

Fraser, N. (1992) 'Rethinking the Public Sphere: A Contribution to the Critique of Actually Existing Democracy,' in C. Calhoun (ed.), *Habermas and the Public Sphere*. Cambridge (MA): The MIT Press, 109–42.

Gardiner, M. (1992) *The Dialogics of Critique: M. M. Bakhtin and the Theory of Ideology*. London: Routledge.

Gardiner, M. (1993) 'Bakhtin's Carnival: Utopia as Critique,' in D. Shepherd (ed.), *Bakhtin: Carnival and Other Subjects*. Amsterdam: Rodopi, 20–47.

Gardiner, M. (1996) 'Foucault, Ethics and Dialogue,' *History of the Human Sciences* 9, 3, 27–46.

Gardiner, M. (2000) *Critiques of Everyday Life*. London and New York: Routledge.

Gardiner, M. (2002) 'Bakhtin and Prosaics: A Critical Interrogation,' in B. Zylko (ed.), *Bakhtin and His Intellectual Ambience*. Gdansk: Wydawnictwo Uniwersytetu Gdanskiego, 2002: 109–19.

Gardiner, M. (2003) 'Introduction,' *Mikhail Bakhtin: Masters of Modern Thought*, Four Volumes. London and Thousand Oaks: Sage Ltd, ix–xxx.

Garvey, T. G. (2000) 'The Value of Opacity: A Bakhtinian Analysis of Habermas's Discourse Ethics,' *Philosophy and Rhetoric* 33, 4: 370–90.

Giddens, A. (1991) *Modernity and Self-Identity: Self and Society in the Late Modern Age*. Stanford, Stanford University Press.

Gouldner, A. (1975) 'Sociology and the Everyday Life,' in L. A. Coser (ed.), *The Idea of Social Structure: Papers in Honor of Robert K. Merton*. New York: Harcourt Brace Jovanovich, 417–32.

Habermas, J. (1978) *Knowledge and Human Interests*. 2nd edition, trans. J. Shapiro, London: Heinemann.

Habermas, J. (1979) *Communication and the Evolution of Society*. London: Heinemann.

Habermas, J. (1987) *The Theory of Communicative Action: Vol. II*. Boston: Beacon Press.

Habermas, J. (1989) *The Structural Transformation of the Public Sphere*. Cambridge (Mass.): The MIT Press.

Habermas, J. (1990) *Moral Consciousness and Communicative Action*, Cambridge (Mass.): The MIT Press.

Habermas, J. (1992a) 'Further Reflections on the Public Sphere,' in C. Calhoun (ed.), *Habermas and the Public Sphere*. Cambridge (MA): The MIT Press, 421–61.

Habermas, J. (1992b) *Autonomy and Solidarity: Interviews with Jürgen Habermas*, rev. edn. P. Dews (ed.). London: Verso.

Heller, A. (1982) 'Habermas and Marxism,' in J. Thompson and D. Held (eds), *Habermas: Critical Debates*. Cambridge (MA): The MIT Press, 21–41.

Hill, M., and Montag, W. (2000) 'Introduction: What Was, What Is, the Public Sphere? Post-Cold War Reflections,' in M. Hill and W. Montag (eds), *Masses, Classes and the Public Sphere*. London and New York: Verso, 1–10.

Hirschkop, K. (1999) *Mikhail Bakhtin: An Aesthetic for Democracy*, New York: Oxford University Press.

Hirschkop, K. (2000) 'It's Too Good To Talk: Myths of Dialogue in Bakhtin and Habermas,' *New Formations* 41, 83–93.

Jung, H. J. (1990) 'Mikhail Bakhtin's Body Politic: A Phenomenological Dialogics,' *Man and World* 23, 85–99.

Kosík, K. (1976) *Dialectics of the Concrete: A Study on Problems of Man and World*. Boston and Dordrecht: D. Reidel Publishing Company.

Lyotard, J.-F. (1984) *The Post-Modern Condition: A Report on Knowledge*. Manchester: Manchester University Press.

McCarthy, T. (1981) *The Critical Theory of Jürgen Habermas*. Cambridge (Mass.) and London: The MIT Press.

Maffesoli, M. (1989) 'The Sociology of Everyday Life (Epistemological Elements),' *Current Sociology* 37, 1, 1–16.

Melucci, A. (1988) 'Social Movements and the Democratization of Everyday Life,' in J. Keane (ed.), *Civil Society and the State: New European Perspectives*. London: Verso, 245–60.

Montag, W. (2000) 'The Pressure of the Street: Habermas' Fear of the Masses,' M. Hill and W. Montag (eds), *Masses, Classes and the Public Sphere*. London and New York: Verso, 132–45.

Morson, G. S. and Emerson, C. (1990) *Mikhail Bakhtin: Creation of a Prosaics*. Stanford: Stanford University Press.

Nielsen, G. (1995) 'Bakhtin and Habermas: Towards a Transcultural Ethics,' *Theory and Society* 24, 6, 803–35.

Nielsen, G. (2002) *The Norms of Answerability: Social Theory Between Bakhtin and Habermas*. Albany: State University of New York Press.

Outhwaite, W. (1994) *Habermas: A Critical Introduction*. Stanford: Stanford University Press.

Robbins, B. (1993) 'Introduction: The Public as Phantom,' in B. Robbins (ed.), *The Phantom Public Sphere*. Minneapolis: University of Minnesota Press, vii–xxvi.

Stolze, T. (2000) 'A Misplaced Transition: Habermas on the Public Sphere,' in M. Hill and W. Montag (eds), *Masses, Classes and the Public Sphere*, London and New York: Verso, 146–57.

Thornton, W. H. (1994) 'Cultural Prosaics as Counterdiscourse: A Direction for Cultural Studies After Bakhtin,' *Prose Studies* 17, 2, 74–93.

Warner, M. (2002) *Publics and Counterpublics*. New York: Zone Books.

Young, M. I. (1987) 'Impartiality and the Civic Public: Some Implications of Feminist Critiques of Moral and Political Theory,' in S. Benhabib and D. Cornell (eds), *Feminism as Critique: On the Politics of Gender In Late Capitalist Societies*. Cambridge: Polity Press, 57–76.

Justice and drama: on Bakhtin as a complement to Habermas

Ken Hirschkop

Introduction: suspicion of the public sphere

The most surprising moment in Habermas's *Between Facts and Norms* is surely when, discussing the differentiation of public spheres in modern societies, Habermas uses as an example the '*occasional* or arranged publics of particular presentations and events such as theatre performances, rock concerts. . .' (Habermas 1996: 374). Rock concerts? Habermas? I'm sure many people's first reaction, however trivial or foolish, was to wonder whether Professor Habermas had ever *been* to a rock concert. But Habermas' choice of examples and the incongruity of the choice aren't accidental: they tell us something interesting about the reception the concept of the public sphere has had in the English-speaking world and about the pressure Habermas has been under since the translation of *The Structural Transformation of the Public Sphere* into English in 1989. Volumes like the present one testify to the ambiguous impact of Habermas' book in the 1990s, which has been welcomed, but also treated with a certain degree of suspicion.

Just as there are romances which never happen because the right people meet at the wrong time, so there are books which arrive too early or too late on the scene to have the impact they should have. When Habermas first published *The Structural Transformation of the Public* Sphere in 1962, he didn't have cultural studies in mind. His argument that the 'public use of reason', first institutionalized in eighteenth-century Britain and France, changed the very basis of legitimacy and state rule, had two obvious targets. On the one hand, Habermas knew that the social welfare state that had emerged after the Second World War was the breeding ground for a 'technocratic' conception of liberal democracy, according to which all significant public decision-making was a matter of technical discussion best left to experts and relevant professionals. Against this 'scientization of politics', which Habermas would address directly in the later volume *Technik und Wissenschaft als 'Ideologie'*, Habermas argued that all societies depended on symbolic integration and mutual understanding, on a norm-governed form of interaction, which could only be legitimately produced through rational-critical public debate. On the other hand, Habermas knew there were also plenty of 'democrats' in thrall to Carl Schmitt's *populist* conception of democracy, which saw democracy as no more than the expression of cultural norms shared by a substantively unified 'people': a people we can assume would be substantively unified by violence if they were not already so in fact. Schmitt sundered democracy, as the rule of the majority, from liberal parliamentary 'discussion', and thereby ensured that practical questions were removed from the sphere of reasoning.

On the one hand, populist 'mass' democracy, embodied in Germany in the Nazi regime; on the other, the technocracy of postwar West Germany which, in a different fashion, reduced democracy to a process of acclamation. These were shrewdly chosen targets in the early 1960s, and Habermas' argument that the work of reason depended on democracy rather than state technocrats was a master stroke. But the environment in which the English translation arrived in 1989 was very different. In the wake of the 'postmodern' accusation that reason itself had an authoritarian edge, no one was likely to warm to the idea that a self-confessed 'category of bourgeois society' with a 'rational' core could be usefully rehabilitated. At the same time, the so-called 'cultural left' of the American university system was well aware that its political aspirations needed something a little firmer than textual politics to ground it. So the idea of the 'public sphere' was taken up, enthusiastically but in a strangely self-defeating way.

In collections like Craig Calhoun's *Habermas and the Public Sphere* (1992) and Social Text's *The Phantom Public Sphere* (Robbins, 1993), the public sphere became fruitful and multiplied. Rather than focus on *the* public sphere as a distinctive form, these volumes committed themselves to a 'plurality of competing publics', each the articulate point of a social movement or group defined by gender, class, ethnicity or some other subaltern status (Fraser, 1992: 125). At a time when the tendency was, in Francis Mulhern's words, 'to subsume the political under the cultural, to undo the rationality of politics as a determinate social form', an argument that distinguished high bourgeois politics from everything else hadn't a chance (Mulhern, 2000, 151).[1] A visible keenness to adopt the notion that certain forms of language could acquire a distinctive, institutionalized force was combined with the prevalent belief that politics was a struggle for power without any privileged arena. Under the weight of this most recent of cultural revolutions, it seemed best to let a thousand public spheres bloom.

Quantity, however, found itself transformed into quality. Habermas had defined the public sphere in two dimensions: empirical and normative. On the one hand, the public sphere was a distinct, institutionalized form of verbal and written interaction, distinct by virtue of its taking place in public fora and in print. One the other hand, as a lengthy excursus of the meaning of 'public' in the volume made clear, the public sphere was defined as a forum in which people without official power 'readied themselves to compel public authority to legitimate itself before public opinion'—a public opinion whose authority depended on its mode of open argument (Habermas, 1989: 25). One can discover public spheres in every nook and cranny of popular culture only if one is willing to drop the normative claim that made the public sphere powerful and compelling. As the editor of one of these volumes admitted in his introduction: 'Even if we grant that the problem-solving functions of the public sphere are being performed less well than in the past, this does not mean that public discourse has ceased to be at least as vibrant a source of understanding, including self-understanding' (Calhoun, 1992: 34). Fine, if what one wants is 'self-understanding', but something has been sacrificed. In the course of a discussion transcribed as the 'Concluding Remarks' of the Calhoun volume Habermas noted the price to be paid:

> There is no longer any attempt to link such an analysis with any remnants of a normative political theory. That is okay, but one has to distinguish what one is doing. This type of analysis, as far as I understand it, . . . is part of a social psychological approach to some sort of an analysis of an expressivist, somehow aesthetic need for self-representation in public space. I don't think this can lead back to a theory of democracy, and to be fair, it is not intended in this way (Habermas, 1992b: 465–6).

Yet Habermas himself had not remained immune to the tendency to disperse publicness into the myriad capillaries of the social system.

The public sphere in Habermas's initial formulation was the compact historical achievement of a particular class. As time went by, however, the concept of the public sphere was 'linguistified', made fluid and mobile to the point where it was not a space in which a certain kind of communication could take place, but a space generated by a certain kind of communication. 'Every encounter in which actors do not just observe each other but take a second-person attitude, reciprocally attributing communicative freedom to each other, unfolds in a *linguistically constituted* public space' (Habermas, 1996: 361; emphasis mine). The linguistification of the public sphere coincided with Habermas' recasting of the normative basis of his social theory. As he moved towards grounding resistance to the 'systemic imperatives' of the capitalist economy and the modern state in the structures of communicative action, the public sphere itself became less a distinctive political accomplishment than a potential situation or institution, always threatening to emerge from the pressure exerted by the communicative structures of ordinary language. Although it's tempting to think of Habermas' conception of the public sphere as adjusting to his larger theoretical change of heart, it's as likely that the shift towards a 'theory of communicative action' or 'discourse ethics' responded to manifest changes in the public sphere. Much of the most articulate opposition to capitalism and the militarism of modern nation-states in the 1960s came from the so-called new social movements, all of which were marked by an organizational fluidity and spontaneity absent from the established institutions of the labour movement. It's striking that in the 1980s Habermas' paradigm case of the public sphere was the civil disobedience of the peace movement, a tactic more typical of new social movements than the trade unions, and one aimed at a symbolic intervention in public space rather than at a rational-critical debate on policy (Habermas, 1985).

51

The new emphasis on organizational spontaneity might have been a problem if the public sphere was intended to be the nucleus or embryo of an alternative state structure. But as Habermas has himself admitted, by 1981 he had given up on the hope that the economy and the state could be 'transformed democratically from within' (Habermas, 1992a: 444). The public sphere thereby became a 'sounding board for problems that must be processed by the political system' (Habermas, 1996: 359) and was effectively relieved of the burden of defining public policy. No longer required to shape society as a whole, the public sphere could make spontaneity rather than centralism is defining feature and its signal advantage. As Habermas is keen to emphasize throughout *Between Facts and Norms*, the strength of the public sphere lies in its non-specialization and its rootedness in lifeworld structures which can't be reproduced by the state or the economy (thus taking up an argument first mooted in *Legitimation Crisis*). The public sphere can do its work 'only insofar as the networks of noninstitutionalized public communication make possible *spontaneous* processes of opinion-formation' (Habermas, 1996: 358).

How then, can these spontaneous processes of communicative action punch their weight in the hard-headed strategic world of state politics? Habermas' hesitation over the degree to which mere facts of reason can exercise compelling force leads him to a slightly more theatrical and symbolic sense of the public sphere. The public sphere may be expert at perceiving problems in the lifeworld. But it must 'in addition, amplify the pressure of problems, that is, not only detect and identify problems but also convincingly and *influentially* thematize them, furnish them with possible solutions and dramatize them in such a way that they are taken up and dealt with by parliamentary complexes' (Habermas, 1996: 359). Hence rock concerts, and other popular forms sharing the vibrancy Habermas' American interpreters were so enthusiastic about, even if this vibrancy is directed at the interpretation of social problems rather then the formation of identities. Hence also, Mikhail Bakhtin.

Bakhtin: public squares and public spheres

If a 'dramatic' publicness is what is called for, then Bakhtin is an obvious source. Bakhtin was a theorist of the novel and a philosopher, not a social or political theorist, yet one of the most striking features of much of his writing is its openly political tone and vocabulary. In his theory of the novel—written out in the 1930s, while Bakhtin was in 'internal' exile for a notionally political crime—language is wrought into shape and given life by political structures and forces, even though these structures and forces are never themselves the objects of theoretical reflection.[2] But despite his lack of political sophistication, cultural theorists willing to engage in political speculation and looking for an alternative to Habermas—and there are a striking number of these—have been quick to light on Bakhtin as their likeliest provider.

Public discourse can't help being dramatic and vibrant, according to this theory, because discourse acquires vibrancy in exact proportion to its public, social quality. Which might seem a strange thing for a man to write in the Soviet 1930s, at the very time when the life is being squeezed out of public dialogue and the civil society on which it depends is being crushed. Bakhtin had no wish or reason to deny this obvious fact. His riposte was that the 'official' discourse of the state and its associated cultural institutions was in fact private and individualistic, appearances and claims notwithstanding. Public, social discourse, on the contrary was to be found not in the lofty speech of elite institutions, but in the 'low genres' of public life, and most particularly in the lowest genre in the literary hierarchy, the 'prosaic' novel. Now novels, of course, have often included recognizably public discourse in their linguistic repertoire and have put recognizable political events in either the background or foreground of the stories they have to tell. But in the modern European version Bakhtin had in mind novels typically focus on the individual life-story—classically, that part of the life-story canonized in the *Bildungsroman*—or on a series of episodes taken from the individual life. And the critical events and discussions which resolve such stories are rarely public in the usual sense of the term. The protagonist, having mastered the obstacles in his or her path, does not enter office or choose political sides in the final scene, but gets married, learns indispensable lessons about love or friendship, or achieves a long fought-for success in business or society.

This didn't matter. For what made language public was not the topics it covered or the places in which it circulated, but the *style* of it. In the novel language resonated differently because it was dramatized, provided with a setting, a context, a narrative frame. This applied obviously to the language spoken by characters, but equally to the kinds of anonymous generic language cited in novels and to the language of the narrative itself. An epistolary novel, set in the form of a series of letters, for example, implicitly provides a narrative setting for the writing of the letters: it provides us with motivations for their composition, establishes their succession as a meaningful sequence of events, informs us about the social context surrounding them, and so forth (likewise for novels which are set as diaries, chronicles, or tales told by a storyteller). Narrators themselves, whether or not they are provided with a name and a place in the story they relate, are also 'framed' by their own narratives, which frequently tell us more about the narrators then they themselves intend. In each such case, the dramatizing of discourse makes it 'dialogical' or 'double-voiced': its meaning and intonation depends on both the expressive intentions of the one speaking or writing (whether character or narrator) *and* on the narrative context or frame in which it is set. At its extreme, such double-voicedness can become parody, which means that the narrative context completely undermines or questions the meaning intended by the speaker. The underlying stylistic feature of all such language, however, is that in its presence discourse 'not only represents, but is itself represented' (Bakhtin, 1975b: 149/336): language conveys or expresses the intentions of a speaker and it is itself presented as a narrative event, with causes or motivations, a social context, consequences, and so on. To adapt a terminology familiar to Habermas, in the novel every utterance, even those of an anonymous narrator, appears as the bearer of both a propositional, moral or expressive content and as an action, a performative utterance with illocutionary force.

The theatre, rather than the debating chamber, therefore serves as the model for the public sphere: to become public means to be put on stage rather than to assume the podium. In this sense, even the most resounding utterance spoken by a sovereign or head of state remains 'private' and individualistic so far as it strives only to express the contents of a single or collective interiority. The 'official seriousness' of which Bakhtin was wholly contemptuous relies on a straightahead gaze and directness of speech. But Bakhtin was convinced that modernity had extinguished the force of all such commanding authority:

> The speech subjects of the high, pontificating genres—the priests, prophets, preachers, judges, leaders, patriarchal fathers, and the like—have passed from life. The writer has replaced them all, simply the writer who has become the heir to their styles. He either stylizes them (that is, assumes the pose of a prophet, a preacher, and so on) or parodies them (to a greater or lesser degree) (Bakhtin, 1986a: 355/132).

The Renaissance marks the turning point in this development, and it can furnish us with a convenient illustration of Bakhtin's thesis. Early seventeenth-century England is distinguished both by political absolutism and by the significance of theatre in its cultural life. In the context of the former, kings and queens speak with absolute authority and furnish the symbolic centre of political power. Their language, rhetorically shaped as it must be, is nevertheless endowed with aura and authority. Monarchs also speak in Elizabethan and Jacobean tragedy. But when put on stage, their language acquires a different hue. Set in the context of a dramatic action, words imbued with royal authority may inspire but they inevitably are 'double-voiced', visible as elements of a narrative action which endows them with a new layer of meaning. The words of Henry IV, Richard III or Macbeth both represent and are represented, and the very fact that royal discourse appears in theatrical guise at once undermines its absolutist claims.

Bakhtin himself, however, was suspicious of dramatic 'double-voicedness', for reasons which are interesting, if not entirely convincing. The tension evident in the double-voicedness of drama was, to his mind, local and resolvable. In the narrative proper to dramatic texts, he argued, the unspoken context provided by the dramatic action itself is absolutely secure; so secure, in fact, that it turns the intentions and discourse of the dramatis personae into mere instruments of its own overarching design. There has been a reasonable amount of dispute about this generalization in Bakhtin scholarship and Bakhtin himself makes clear that by drama he means not every instance of theatre without exception (he makes exceptions for Ibsen and Shakespeare, among others) but the ideal type of drama propounded in genre theory. But the distinctiveness he attributes to the novel in his account is important for our discussion:

> Prosaic double-voicedness is different. There—on the ground of novelistic prose—double-voicedness draws its energy, its dialogized ambiguity, not from individual

differences, misunderstandings and contradictions (however tragic, however firmly grounded in individual destinies); in the novel this double-voicedness sinks its roots deep into what is essentially a socio-linguistic diversity of speech and language. True, in the novel linguistic diversity is basically always personified, incarnated in individualized human figures who have individualized disagreements and contradictions. But in the novel these contradictions between individual wills and minds are submerged in the social diversity of language: they are reinterpreted through it. Contradictions between individuals in the novel are only the surface crests of the elemental force of social linguistic diversity, an elemental force which plays through them and imperiously deepens their contradictoriness, populating their consciousnesses and words with its own essential diverse character (Bakhtin, 1975b: 139: 325–6).[3]

In the novel, double-voicedness spreads from the individual characters outwards into the narrative design itself, which thereby loses its anchoring function. The reason is, at one level, obvious: unlike in drama, in the novel the contextualizing narrative is made of the same linguistic stuff as the discourse it contextualizes. But this reason only makes sense when you realize that for Bakhtin novelistic discourse is the paradigm of all linguistic expression.

In the inherited version of linguistics, natural languages (French, English, Latin, Punjabi, and so on) are understood as unified, if complex, structures that can be codified in metalinguistic texts like dictionaries and grammars. The conventions of grammar and the structured vocabulary these metalinguistic texts describe can be put into play by actual speaking subjects. On this account, style is the individual manner in which a subject, either singular (Flaubert) or collective (the Baroque), expresses itself in generally available linguistic forms. Like Habermas, Bakhtin believes a theoretical description of a language must be supplemented by some kind of 'universal pragmatics', if we are to understand how successful communication is possible.[4] Habermas, as we know, described the reciprocal expectations that speakers had to make in order for theoretical, moral and aesthetic utterances to be accepted as such. Bakhtin points to narrative. Because every utterance is simultaneously 'born in dialogue as a living reply within it' and 'directed towards an answer and cannot escape the profound influence of the answering word it anticipates' (Bakhtin, 1975b: 93/279–93/280), it cannot be understood in even the most ordinary sense unless you grasp its place in the narrative constituted by every conversation, every exchange of discourse. The point has been made with customary eloquence in another philosophical work indebted to narrative, Alasdair MacIntyre's *After Virtue*:

If I listen to a conversation between two people my ability to grasp the thread of the conversation will involve an ability to bring it under some one out of a set of descriptions in which the degree and kind of coherence in the conversation is brought out: 'a drunken, rambling quarrel', 'a serious intellectual disagreement', 'a tragic misunderstanding of each other', 'a comic, even farcical misconstrual of each other's motives', 'a penetrating interchange of views', 'a struggle to dominate each other', 'a trivial exchange of gossip'.

The use of such words as 'tragic', 'comic' and 'farcical' is not marginal to such evaluations. We allocate conversations to genres, just as we do literary narratives.

> Indeed a conversation is a dramatic event, even if a very short one, in which the participants are not only the actors, but also the joint authors, working out in agreement or disagreement the mode of their production. For it is not just that conversations belong to genres in just the way that plays and novels do; but they have beginnings, middles and endings just as do literary works. They embody reversals and recognitions; they move towards and away from climaxes. There may within a longer conversation be digressions and subplots, indeed digressions within digressions and subplots within subplots (MacIntyre, 1985, 211).

When we speak, we narrate. Not in the sense that we tell a story but in the sense that we participate in creating the narrative which we need in order for a conversation (or any other linguistic exchange) to take place. To accomplish this we must not only respond to others in a second-person attitude but, simultaneously, take a third-person view of the conversation itself, just as if we were characters in a novel and the author of that novel at one and the same time. Discourse entails an exchange of utterances which is at the same time the mutual elaboration of a narrative.

'The task', Bakhtin commented, 'consists of forcing the *thing-like* environment, acting mechanically on the personality, to speak, that is, to disclose within it a potential discourse and tone, to transform it into the semantic context of a thinking, speaking and acting (in this sense, creating) personality' (Bakhtin, 1986: 387/164). Which is to say: the task is to force one's way into the process of elaborating the narrative that controls the sense and significance of one's own discourse. But once you have broken down the barrier between your own discourse and the narrative that frames it, between your second-person address to others and your third-person perception of the conversation as narrative or drama, linguistic structures are bound to look different. Your own language and the language spoken or written by others means more than you intended, for it is now part of a necessarily social action ('Every word', Bakhtin once said, 'tastes of the context and contexts in which it has lived its socially tensed life' (Bakhtin, 1975b: 106/293)). Conversely, natural languages begin to appear as a collocation of possible narrative structures, which will often collide and conflict with one another. The consciousness that has successfully novelized its world 'finds not language, but "languages". It confronts the necessity of having to *choose a language*' (Bakhtin, 1975b, 108/295). This forced choice is the precondition of modern novelistic style:

> The internal stratification of a unified national language into social dialects, group manners, professional jargons, generic languages, the languages of generations and age groups, the languages of tendencies, the languages of authorities, the languages of intellectual circles and passing fashions, the languages of socio-political days and even hours (for each day has its own slogan, its own vocabulary, its own accents), this internal stratification of every language at every given moment of its historical existence, is the necessary prerequisite for the novel as a genre: the novel orchestrates all its themes, its entire represented and expressed object world by means of this social heteroglossia and the multiple individual voices growing on its soil (Bakhtin, 1975b/1981: 76/262–3).

These 'socio-ideological languages' are not expressions of collective subjects but contextualized modes of speaking and acting. Novels do not merely represent this 'social heteroglossia' (a neologism which I translated in the earlier quotation as 'social diversity of language'): they embody it, because they demonstrate how the progress of a discourse creates its own narrative scaffolding. All a responsible and democratic citizenry need do is follow their example.

And that, of course, is the problem. The modern novel, which relentlessly scrutinizes the details of everyday linguistic usage, obsessively connects these to contemporary forms of social classification, and represents these social forms of linguistic exchange through the extensive deployment of irony and parody, did not emerge fully-grown from the womb of natural language. There has always been narrative and there has always been discourse, but the dialogical intertwining of the two that one finds in the novel is as much a distinctively modern achievement as the postconventional morality so highly prized by Habermas. Bakhtin claims novelistic style demands a 'conscious awareness of the historical and social concreteness and relatedness of living discourse, of its participation in historical becoming and social struggle' (Bakhtin, 1975b: 144/331) but he does not acknowledge that such a consciousness of language is itself something socially and historically concrete: it emerges, like the public sphere itself, in the course of the struggles that put an end to the European *ancien regime*. The dialogical novel combines a distinctively modern kind of narrative—in which the future is constitutively open and uncertain, fashioned by human efforts—with a distinctly modern form of language.

What makes the language of the novel 'modern'? Three historical changes define it. The first is the replacement of Latin as an official language by the European vernaculars in the period just before and during the Renaissance. When Bakhtin speaks of the 'fundamental liberation of cultural-semantic and expressive intentions from the power of a single, unified language' (Bakhtin, 1975b: 178/367) he is thinking of the dethroning of Latin which, in the European Middle Ages, served as a distinct and authoritative 'language of truth', distant from the socially coloured and variegated discourse of the not yet nationalized vernaculars. For the language world as a whole to function as 'heteroglossia', and for the novel's narrative to blend with its constituent voices, it's essential that no part of it is able to establish an ersatz authority based on its apparent resistance to change or its location in the most powerful cultural and political institutions. The second, and related, consideration is the rise of print culture and its effects on the written form of language. Print consolidated the triumph of the European vernaculars as the dominant media for political, scientific, religious and artistic discourse, but it also created a discursive space within which different kinds of language could jostle and intersect. Finally, the rise of a distinctly historical consciousness in Europe at the time of the Renaissance made a new sense of the mutability of language possible, which eventually put paid to the notion that all language change represented decline from an Adamic, pristine initial state.

Bakhtin did not give these factors their due weight in his analysis: he wanted to present the dialogical novel as the flowering of tendencies innate in *any* language and no doubt thought that binding its achievement to the contingencies of European history would undermine his case. But the more we examine his theory with distinctively twenty-first century eyes, the more shrewd and useful it appears to be. Unlike Habermas' work, Bakhtin's waited until just the right moment to make its translated appearance in the capitalist West.

The expression of suffering

When Habermas demoted the public sphere to the status of a 'warning system with sensors that, though unspecialized, are sensitive throughout society' (Habermas, 1996: 359) he explicitly relieved it of the burden of having to solve problems, that is, of having to produce a rational solution to questions of social policy, based on debate, the accumulation of evidence and so forth. These, in his more sober later writing, are reserved for political institutions in the strict sense. But what looks like an admission of defeat here may in fact be a very shrewd move. For what the public sphere loses in terms of decision-making power it more than compensates for in terms of its ability to track the problems of capitalism down to their private lair. In its revised form, the public sphere 'draws its impulses from the private handling of social problems that resonate in life histories' (Habermas, 1996: 366), which means it becomes the point at which politics and the life histories of individuals intersect:

> (I)n the diverse voices of this public, one hears the echoes of private experiences that are caused throughout society by the externalities (and internal disturbances) of various functional systems—and even by the very state apparatus on whose regulatory activities the complex and poorly coordinated sub-systems depend. Systemic deficiencies are experienced in the context of individual life histories; such burdens accumulate in the lifeworld. The latter has the appropriate antennae, for in its horizon are intermeshed the private life histories of the 'clients' of functional systems that might be failing in their delivery of services . . . Besides religion, art, and literature, only the spheres of 'private' life have an existential language at their disposal, in which such socially generated problems can be *assessed in terms of one's own life history.* (Habermas, 1996: 365).

'Systemic deficiencies' and failure in the 'delivery of services': Habermas's functionalist idiom is polite language for the ruthless exploitation of workers, the impoverishment of families and individuals, and the brutality with which powerless people in liberal capitalist states are denied even the most basic human dignities. The public sphere is uniquely suited to the demystifying of these problems in liberal capitalist societies. In contrast to theories of ideology, theories of the public sphere do not have to explain how capitalist societies manage to gain the consent of those who stand to lose the most in them. No matter how sophisticated a theory of ideology may be, it still sets itself the task of demonstrating how a certain worldview or social horizon triumphs in the consciousness of the many: it assumes that social stability means consent. But liberal capitalism does not need blanket consent to function, nor does it need to persuade majority opinion of its virtues. It only needs to ensure that dissatisfaction with the course of one's life never becomes a focus for politically-orientated action. The secret weapon of its ruling class is the ability to 'externalize' problems, that is, to separate the misery and dissatisfaction caused by political and economic arrangements from the system itself and to anchor them in the cut-off sphere of individual life-histories. Recent discussions of the triumph of capitalism contrast the clearly-expressed dissatisfaction of those who lived under historical Communism with the consent of liberal-capitalist citizens. But this demonstrates not so much that liberal capitalism has produced a contented citizenry as that it has managed to ensure that the unhappiness and discontent it produces is systematically dissociated from the business of politics.

The social suffering inflicted on the citizens and migrants of liberal capitalist societies is well enough documented (see, for example, Bourdieu *et al*, 1999). And certainly one sees this suffering represented on a regular basis on television, at the cinema, while reading the newspaper or listening to music. It's a striking and distinctive feature of these societies in the late twentieth and early twenty-first centuries that they are far more 'democratic', far less censored, in the range of what they represent in the media, than previously (although it remains the case that in the US in particular, the subject matter is skewed towards a phantasmatic version of 'middle class' existence, *Roseanne* and Jerry Springer notwithstanding). But the limit of this democracy is found in the narrative shape of the stories that are told and in the style in which suffering is expressed and described.

Raymond Williams once commented that today drama is 'built into the rhythms of everyday life . . . What we have now is drama as habitual experience; more in a week, in many cases, than most human beings would previously have seen in a lifetime' (Williams, 1989: 4). But this ever present drama has not been worked out from the ground up: it's largely a creature of the broadcasting industry. As a consequence, it tends to lack the 'openness' and uncertainty characteristic of narrative forms that presuppose a mutual effort of elaboration. The novel is permeated with 'the spontaneity of the unfinished present' (Bakhtin, 1975a: 471/27) precisely to the extent that it mimics the mutual elaboration of narrative in conversation. Although novels are not dialogues, when they are 'double-voiced' they offer up their discourse as something incomplete, which refers outward to the reader, so to speak, for his or her response. The reader who realizes that a narrator is, to use the traditional terminology, 'unreliable', for whom none of the language in the novel can be taken on faith (because all of its is held at a distance by the novel itself), must ascertain the truth without the help of an authoritative discourse to guide her or him. But 'systemic deficiencies' and the suffering they entail are generally dramatized in a different manner. The dominant tendency of the last twenty years has not been to hide humiliation and suffering, but to display it in an increasingly 'confessional' and melodramatic manner. This suffering, however, appears in the narrative (and this applies to 'human interest' stories in the news as much as to fiction) as an experience which exists only to spur on the protagonist's moral development or self-improvement, as a lesson from which the one who suffers must draw a usually rather moralizing conclusion. The expression of the suffering itself is thus characteristically 'single-voiced', in so far as it strives to present itself as only the externalization of a raw, isolated subjectivity. But as Bakhtin has shrewdly observed, we can only encounter the external signs of another's subjectivity in the form of something worldly, as signs or representations, bodily movements and facial expressions. As a result the raw expressions of feeling we are likely to confront in most of the drama we consume week in and week out has an object-like character for us. This is hardly surprising, if we bear in mind that however much contemporary drama may dwell on the pseudo-immediacy of the suffering it represents to us, the path of development its narratives trace has nothing spontaneous about it. Characters do not really develop in Anglo-American dramatic culture—they conform to a prescribed model, and the suffering they undergo is always calculated to lead them to a predetermined state of emotional or psychological 'maturity'. However strikingly expressed, the indignities, anxieties and humiliations displayed in this manner have soft edges, because in the end they figure not as problems which a narrative must explore, but as a leash that guides characters to an ending that reassures everybody.

By ensuring that little is at stake in socially induced suffering, the culture of liberal capitalist regimes keeps painful 'systemic deficiencies' at arm's length. The public sphere Habermas has in mind counterattacks by allowing citizens to question one another about their experiences, motives and reasons for action (in which case, Jerry Springer, minus the staged confrontations, might just qualify). It 'floats' the existential commitments we make on the tide of language by taking advantage of the fact that claims to be speaking truthfully, appropriately, and the truth can always be asked to produce reasons or behaviour to back them up. Through the crevices in discourse which allow one to 'open up' the discussion of life experiences, citizens are able to connect problems experienced in individual life histories to wider social structures. But the weaknesses of this approach to the broadening of perspectives are familiar enough to make us wonder whether other tactics might occasionally come in handy. The approach of discursive reason often fails because it cannot short-circuit the economy of an expressive language that, however self-deluding, still satisfies its customers. When self-dramatization is too powerful a genre, its grip might be loosened by 'novelizing' the material, rather than trying to force it into the mould of explicitly political discourse. The imaginative reshaping of ordinary language, its stylization through the provision of unexpected contexts, aims to restore to it an element of spontaneity. Bakhtin correctly intuited that to 'represent' the language one used, *while using it*, meant getting into a new relation with language, exemplified by the kind of aesthetic distance novelistic writing could put between the reader and its expressive discourse. If dialogism is successful, a familiar language ought to *sound* different. But a language held at a distance in this fashion is also, ironically, a language in a position to shape its own context and narrative. Connecting lifeworld problems and the suffering they induce with political and economic arrangements—which amounts to recognizing systemic deficiencies *as* systemic deficiencies—entails bridging the gap between the language of our suffering and the narrative which determines its 'place'. This gap isn't bridged by a new vocabulary, or by a shrewd combination of words. It depends on a different *style* of discourse, in which the narrative of our social history emerges out of the various languages we use rather than serving as their mute, but all-powerful background.

The weakness of ordinary language

The public sphere makes itself felt in every encounter 'in which actors do not just observe each other but take a second-person attitude, reciprocally attributing communicative freedom to each other' (Habermas, 1996: 361). For all Bakhtin's talk of 'dialogue', he has in mind something rather different: not the equitable and symmetrical situation of conversation (which Bakhtin, in fact, hardly ever mentions), but the asymmetrical relationship between a novel and its constituent 'voices'. The stylization of public and ordinary language cannot rely on the unplanned efforts of ordinary conversation: it requires an imaginative, 'carnivalesque', if you like, re-dramatization of language, which usually depends upon larger structures, in particular the narratives we encounter in print and in the visual media. Bakhtin rather unconvincingly argued that the structures of the novel are extrapolations of tendencies located at the heart of ordinary language, that novelistic 'dialogism' is ordinary dialogue writ large. But the relationship he hit upon was in fact the reverse: in a complex society, with advanced forms of print and visual media, the distinction between ordinary and second-level discourse begins to blur, as we embed the narrative and stylistic techniques we find beyond ourselves in our everyday language and the narrative models that drive it. All of which amounts to the recognition that in the liberal capitalist societies, one has to fight fire with fire.

Ordinary language, by virtue of the pragmatic presuppositions on which its employment depends, does indeed possess the potential to create linguistically constituted spaces of communication. But the time has long passed when it could claim a style or form distinctly its own. Since the advent of a democratizing culture industry, willing to frame and broadcast ordinary language back to its source—the population at large—ordinary language has itself felt the influence of the specialized media beyond it. It's no longer a law unto itself: today, the existential language of our life histories takes much of its form, syntax and vocabulary from the print and visual media which claim merely to represent it. In this context, the task of a public sphere is not only to set ordinary language in motion, but to restore to it a fluidity which popular culture systematically threatens. Which is to say that when 'sociability has become a compulsory universal initiation rite; when *dialogue*, withered to unimpeachable propriety, lacks the logos, lacks the individual, and, lacking these, lacks—dialogue' (Jarvis, 2000: 22) it may be that democracy depends on something a little less spur-of-the-moment and a little more artful than we might have supposed. When ordinary, everyday language has been penetrated by the rhythms and intonation of the culture industry which relentlessly surrounds it, it needs a push to get the engine of public opinion going.

Habermas is himself not unaware of the peculiar status of cultural discourse. Discussing civil society and the public sphere, he singles out religion, art and literature for sharing, with private life, an 'existential language'. At the same time, however, he is aware that this existential language circulates through what are in fact highly specialized, functionally differentiated institutions: 'To the extent that these experiences [of socially generated problems, KH] find their concise expression in the languages of religion, art, and literature, the 'literary public sphere' in the broader sense, which is specialized for the articulation of values and world disclosure, is intertwined with the political public sphere' (Habermas, 1996: 365). But in assigning literature the role of way-station between private life-history and politics, Habermas has passed over the problematic and distinctive features of artistic discourse (in its print and its electronic forms), which have consequences not only for its own role, but for the operation of the political public sphere 'at the summit' as well.

In fact, artistic prose as we find it in print, film and television entails both a specialized and an ordinary form of discourse. As a craft and a multi-billion pound industry it entails a highly specialized critical, business and technical language, which reaches an apogee of sorts in the current practice of academic literary and film criticism. But the 'product' of this discourse is, as we know, couched in a concise, reworked form of the 'existential language' in which people interpret their own life-histories. Even thirty years ago, Enzensberger pointed out that the democratizing of the media entailed not the denial of 'artistic' or 'professional' specialization, but the harnessing of it to the socialist project (Enzensberger, 1970). An artistic prose capable of transforming our existential language into something with narrative force is unlikely to emerge from the interaction of well-intentioned citizens alone: it would require a specialized and organized practice consciously aimed at the emancipation of the existential language currently in circulation, which is itself in large part a product of the culture industry.

Justice and the future

In novelistic prose, time exists as 'becoming, as uninterrupted movement into a real future' (Bakhtin, 1975a: 473/30). Such an open future cannot be willed into existence by even the most talented writer or intellectual: it depends on democratic convictions that value the idea that we should mutually elaborate our interpretation of the past and cooperatively determine the directions in which we intend to proceed.

Nevertheless, the point of a novelistic public sphere is not merely to drama-tize issues and problems so that they can then be properly processed by politi-cal reason. The dramatic qualities a public sphere needs bear on the substance of the public sphere as well: they show us the weaknesses and limitations of a public sphere based on discourse ethics. Habermas believes the public sphere is capable of unleashing a procedural rationality embedded in the pragmatics of everyday language, but he is careful to point out that such a rationality can only decide questions of justice: moral questions which admit of universalist answers. At one point Habermas went so far as to claim that if you could not sufficiently distance yourself from the contingencies of your lifeworld to make principled argument possible, this demonstrated that the question you were contemplating was not a moral, but an ethical one (see Habermas, 1993: 1–18 and 165–76). But why the subject should launch itself into the decentred space of procedural ratio-nality remained an unsolved question, and the most pragmatic limitation of Habermas's otherwise shrewdly practical theory. Once Habermas abandoned the notion of an emancipatory interest in the 1960s, he was stuck with the tradi-tional and time-honoured difficulty of all Kantian ethics: how to motivate the subject to act rationally, when acting rationally means self-regulation, that is, acting against your own inclinations and desires.

Habermas sought an answer that would not compromise the purity of prac-tical reason:

> This much is true: any universalistic morality is dependent upon a form of life that *meets it halfway*. There has to be a modicum of congruence between morality and the practices of socialization and education. The latter must promote the requisite inter-nalization of superego controls and the abstractness of ego identities. In addition, there must be a modicum of fit between morality and socio-political institutions. Not just any institutions will do. Morality thrives only in an environment in which post-conventional ideas about law and morality have already been institutionalised to a certain extent (Habermas, 1990, 208–9).

Which is reasonable enough (pardon the pun), but begs the question of why subjects would institutionalize a Kantian, universalist morality in the first place. That this answer does not quite do the trick has been recognized by Habermas and others committed, at least in part, to discourse ethics. Claus Offe, noting the weakness of all strategies of self-limitation (and bearing in mind the with-ering critique of Adorno on this score), suggested that civil society had to encourage or foster institutional and associational designs that would make acting on universalist precepts less risky for the individual subject (Offe, 1992). For his part, Habermas has turned to modern law for help. Acknowledging that rationally arrived at convictions cannot be the basis of all behaviour, Habermas argues that the facticity of modern law, its astute combination of 'de facto con-straint and rational validity' (Habermas, 1996: 27) allows it to step into the void. Law 'removes tasks of social integration from actors who are already overbur-dened in their efforts at reaching understanding' (Habermas, 1996: 38). By setting up rational norms which can also be viewed as enforceable facts, the legal

63

system establishes a normative world with which subjects can go along with the simple motive of wanting a quiet life. In this respect, Habermas has not suggested any new kind of motivation for rational conduct: he merely suggests that the enforceability of law means that citizens can obey it for purely strategic, self-interested reasons when they can't bring themselves to obey it for 'real' reasons.

But there may be other kinds of motivation that can be brought to bear. If the legacy of modernity includes not only procedural rationality but also the notion of an open history that nevertheless hangs together as narrative, then perhaps a certain desire for stories will also lead us to demand a different role in the determining of social priorities. Just as 'modern' subjects cannot do without certain pragmatic presuppositions when they argue, so they are unwilling to limit themselves to an existential language that is merely and solely private and expressive. We need life-histories with a satisfying shape, and two requirements of that shape are an open uncertain future and a sense of connection with larger stories: stories of families, nations, movements or whatever. Modern states spare no effort to provide national stories in which their citizens can embed their private histories. Sometimes these stories are decidedly ethnic and involve no more than the expression of given national characteristics over long stretches of history. At other times they rely on principles (as embodied in a declaration or constitution) the continual re-enactment of which provides a sense of continuity. But in nearly every case, the future evoked in such collective histories is 'monumental', as Bakhtin might have put it, not a real future, but the future memory of the past, that is, the desire for a future that will remember the sacrifices made now, today, in its name and commemorate those sacrifices by remaining true to their unchanging cause.

The systemic deficiencies of a liberal capitalist order create unjust outcomes, but they also make successful life-histories difficult. And just as no one can act strategically all of the time, so no one can be satisfied with a life which is no more than one damn thing after another. To harness the demand for stories to a democratic project we need to focus on the narrative 'disappointment' experienced by so many citizens and migrants and on the false narrative isolation of lifeworld problems from larger structures. A public sphere that willingly takes up this task will not surrender the cause of justice. But the justice it speaks of will be one that remembers enslaved grandparents, anticipates liberated grandchildren, and draws their emancipation together in a compelling narrative.

Notes

1 Mulhern is speaking of the British 'New Times' project led by reforming elements in the Communist Party, but the phrase applies more generally.

2 This political tone and vocabulary is the object of a good deal of critical dispute in Bakhtin scholarship. There is a body of Bakhtin commentary which argues vociferously that Bakhtin never intended to write in an 'ethical' or 'moral' idiom (he wrote fragments of a never-finished work of 'ethical philosophy' sometime in the 1920s) and that the political tone of the later work is merely a shell or disguise forced on him as an accommodation to Stalinism. Although this line is prin-

cipally argued by Russian commentators, it has American devotées in the persons of Gary Saul Morson and Caryl Emerson (Morson and Emerson, 1990). For a Russian version of the argument see Bocharov (1994).

3 References to Bakhtin include a page reference to the original Russian followed by a page reference to the published English translation. The translations which appear in this text are my own, and will differ slightly from the existing published versions.

4 According to their accepted profiles, Bakhtin and Habermas occupy opposite ends of the intellectual spectrum: Habermas is the dry rationalist and systematic philosopher who takes sociology very seriously, while Bakhtin is the wild spiritualist essayist who trusts language to knock down every system in its way. The contrast has some truth to it, but it obscures their shared origins and continued devotion to neo-Kantian thought. This isn't just a matter of Bakhtin's professed devotions to the neo-Kantian cause (which he reiterated until the very end of his life), but the inner structure of his argument, which often merely translates the project of neo-Kantian culture philosophy into the discourse of linguistics.

Bibliography

Bakhtin, M. M. (1929) *Problemy tvorchestva Dostoevskogo*. Leningrad: Priboi. Translation: As Appendix to *Problems of Dostoevsky's Poetics* (1984), translated by C. Emerson. Minneapolis: University of Minnesota Press.

Bakhtin, M. M. (1975a) 'Epos i roman' in *Voprosy literatury i estetiki*, Moscow: Khudozhestvennaia literatura. Translation: 'Epic and Novel' in *The Dialogic Imagination* (1981), translated by M. Holquist and C. Emerson. Austin, Texas and London: University of Texas Press.

Bakhtin, M. M. (1975b) 'Slovo v romane' [1934–35] in *Voprosy literatury i estetiki*. Moscow: Khudozhestvennaia literatura. Translation: 'Discourse in the Novel' in *The Dialogic Imagination* (1981), translated by M. Holquist and C. Emerson. Austin, Texas and London: University of Texas Press.

Bakhtin, M. M. (1986a) 'Iz zapisei 1970–1971 godov' ['From the Notes of 1970–1971'] in *Estetika slovesnogo tvorchestva*, 2nd edition. Moscow: Isskustvo, 355–80. Translation: *Speech Genres and Other Late Essays* (1986), edited by M. Holquist and C. Emerson, translated by V. W. McGee. Austin, Texas: University of Texas Press.

Bakhtin, Mikhail (1986b) 'K metodologii gumanitarnykh nauk' ['Towards a Methodology of the Human Sciences'], in *Estetika slovesnogo tvorchestva*, 2nd edition, Moscow: Isskustvo, 381–93. Translation: *Speech Genres and Other Late Essays* (1986). Edited by M. Holquist and C. Emerson. Translated by V. W. McGee. Austin, Texas: University of Texas Press.

Bakhtin, M. M. (1990) *Tvorchestvo Fransua Rable i narodnaia kul'tura srednekov'ia i renessansa*, Moscow: Khudozhestvennaia literatura. Translation: *Rabelais and His World* (1986), translated by H. Iswolsky. Cambridge, Mass.: MIT Press.

Bakhtin, M. M. (1996a) 'Dopolneniia i izmeneniia k *Rable*' ['Additions and Amendments to *Rabelais*'] in *Sobranie sochinenii v semi tomakh, tom 5, Raboty 1940-kh—nachala 1960-kh godov* [*Collected Works in seven volumes, Vol. 5, Works from the 1940s to the beginning of the 1960s*], edited by S. G. Bocharov and L. A. Gogotishvili. Moscow: Russkie slovari: 80–129.

Bakhtin, M. M. (1996b) 'Iazyk v khudozhesvennoi literature' ['Language in Artistic Literature'] in *Sobranie sochinenii v semi tomakh, tom 5, Raboty 1940-kh—nachala 1960-kh godov* [*Collected Works in seven volumes, Vol. 5, Works from the 1940s to the beginning of the 1960s*], edited by S. G. Bocharov and L. A. Gogotishvili, Moscow: Russkie slovari: 287–97.

Bocharov, S. (1994) 'Conversations with Bakhtin', *PMLA* 109: 5, 1009–24.

Bourdieu, P. *et al* (1999) *The Weight of the World: Social Suffering in Contemporary Society*, translated by P. P. Ferguson, S. Emanuel, J. Johnson and S. Y. Waryn. Cambridge: Polity Press.

Calhoun, C. (1992) 'Introduction: Habermas and the Public Sphere' in C. Calhoun (ed.) *Habermas and the Public Sphere*. Cambridge, Mass.: MIT Press: 1–48.

Enzensberger, H. M. (1970) 'Constituents of a Theory of the Media', *New Left Review* 64: 13–36.

Fraser, N. (1992) 'Rethinking the Public Sphere: A Contribution to the Critique of Actually Existing Democracy' in C. Calhoun (ed.) *Habermas and the Public Sphere*. Cambridge, Mass.: MIT Press: 109–42.

Habermas, J. (1985) 'Right and Violence—A German Trauma', *Cultural Critique* 1: 125–39.

Habermas, J. (1987) *The Philosophical Discourse of Modernity*, translated by F. Lawrence. Cambridge: Polity Press.

Habermas, J. (1989) *The Structural Transformation of the Public Sphere: An Inquiry into a Category of Bourgeois Society*, translated by T. Burger and F. Lawrence. Cambridge, Mass. and London: MIT Press.

Habermas, J. (1990) 'Morality and Ethical Life: Does Hegel's Critique of Kant Apply to Discourse Ethics? in *Moral Consciousness and Communicative Action*, translated by C. Lenhardt and S. W. Nicholson. Cambridge, Mass: MIT Press: 195–215.

Habermas, J. (1992a) 'Further Reflections on the Public Sphere' in C. Calhoun (ed.) *Habermas and the Public Sphere*. Cambridge, Mass.: MIT Press: 421–61.

Habermas, J. (1992b) 'Concluding Remarks' in C. Calhoun (ed.) *Habermas and the Public Sphere*. Cambridge, Mass.: MIT Press: 462–79.

Habermas, J. (1993) *Justification and Application: Remarks on Discourse Ethics*, translated by C. P. Cronin. Cambridge, Mass.: MIT Press.

Habermas, J. (1996) *Between Facts and Norms: Contributions to a Discourse Theory of Law and Democracy*, translated by W. Rehg. Cambridge: Polity Press.

Hirschkop, K. (2000) 'It's Too Good to Talk: Myths of Dialogue in Bakhtin and Habermas', *New Formations* 41: 83–93.

Jarvis, S. (2000) 'The Future of Monologue', *New Formations* 41: 21–30.

MacIntyre, A. (1985) *After Virtue*, 2nd edition. London: Duckworth.

Morson, G. S. and C. Emerson (1990) *Mikhail Bakhtin: The Creation of a Prosaics*. Stanford, Ca.: Stanford University Press.

Mulhern, F. (2000) *Culture/Metaculture*. London and New York: Routledge.

Offe, C. (1992) 'Bindings, Shackles, Brakes: On Self-Limitation Strategies' in A. Honneth, T. McCarthy, C. Offe, C. and A. Wellmer (eds). *Cultural-Political Interventions in the Unfinished Project of Enlightenment*, translated by B. Fultner. Cambridge, Mass.: MIT Press: 63–94.

Robbins, B. (ed.) (1993) *The Phantom Public Sphere*, Cultural Politics Series, vol. 5. Minneapolis and London: University of Minnesota Press.

Voloshinov, V. N. (1973) *Marxism and the Philosophy of Language*, translated by L. Matejka. New York: Seminar Press.

Williams, R. (1989) 'Drama in a Dramatised Society' in *Raymond Williams on Television*, edited by A. O'Connor. London: Routledge.

John Stuart Mill, free speech and the public sphere: a Bakhtinian critique

John Michael Roberts

Introduction

John Stuart Mill is often regarded as one of the modern founders of a theory of free speech as is clearly seen in his theory of the liberty of thought and discussion (see Baum, 2001; Haworth, 1998; O'Rourke, 2001). What I want to demonstrate in this chapter, however, is that Mill constructs not so much a rationale for free speech as a defence of the liberal form of the bourgeois public sphere. This defence is predicated upon a peculiar aesthetic of cultivated intelligence that is itself based upon what Mill terms as the pursuit of 'higher pleasures'. By recourse to the dialogic theory of the Bakhtin Circle I argue that, *in reality*, such a standpoint is highly restrictive because it serves to silence public utterances of a majority of individuals. Moreover it legitimates an ideological form of the capitalist state, namely the liberal form of the state. Thus, those public spheres which do not practise higher pleasures can expect their utterances to be regulated through the coercive body of the liberal state. I illustrate these points by showing how Mill constructs his theory of the liberty of thought and discussion through an implicit dialogue with Chartist public spheres. I begin the chapter by explaining the term 'public dialogue' by expanding upon the insights of the Bakhtin Circle.

The Bakhtin Circle and public dialogic

The dialogic theory of Mikhail Bakhtin and his colleagues, known collectively as the Bakhtin Circle, and including P. N. Medvedev and V. N. Voloshinov, can be explored through a number of interlocking points. First, according to the Bakhtin Circle, dialogue always operates within specific historical social relations such as capitalism. Further, some in the Circle argue that the different forms that social relations assume are mediated through the determining moment of a mode of production. This determining moment reacts upon other social forms of life and *vice versa*. Thus the Bakhtin Circle rejects a 'mechanical causality' that reduces social life to the dictates of the socio-economic base.

Rather the Bakhtin Circle argues that each social form is an ideological and unified whole in its own right that nevertheless refracts the determinations of socio-economic relations. Thus changes in an ideological form may prove problematic for the reproduction of socio-economic relations. 'Therefore any explanation must preserve *all the qualitative differences* between interacting domains and must trace all the various stages through which change travels' (Voloshinov, 1973: 18). That is to say, a social form not only reflects socio-economic relations, it also refracts socio-economic relations, as well as other social forms, in its own unique way (see Bakhtin, 1981: 326; Bakhtin and Medvedev, 1978: 16 ff.; Voloshinov, 1973: 23; for a discussion of 'refraction' in Marxist theory see Roberts, 2002).

Second, the Bakhtin Circle insist that a theory of dialogue must aim to capture the conflicts and contradictions internal to a set of social relations. At a transcendental level Voloshinov (1973) argues that this can be achieved by first locating the 'unit' of dialogue that will represent a starting point to understand the developed dialogic whole of historical social relations such as capitalist social relations. Voloshinov discovers this starting point of analysis in the word. Voloshinov notes that the word is the most suitable starting point for a dialogic analysis of the internal relationship between 'base' and 'superstructure' because the word is present in each and every act of understanding. Standing as 'the purest and most sensitive medium of social intercourse', the word is a 'neutral' sign to the extent that it can transform its ideological allegiance across a whole spectrum of ideological fields such as science, art, religion, politics and so forth. A word, therefore, is a crucial medium for the ideological organization of social life (Voloshinov, 1973: 14).

Third, the Bakhtin Circle's theory of dialogue is integrally related to time. A word is the most 'sensitive index of social changes' and can register 'all the transitory, delicate, momentary phases of social change' (Voloshinov, 1973: 19). Thus for the Bakhtin Circle a word contains social evaluations which then acquire new evaluations within a given community of speakers in a given context. By appropriating particular words, a community of speakers will endow them with new evaluations. Thus each word contains both 'concrete' and 'abstract' moments because it will have relatively autonomous evaluations which can be appropriated within specific contexts.

Fourth, this theory of dialogue suggests that each word contains an 'inner dialectic quality'. This dialectical quality relates to the manner by which a word refracts the contradictory nature of the world. For this reason a word will acquire different 'accents' composed of different evaluations. A word is thereby, at the same, an *utterance* structured by evaluative expressions that establish hierarchical relationships between speaker and listener in particular contexts. To put the point another way, utterances represent the sedimented and ideological expression of past interaction between a community of speakers located in a temporal and spatial context. These utterances become dislodged from a particular dialogical context and are transformed into 'public property' to the extent that past accents can be appropriated by a new community of speakers and 're-accented'. The *potential* for specific ideological conflict is therefore embedded within the very form of the word. Consequently the utterance represents the 'generative' moment of speech because it denotes the 'real units that make up the stream of language-speech' (Voloshinov, 1973: 96). That is to say, utterances render explicit the dialogic relationship between speaker and listener as well as the evaluational rank through which dialogue between participants is embedded. Yet this special property of utterances is already contained within a single word.

Fifth, dialectical utterances encapsulated within a word are transformed into speech performance and speech genre. The former refers to everyday interaction of 'unofficial discussions, exchanges of opinion at theatre or a concert or at various types of social gatherings, etc.' The latter refers to those evaluative accents embedded in the form of speech employed by particular social groups. Speech genres are associated with 'fixed social custom' that 'commands a particular kind of organization of audience and, hence, a particular repertoire of little behavioural genres' (Voloshinov, 1973: 97). From speech performance and speech genre Voloshinov derives the theme and meaning of an utterance. The theme of an utterance refers to the unitary significance of an utterance. Theme is 'the concrete, historical situation that engendered the utterance' (Voloshinov, 1973: 99). To understand the theme of an utterance is to also understand something about the historical instant to which the utterance belongs. Theme cannot therefore be reproduced to other contexts. Meaning, on the other hand, refers to reproduction of a theme within a variety of dialogic contexts. One word can therefore have a number of meanings but only one theme. By understanding the dialectical relationship between theme and meaning we begin to gain an insight into the unique forms of specific speech performance and speech genre (Voloshinov, 1973: 20).

Sixth, dialogism draws our attention to the dialogic conflict that ensues between a social group aiming for dominance and hegemony over another social group. The important terms in this respect are *monologue* and *heteroglossia*. According to Voloshinov the most insidious ideas are those linked with ruling-class ideas. In particular he is critical of those who develop an 'abstract objectivist' approach to the study of language. This approach views language as comprising the '*isolated, finished, monologic utterance*, divorced from its verbal and actual context and standing open not to any sort of active response but to passive understanding on the part of a philologist . . .' (Voloshinov, 1973: 73). That is to say, the monologic utterance represents the dominance of abstract, alienated and dead language over the inner dialectical quality of utterances (see Bakhtin, 1984: 79).

Against the centralizing forces of monologic discourse the Bakhtin Circle counterposes heteroglossic dialogue. Heteroglossia is a centrifugal dialogue that strives to make visible the multiaccentual, and thereby inner-dialectical, nature of words. Heteroglossia seeks to overcome the uniaccentual meaning of monologic words. The reason for this requirement is clear. Language enables self-reflection and the formation of a self-critical consciousness. Utterances imply evaluation and evaluation denotes the potential for dialogism about particular right-claims, powers, and immunities of subordinate groups. Heteroglossia is thus the constant dialogic means of rendering visible the contradictory social mediation of monologic dialogue. In order to quell the thirst for antagonism, monologic discourse must penetrate the 'languages' of heteroglossia and resonate an internally persuasive agenda (see Voloshinov, 1973: 23).

Seventh, dialogic struggle develops devices to represent and organize the ideological themes that emanate from these struggles. These 'devices' operate along different lines depending upon whether they are mediated through monologic or heteroglossic discourse. Monologic discourse seeks to separate device from ideological material. Indeed, material is seen as being ready-made and as existing outside of the organizing force of device. Material is therefore a mere motivation for device and is completely replaceable by it (Bakhtin and Medvedev, 1978: 110). As a result device is positioned as being 'ideologically neutral' due to its separation from the ideology of material. Heteroglossic discourse sees device and meaning as dialectically fused. It is just not the case that device can simply appropriate material and use it for its own purposes. Thus the device used to represent and organize material contain specific evaluations. At a minimum this implies that a device chosen simultaneously 'defines the choice of subject, word, form, and their individual combination within the bounds of a given utterance' (Bakhtin and Medvedev, 1978: 121).

Seventh, struggles around an utterance create 'a compact and singular phonetic unity' (Bakhtin and Medvedev, 1978: 101) unique to the utterance in question. That is to say, sound enters into a relationship with meaning through an ideological context in which a sound gains a unique and non-repeatable identity. Sound is therefore a socially meaningful moment of dialogic interaction between those in a specific social audience. Sound is at the same time concerned 'with the mutual organization of the speaker and the listener, and the hierarchical distance between them' (Bakhtin and Medvedev, 1978: 102).

Finally because dialogue operates within an interconnected 'concrete whole', or social relations, it '*belongs to the whole people*, it is *universal, everyone* must participate in its familiar contact' (Bakhtin, 1984: 128; emphasis in original). Within refracted social forms, therefore, communal public spaces open up in which people can participate in dialogue. These spaces become 'meeting- and contacting-points for heterogeneous people' (Bakhtin, 1984: 128). They are familiar spaces for the articulation of heteroglossic utterances within specific social forms. As such the content of heteroglossic utterances are unique to a refracted social context, or social form, and are mediated through specific speech genres and speech performances. In turn speech genres enable 'themes' to emerge that give rise to the compositional dialogic unity of a social form: 'to particular types of construction of the whole, types of its completion, and types of relations between the speaker and other participants in speech communication . . .' (Bakhtin, 1987: 64). Speech genres are however 'doubly orientated' to the extent that they exist in both wider social relations and within specific social forms. Thus, and for whatever reason, heteroglossic genres may become linked

to heteroglossic utterances and genres in other social forms. A heterogl
chain of speech communication may then emerge across different social forms
(cf. Bakhtin, 1987: 93).

Having outlined the ideas of the Bakhtin Circle I am now in position to
evaluate critically John Stuart Mill's defence of the liberty of thought and
discussion.

The public sphere and the liberty of thought and discussion

In *On Liberty* (originally published in 1859) Mill provides four 'grounds'
through which the 'liberty of thought and discussion' might flourish. These
'grounds' are: (i) the recognition that an opinion could be fallible; (ii) the necessity for the collision of different opinions to establish truth; (iii) that prejudice
should be eliminated; (iv) and that dogma should also be eliminated. I now focus
in more detail upon each 'ground'.

The fallibility of opinions

The first argument put forward by Mill in favour of the liberty of thought and
discussion is that human beings are fallible creatures. According to Mill, no view
is obviously false because human beings develop their mental faculties for debate
and discussion. History often shows us that an opinion once thought as infalli-
ble can gradually be shown to be fallible through accumulated evidence.

> (I)t is as certain that many opinions, now general, will be rejected by future ages, as
> it is that many, once general, are rejected by the present (Mill, 1998a: 23).

Thus Mill holds strongly to the view that each person should be given the opportunity to revise and reject opinions that were once thought of as being infalli-
ble. It is therefore unacceptable to suppress an opinion.

This is in line with Mill's idea that human nature is not static and calculable
as previous liberal thinkers had suggested. Instead human nature is 'capable, . . .
in a certain small degree, of springing up spontaneously; and susceptible of being
brought by cultivation to a high degree of development' (Mill, 1998b: 163).
According to Mill the very fact that human nature develops through concrete and
contingent circumstances means that each individual also has the ability to
develop a taste for 'higher pleasures'. By employing the term 'higher pleasures'
Mill is drawing attention to the idea that an individual, through their experiences,
will settle for a particular action because it advances their own unique higher faculties and capacities. Higher pleasures, by developing 'in proportion to . . . higher
faculties', will simultaneously bring happiness to a person and contribute 'to a
sense of dignity' (Mill, 1998b: 140). Higher pleasures contribute to a sense of
dignity because they call on individuals to engage in a complex process of deliberation about the relevance of particular action towards promoting happiness.
By engaging in this deliberative process a person can discover their inner nature
and thus discover their own unique individual 'essence'.

Thus, for Mill, liberty is defined by the ability of an individual to increase his or her wants in a wide variety of ways. To assess the rational desirability of these wants a person requires a realm of autonomy. Accordingly Mill suggests that personal autonomy implies freedom from restrictions so that an individual can reflect upon their 'self-regarding' actions to implement 'successive plans of life'. The only interference permissible upon this realm of autonomy is self-protection or the prevention of harm to others. These two prerequisites, auto-nomy and security, are, Mill tells us, liberty's 'vital interests' which are 'grounded on the permanent interests of man as a progressive being' (Mill, 1998a: 15). So, public deliberation helps to develop the sort of enquiring and cultivated mind amenable for liberty. To be 'fallible' is to seek higher pleasures and to cultivate one's own unique sense of self, to cherish a realm of autonomy, and to engage in public discussion with others in order to challenge the truthfulness of their own individual opinions (Mill, 1998a: 25).

The collision of opinions to establish truth

By the phrase, 'collision of opinions', Mill is drawing our attention to a practi-cal mode of discussion in which ideas 'bounce off' one another, or are 'thrown about' (Haworth, 1998: 68–9). Mill strengthens his position here by stating that a collision of opinions encourages an active engagement with an opponent's argument and a willingness to hear and understand both sides of an argument. This is because, as is frequently the case, '. . . conflicting doctrines, instead of being one true and the other false, share the truth between them' (Mill, 1998a: 52). In other words, the 'truthful aspects' of conflicting doctrines are brought together to develop a new truthful doctrine. This leads Mill to say that '(t)ruth, in the great practical concerns of life, is so much a question of the reconcil-ing and combining of opposites . . .' (Mill, 1998a: 54). And the collision of opinions activate that form of individuality bound up with the development of higher pleasures (see Mill, 1998a: 46).

The elimination of prejudice

Mill's third ground for the liberty of thought and discussion relates to the neces-sity to eliminate prejudice. Specifically, Mill holds that even if a belief is true it must still nevertheless be challenged and criticized. Otherwise a person will hold a certain belief without appreciating the reasons for why they do so. If this is the case then 'their conclusion may be true, but it might be false for anything they know' (Mill, 1998a: 42). Thus a conclusion 'might be false' because the person in question could accept the reasons for a belief without at the same time exploring conflicting opinions surrounding the belief in question. We must, in other words, examine the other side of an argument, to know its basis for truth and understanding, and to make judgements on the knowledge we acquire of it. Unless we learn the other side of an argument as is fully possible then we have no choice than to suspend judgement on the truth of an argument. Indeed,

Mill dabbles in hermeneutics here when he says that an individual should throw 'themselves into the mental position of those who think differently from them' and consider 'what such persons may have to say' (Mill, 1998a: 42). The most satisfactory way to eliminate prejudices, in this regard, is actually to hear the opposite side of the case from an adversary. And this is achieved by bringing other arguments 'into real contact with his own mind'. This real contact can be accomplished, Mill continues, by witnessing other arguments as they are actually being spoken by the person who believes them (Mill, 1998a: 42). If an opponent can not be found then it will be necessary to play devil's advocate in order to 'conjure up' the strongest arguments of a possible opponent.

The elimination of dogma 教条

Finally, Mill argues that a dogmatic adherence to an opinion must be rejected. As an empiricist Mill argues dogmatic opinions are in no meaningful way based upon personal experience. This being the case dogmatic words spoken in free discussion 'cease to suggest ideas, or suggest only a small portion of those they were originally employed to communicate' (Mill, 1998a: 45). Unless an opinion is linked with a living belief, then opinions become like fossils and are learnt merely by rote. An opinion is thereby transformed into dogma when 'the finer essence' of an opinion is lost in favour of 'the shell and husk'. The problem becomes more astute when we realize, with Mill, that those who hold dogmatic beliefs often look to keepers of a formulaic faith to confirm an opinion rather than discuss the basis of the opinion themselves. In other words, they hold on to a belief in an habitual manner and with 'no feeling which spreads from the words to the things signified, and forces the mind to take *them* in, and make them confirm to the formula' (Mill, 1998a: 47–8). Now that I have outlined Mill's four grounds for the Liberty of Thought and Discussion I begin critically to unpack them through the dialogic theory set out by the Bakhtin Circle. By using the Bakhtin Circle I try to show that Mill implicitly addresses more radical, heteroglossic utterances as articulated by Chartist utterances.

Mill and Chartism

According to contemporary supporters, Mill demonstrates an acute under-standing of the need for a robust public sphere of thought and discussion in modern societies. Baum (2001), for example, argues that Mill is alert to the inequalities prevalent in modern societies concerning who can and who cannot have access to the public sphere. Indeed, the four grounds to establish an inclu-sive public sphere would seem, by their very nature, to encourage inclusive public debate and discussion. But a more critical standpoint would suggest that Mill is not interested in setting out an argument for democracy as such, but he is rather more interested in setting out the necessary prerequisites for a robust *liberal* democracy to take account of radical social movements in nineteenth century Britain.

A clue to this alternative, more critical, take on Mill's thinking can be found in the following quote from his *Principles of Political Economy*. Here Mill states that:

> of the working men, at least in the more advanced countries of Europe, it may be pronounced certain, that the patriarchal or paternal system of government is one to which they will not again be subject (Mill, 1985: 121–2).

This quote serves as recognition on Mill's part that the early- and mid-nineteenth century had witnessed an unprecedented outpouring of radical and socialist heteroglossic utterances in working-class public spheres. The most important public sphere established in this respect belonged to the Chartist social movement, arguably the world's first organized socialist political party.

After 1830 many co-operative newspapers such as the *Trades Newspaper* and *The Poor Man's Advocate* began to discuss the issue of economic exploitation as this occurred within the production process itself (Hollis, 1970; Thompson, 1984). Government attempts to curb these radical public spheres by introducing a 4d stamp duty on all press merely served to exasperate matters. For this excessive measure meant that, in order to survive, the working-class press had to forego the stamp, publish illegally and effectively embark upon 'the great war of the unstamped'. Outlawed working-class press thrived and established a circulation that exceeded 'respectable' stamped press (Wright, 1988: 95–8). In London the Society for the Promotion of the Repeal of the Stamp Duties (SPRSD) was soon to displace its more middle-class members and campaign openly for working class press. By June 1836 the SPRSD was transformed into the London Working Men's Association (LWMA). The Association was later to sponsor the *Charter*, the 'declaration of working-class rights' in nineteenth century Britain. Encouraging the growth of public spheres in the guise of discussion groups in liaison with radical newspapers, organisers ensured that LWMA membership grew to one hundred with 35 honorary members merely within a year. On the whole, membership reflected the wants of skilled artisans and respectability was a prized asset (Hollis, 1970: 77; Prothero, 1979: 310–18). By January 1837 the LWMA drafted an address to Parliament that was to become known as 'The People's Charter'. Based around six points—universal suffrage, no property qualifications, annual parliaments, equal representation, payment of MPs, and vote by ballot—the Charter set the tone for working-class political activity for well over a decade.

In many respects Mill's defence of the liberty of thought and discussion can be seen as inhering within an inner dialectical dialogue with Chartists, even if he does not mention them explicitly. For Mill was more than aware that the old paternalist way of thinking was outdated because the labouring classes no longer accept its ideological basis. As a result of working-class political activity, of which the Chartists were the most prominent, the consciousness of workers had significantly altered in form to those that classical liberalism once sought to address. According to Mill:

The working classes have taken their interests into their own hands, and are perpetually showing that they think the interests of their employer not identical with their own, but opposite to them (Mill, 1985: 122).

The working class, Mill concludes, was sufficiently organized to be recognized as a social force with its 'own qualities'; a force that could 'no longer be governed or treated like children'. Indeed Mill holds forcibly to the belief that the working classes of his day articulate socialist ideas through new and powerful public spheres. As he says in regard to the self-education of the labouring population:

> The instruction obtained from newspapers and political tracts may not be the most solid kind of instruction, but it is an immense improvement upon none at all . . . The institutions for lectures and discussion, the collective deliberations on questions of common interest, the trades unions, the political agitation, all serve to awaken public spirit, to diffuse variety of ideas among the mass, and to excite thought and reflection in the more intelligent . . . The working classes are now part of the public; in all discussions on matters of general interest they, or a portion of them, are now partakers; all those who use the press as an instrument may, if it so happens, have them for an audience; the avenues of instruction through which the middle classes acquire such ideas as they have, are accessible to, at least, the operatives in the town (Mill, 1985: 124).

Through the example of Chartism, I show in the next section how Mill's defence of the liberty of thought and discussion denies the multiaccentual nature of its own ideological form. Ultimately, proletarian heteroglossic utterances haunt Mill's own words and cause him to defend a mode of regulating radical public spheres through monologic dialogue that is complicit with an ideological form of the capitalist state, namely a liberal form of the capitalist state.

The monologic form of the Millian public sphere

To begin this critique, I return first to Mill's observation that people are fallible creatures. As we have seen, Mill links fallibility with the idea that each individual develops his or her own human nature and that we can only be certain of the validity of an opinion through both experience and discussion. Thus opinions can be shown to be half-truths by being brought into contact with another opinion. However, from a Bakhtinian standpoint, an 'opinion' is not a self-contained unit of meaning that gains a new meaning *after* it enters into a relationship with another opinion. Such a view effectively views speakers as selecting particular linguistic forms that are then combined in novel ways. Moreover, such a view insists that opinions represent relatively stable syntactic intonations coloured by a logical scheme of meaning. But this misses the crucial point that opinions in fact contain an 'inner dialectical quality' because they refract a number of accents at a number of levels of abstraction. Thus, according to the Bakhtin Circle, each utterance has a contradictory meaning which then obtains a new contradictory theme depending upon its initial context and depending upon the social mediations it has gone through to reach the context in question. For example, one of the great influencing figures upon Mill, Jeremy Bentham, argued that the utility of human action should simply rest content with the pursuit of happiness and pleasure (or well-being and welfare) and the avoidance of pain. By reconfiguring human action around a happiness principle, Bentham also insisted that moral decisions about a person's 'best interests' as regards happiness lies with individual judgement. Socialist political economists, however, recognized the subversive, heteroglossic, meaning inherent in Bentham's ideas. William Thompson, a pupil of Robert Owen and a leading light in British socialist theory in the early nineteenth century, subverted Bentham's supreme principle of 'the greatest happiness for the greatest number' by arguing that 'equality' should be the mainstay of utilitarian philosophy. But Thompson added an important caveat. He insisted that 'as *near an approach as possible* to equality' should be the guiding principle, 'as near as is consistent with the greatest production'. And for Thompson 'the strongest stimulus to production' would be achieved by ensuring that 'the *entire use* of the products of labour' went 'to those who produce them' (cited in McNally, 1993: 122). 'With a twist', claims McNally (1993: 122), 'Benthamite utilitarianism could be employed as the theoretical support for a radical critique of established political economy'. By subverting Bentham's ideas in this manner, socialists like Thompson focused upon what might be termed as the 'inner dialectical quality' of Benthamite utilitarianism. That is to say, Thompson engaged (indirectly) in a process of public dialogue with Bentham in order to expose his ideas as a means to ideologically justify the subordination of labour to capital. By accomplishing this task Thompson rendered visible an alternative meaning of utilitarian philosophy which Bentham had pushed to the foreground. And this alternative meaning could then produce new themes about how to remedy exploitation within specific proletarian public spheres.

By conceptualizing opinions as relative stable syntactic forms, however, Mill constructs a *device* through the liberty of thought and discussion that is seen to encourage the collision of opinions so as to avoid the infallibility of dogmatic opinions. Thus by focusing upon stable forms of opinions rather than their inner-dialectical quality, the primary task Mill sets himself is to 'discover' a device to show how these stable forms interact. He is thus less interested in discovering how device is dialectically entwined with actual everyday 'multiaccentual' meaning through utterances to produce new material themes. This being the case, Mill separates device from meaning and concentrates upon the former at the expense of the latter. The device to bring about thought and discussion is made an end in itself and consequently, as we will see below, effectively denigrates the ideological and multiaccentual material of 'opinions'.

According to Mill, 'cultivated' opinions are 'truthful' to the extent that they are the *possession* of *neutral* individuals, ie individuals who do not have a political agenda. As he says:

Truth, in the great practical concerns of life, is so much a question of the reconciling and combining of opposites, that very few minds sufficiently capacious and impartial to make the adjustment with an approach to correctness . . . (Mill, 1998a: 54).

When Mill therefore suggests that opinions are 'standing antagonisms of practical life' (Mill, 1998a: 54) he means that different opinions are worthy of debate and discussion only if individuals first bracket the social and historical context through which these opinions have been mediated. Hence the reason why one must be 'impartial' when reflecting upon the 'truth' of an opinion. As a result Mill, also implies that the distinctive multiaccentual evaluations of different opinions must likewise be bracketed. However, and as Bakhtin (1984: 183–5) argues, to insist on this form of bracketing is simultaneously to close down considerably the dialogic relationship between a speaker and a hearer, because we learn little about the social identity of a respective 'author' or 'creator' of opinions. We cannot learn anything of value because the opinions have been abstracted outside of meaningfully real ideological relations. And yet we know that opinions are indeed uttered in real situations, from the mouths of real people, and are refracted through different dialects, language styles, speech genres, power relations, and so on. When a word is uttered it is not merely an individual's identity that is invoked, but also a social and historical whole through which the utterance has been mediated and through which it has gained a specific evaluation.

Again, the Chartists provide us with an illustration of this point. Chartists were aware of a new experience developing within the workshop, an experience refracted through wage-labour and based upon poverty, insecurity and exploitation. With equal insight Chartists were aware that industrial capitalism spelt a form of wage-slavery. Capitalists, as the Chartist McDouall observed, only became interested in the 'body' of the worker 'be for the work it will do' (Kirk, 1987: 30; see also Behagg, 1990). The importance of Chartism, therefore, was that it represented a qualitative *transformation* in working class ideas in the sense that the state came to be viewed less as a remnant of 'Old Corruption' and more as an authoritarian mechanism for the dictatorship over direct producers. 'The people' slowly came to be equated with the working class' (Wood, 1998: 109–10; see also Clarke, 1988: 65; Yeo, 1997: 47–50). As a result Chartists increasingly viewed the state as the institutionalized power of the capitalist class. Unlike their liberal counterparts, therefore, many (though certainly not all) Chartist agitators viewed society as an internally mediated and connected 'whole' in the sense that they advocated a political *and* social transformation in order to remedy society's ills (see Lloyd and Thomas, 1998: 95; Thompson, 1998: 121).

Mill, however, still considers society to be one based upon external relationships between discrete units of life. For example, we have seen that for Mill the meaning of an opinion is acquired through the constant conjunction of an abstract and relatively stable language with individual speakers located in particular social contexts. Taking these points on board involves an obvious question. What exactly does Mill mean by the terms 'liberty', 'thought' and 'discussion'? This is a somewhat awkward question to answer because, as we have seen, Mill *appears* to construct a radical theory of free speech that, *in reality*, belies a more restrictive meaning. As we have also seen, this restrictive meaning is premised upon an individualist defence of the liberty of thought and discussion. Therefore, as O'Rouke (2001: 78) correctly points out, an opinion's evaluation is not of prime importance for Mill. This follows from our point that the meaning of an opinion is of secondary importance to the actual device of the liberty of thought and expression. This being the case, if evaluations and meaning are not highly regarded by Mill then what are the values embedded within his device? O'Rouke (2001: 78–9) argues that the main value of the liberty of thought and discussion relates not to the right of individuals to express an opinion but to the right of others to hear an opinion. In other words, Mill's device values the freedom of individuals to *hear* all sides of an opinion. Mill says on this point:

> But I must feel permitted to observe, that it is not the feeling sure of a doctrine . . . which I call an assumption of infallibility. It is the undertaking to decide that question *for others*, without allowing them to hear what can be said on the contrary side (Mill, 1998a: 28).

Mill's device implicitly suggests that the *right* to thought and discussion rest with the hearer of an opinion. Mill thereby endorses a one-sided defence of thought and discussion that privileges the right of one party in a dialogic act, namely the hearer. But why does Mill defend this one-sided argument? The answer lies with his view of the Principle of Liberty, namely the requirement of each individual to develop their own intellectual capacity so as to enjoy higher pleasures. The right to hear different sides of an opinion contributes significantly to the development of this intellectual capacity.

Mill thereby believes that a cultivated mind is one that thinks in a contemplative manner. But the speech performance conjured up by this image is one in which individual desires are subject to 'earnest self-control' in order to discover one's higher pleasures. This is an individual whose impulses are strong and based within 'an energetic character'. Integral is a realm of personal autonomy to guarantee freedom from restrictions so that an individual can reflect upon their 'self-regarding' actions. So, while Mill also suggests that thought and discussion must avoid a 'text-book' approach he nevertheless emphasizes that an individual must avoid those 'lower pleasures' associated with custom and herd mentality. Those unfortunate enough to wallow in the quagmire of custom and lower pleasures are more likely to ask themselves: 'what is suitable to my position? what is usually done by persons of my station and pecuniary circumstances?' Apparently what each of us should ask ourselves is: 'what do I prefer? or, what would suit my character and disposition? or, what would allow the best and highest in me to have fair play, and enable it to grow and thrive?' (Mill, 1998a: 68). But notice here that Mill subtly relates lower pleasures and custom with reflection upon one's social position and, by default, their social environment—

the type of reflection, in fact, carried out by the Chartists. On Mill's under-standing, therefore, only those who reflect upon their individual character irre-spective of their social environment can begin to enjoy higher pleasures. Indeed, Mill goes as far as to say that even those individuals who seek improvements to their social conditions by appealing to virtues such as justice and right could in principle be bound up with custom and therefore be in conflict with liberty and higher pleasures (Mill, 1998a: 78).

As regards speech performance, therefore, a person who manages to gain self-control over lower pleasures by bracketing out the social environment is one who gains mastery over their individual character. Thus there is a strong impulse here towards serious, one might almost say, scholarly, debate. We can appreci-ate the seriousness of this form of discussion in more detail if we look at the speech performance that Mill prefers. Accordingly 'the greatest orator, save one, of antiquity, has left it on record that he always studied his adversary's case with as great, if not with greater, intensity than even his own' (Mill, 1998a: 42). The image conjured up by this speech performance is one probably more at home with the legal profession than it is with everyday life. In other words, it is thoroughly unrealistic and has an in-built bias towards a certain type of disin-terested thinking. Moreover, this liberal standpoint rejects the very basis of heteroglossic utterances as being bound up within popular, everyday culture. And this is the very form that popular public spheres assume. In one important respect, for example, Chartism represented such a powerful social movement in Britain because it managed to embed political demands within popular culture (Eley ,1990: 32; Yeo, 1971: 101, 1982: 349). Of particular significance was the development of working class public spheres via the increasing sophistication through which working-class interests came to be circulated through Chartist newspapers. At the forefront of this development was the establishment of the *Northern Star* by Chartism's most alluring and charismatic leader, Feargus O'Connor. The *Star* had sales of nearly 50,000 copies per week in just two years after its establishment in November 1837. This popularity lay in part with its ability to play a cultural and educational role by employing skilled journalists to articulate the latest political news. Copies were readily available from working class clubs and reading rooms, radical coffee-houses and Chartist taverns. Friends passed on copies or would subscribe together and read aloud in specific spaces such as a home, the workshop or at meetings. The *Star*'s populist report-ing style invited such a response. But above all else, the *Star* reported on local issues to a national audience (Epstein. 1976: 60 ff.). Thus the populist appeal of Chartism lay in the appropriation of distinctive spaces in which to hold meetings, effectively making Chartism a local as well as a national movement (D. Thompson. 1984: 60–61). Between the years 1838–9, for example, O'Con-nor travelled extensively across the UK and spoke publicly at least fifty-six meetings. Conducted with dramatic oratory skills and attracting large crowds, O'Connor marvelled in a belief that such meetings constructed 'a great chain' of working-class radicalism that connected a diverse array of places (Southall, 1996).

Knowing this about Chartism, perhaps it is unsurprising that Mill would want to distance his own elevated device of thought and discussion from what he believed to be dogma found within 'a set of everyday judgements and practices'. According to Mill, dogmatic beliefs:

> have no hold on ordinary believers—are not a power in their minds. They have an habitual respect for the sound of them, but no feeling which spreads from the words to the things signified, and forces the mind to take *them* in, and conform to the formula (Mill, 1998a 47–8).

This quote is interesting because it enables us to see how Mill subtly asserts his own 'authorship' over the right of thought and discussion. In effect Mill imposes his own intentions and evaluations over the utterances of those he dislikes. The truthfulness in the collision between two opinions is thereby decided in advance by Mill through his device of the liberty of thought and discussion. Therefore this only *appears* as a collision because sooner or later Mill will state the mono-logic and uniaccentual dominance of the liberty of thought and discussion (see Bakhtin, 1984: 204).

In the *Principles of Political Economy* Mill provides an example of his mono-logic approach. Here he makes clear that:

> The institutions for lectures and discussion, the collective deliberations on questions of common interest, the trades unions, the political agitation, all serve to awaken public spirit, to diffuse variety of ideas among the mass, and to excite thought and reflection in the more intelligent (Mill, 1985: 124).

Mill's use of particular words in this passage is interesting. First he uses the word 'excite'. This word has a negative (monologic) meaning in bourgeois thought when it is associated with popular public discussion and can be traced back to the word 'mob'. Taken from the Latin expression *mobile vulgus* (the 'excitable' or 'movable' crowd) the word 'mob' first came to be used in the English language to denote rioters in London during the Exclusion Crisis (1678–81). Over the next few decades the term was frequently used to describe disorder in London and helped more generally to establish the 'cultivated mores' of patrician culture at some distance from a plebeian culture (Shoemaker, 1987: 273). Also, however, we see from this passage that Mill equates the 'mass'—those content with lower pleasures—with working-class political agitation. Under-pinning this speech performance in Mill is an apprehension of the 'sound' emanating from the lower classes. It is a sound of defiance towards those institutions that sought to regulate and govern working class culture. But Mill does not satisfactorily account for the connection between sound and meaning here. Rather than explore the specificity of the sound of working-class grievances within the unique ideological form of the proletarian public sphere at this his-torical juncture, Mill merely makes some general observations about some of the practicalities of the 'excitable speech' he highlights. He then compares this sound to his general device of the liberty of thought and discussion. Thus Mill insists that these sounds are an example that the working class is moving towards an appreciation of the 'increase in intelligence, of education, and of the love of independence . . .' (Mill, 1985: 125). But in making these assumptions about the relationship between sound and meaning, Mill really only ever indicates that sound arouses pleasure. After all, Mill says very little about the complex social mediations of 'excitable speech'. Indeed, it is impossible to say anything meaningful about this type of 'excitable speech' because Mill pushes its ideological meaning into the background in favour of the brute practicalities of language. We might well ask why, exactly, does excitable speech arouse lower pleasures and not higher pleasures? Merely talking about 'excitable speech' is to universalize a historically specific moment.

But let us stay with Mill's identification of the working class. It is certainly a social class that worries him immensely. After all, although Mill clearly sees that working-class minds of his day were 'less and less acquiescent in the degree of dependence' upon dominant interests, he also understands that a new form of thinking is required to educate the working classes in 'the virtues of independence'. Indeed he goes as far as to say of the working class that: 'The prospect of the future depends on the degree in which they can be made rational beings' (Mill, 1985: 123). But if Mill is concerned with the minds of the working class, why is this the case?

According to Mill the 'labouring population' of his day, particularly the unskilled, have the least propensity for developing higher pleasures. In particular Mill suggests that the labouring class fail fully to exercise their capacities for political discussion. In *Considerations on Representative Government* (originally published in 1861), for example, Mill insists: 'But political discussions fly over the heads of those who have no votes, and are not endeavouring to acquire them. Their position, in comparison with the electors, is that of the audience in a court of justice, compared with the twelve men in the jury-box' (Mill, 1998c: 328–9). Apparently, this class has no 'inducement' to arrive at meaningful opinions. Mill is careful not to condone class legislation in respect to voting qualifications. In fact he explicitly renounces the link between property and the right to vote (see Mill, 1998c: 335). Yet Mill does retain a normative ground for the right to vote and this, as we have seen, can be found within the educational cultivation of individuals and their ability to engage in thought and discussion. This is why Mill argues (unsurprisingly , perhaps, considering that he is a political philosopher) that the 'liberal professions' endow individuals with 'a still higher degree of instruction' for thought and discussion (Mill, 1998c: 336). Thus we must conclude that those who Mill fears as following customary practices are those who belong to the labouring classes. And, in fact, there is ample evidence between the lines that this is the case. For example, Mill laments 'our habit of combining', of working collectively to improve one's social position, because it merely teaches 'simple minds' those 'obvious grounds of truths' of which 'they have neither knowledge nor talent to resolve every difficulty which can be raised' (Mill, 1998a: 43).

But Mill is disingenuous in his observations here. As we have seen, Chartism produced innovative and sophisticated public spheres through newspapers and the appropriation of public spaces. Many of these public spheres were characterized by an ethic of professionalism. Amongst other things, this implied the systematic collection by Chartists of data concerning the lecturing requirements of different localities. Where one locality was lacking in professional speakers, it was now possible for Chartist agitators to respond promptly. Even so, national Chartist speakers often shared a platform with local and respected Chartist agitators. In order to respond to the growth of local Chartism, Chartists were sensitive towards the need to encourage 'the free flow of ideas and communication' between speakers and the audience (Howell, 1995; see also Howell 1991). In this respect Chartists constructed a chain of heteroglossic speech performances and speech genres from one social context to another so that the form of the radical meanings of words addressed specific themes within particular social contexts.

But perhaps what perturbed Mill was not so much the willingness of working-class speakers to use a populist idiom with which to express political demands, but rather the innovative way in which they used public space for their own heteroglossic speech performances. The national and local character of Chartism exposed gaps in the manner to which law and governance sought monologically to regulate radical heteroglossic speech performances. As a result one of the main problems which the state faced in respect to both the national and local tactics of Chartism was exactly a spatial problem of governance. No trained arm of the law existed to prevent public meetings. The military, being unevenly distributed across the country, was seen by many to be an increasingly ineffective regulatory force. There was also a growing anxiety over whether troops should be called to settle local industrial disputes (Radzinowicz, 1960: 69–78). This anxiety was not helped much by the ability of Chartists to work within the monological limits of the state and thereby bring to the fore heteroglossic traces within regulatory forms. For example, delegates to the Chartist Convention kept within the legal restriction of the 1799 Seditious Meetings Act of not allowing more than fifty people to attend. In the eyes of the law, therefore, the Convention was deemed a legal body whose remit was merely designed to petition various public bodies (Parssinen, 1973: Yeo, 1982). And yet the government and local authorities were not totally inept at regulating Chartist public spheres. Developing a new 'economy in physical force' encapsulating knowledge of the dynamics of crowd behaviour (Mather, 1959: 98), and armed with only truncheons, the police would set about 'dismantling' makeshift public spheres by entering a crowd and removing the ringleaders. In 1839 nearly nine Acts were passed with the aim of improving the police force. Birmingham, Manchester and Bolton all now had a police system modelled on the success of London and this was complemented by legal measures aimed to give police better protection in the face of assault in the course of duty. The base was finally laid for the establishment of constabulary forces in all the counties.

What we might suggest, therefore, is that Mill provides a theoretical complement to this new and emerging monologic regulation of proletarian public spheres. Rather than call for explicit state intervention Mill calls for the implementation of an *ethical* code of conduct. This is a rallying cry for the self-regulation of life through improvement and education. Mill clearly argues for a government that refrains from regulating conduct unless conduct infringes the action of others. Mill also argues, however, that when the intellectual capacity to pursue higher pleasures is not catered for, then the state has a duty to guarantee that this capacity is promoted. Mill's observations on state education are instructive here. He argues that every child should receive an education so that those intellectual capacities congruent with higher pleasures are developed. But Mill is careful to avoid arguing for a universal form of education because this would contravene his commitment to the liberty of the individual. Universal education would always be in danger of 'moulding people to be exactly like one another: and as the mould in which it casts them is that which pleases the predominant power in the government . . . (I)t establishes a despotism over the mind, leading by natural tendency to one over the body' (Mill, 1998a: 117–18). In place of universal education Mill argues that the state should merely ensure that a diversity of education exists and that public examinations should be carried out. Through exams, children would learn 'facts' that 'such and such an opinion is held'. However, the necessity for education for all would only proceed up to a certain 'minimum of general knowledge'. Beyond that minimum, individuals would sit more advanced examinations on a voluntarily basis.

Mill's insights into education enable him to construct a new mode of ethical conduct and one which is based upon the imposition of a new form of bourgeois (monologic) ideology upon a new form of proletarian (heteroglossic) ideology. In *Considerations* Mill unambiguously equates universal education with his class fear that manual labourers would gain a voice in the public sphere. This leads Mill to posit a two-fold danger for society: 'that of too low a standard of political intelligence, and that of class legislation' (Mill, 1998c: 333). In saying this, Mill does not believe that the state should necessarily intervene in civil society to provide a remedy to this situation. Instead Mill prefers a restrictive role for state regulation for three main reasons. First, a restrictive government is necessary simply because individuals are the best judge as to what actions promote their own interests. Second, and following the previous point, by judging their own best interests individuals develop their 'mental education'. Whereas 'government operations tend to be everywhere alike', individuals discussing options between themselves in a voluntary capacity encourage 'varied experiments, and endless diversity of experience'. As such governments should merely 'enable each experimentalist to benefit by the experiments of others'. Third, a restrictive government is beneficial because it acts as a check upon 'adding unnecessarily' to state power (Mill, 1998a: 121–2). But far from expressing a neutral role for the state Mill constructs a defence a particular ideological form of the capitalist state, namely a *liberal form* of the capitalist state.

By the nineteenth century, the state increasingly saw its task as simply regulating civil society 'from afar'. This state form was a reaction to the dissolution of corporate forms of property, as money slowly became the main abstract bearer of property relations and gained value through a circuit of commodity production. In turn the exchange of commodities was regulated by the abstract value of money and the abstract dominance of law. The liberal form of the state thus recognizes that both money and law already exist within the domain of civil society and thereby seeks to enforce the rights of both 'through the legal forms of the person, property and contract and of money as legal tender' (Clarke, 1988: 127). Civil society acts as the precondition for the liberal state form, making the latter see its role negatively as providing administrative support for the abstract content of civil society.

Mill's defence of restrictive government can be seen as being compatible with the liberal state form because it justifies a minimal role for the state in securing the reproduction of capital. First, Mill argues that too much state administration produces too much bureaucracy. And too much bureaucracy unnecessarily adds to the power of the state (see Mill, 1998a: 122). Elsewhere in *Principles of Political Economy* Mill is even more adamant in his belief that 'as a general rule, the business of life is better performed when those who have no immediate interest in it are left to take their own course, uncontrolled either by the mandate of the law or by the meddling of a public functionary' (Mill, 1985: 317). In other words, Mill supports a *laissez-faire* approach which admits that government agencies are far inferior 'in any of the common operations of industry or commerce' (Mill, 1985: 311). While Mill, however, is prepared to say that the state frequently fails to regulate business by a 'maze of technicalities' (Mill, 1985: 244), he also suggests that law fails because it is not coherent, consistent and universal in its pronouncements. For example, law omits 'due evidence of transactions, by a proper registration of legal documents' (Mill, 1985: 245). That is to say, law is too informal in its everyday operation. Moreover, this lack of universal formality hinders the everyday operation of the universal formality of 'purchase and sale', ie, commodity exchange. What would enhance commodity transactions, suggests Mill, would be the increasing expansion of the circuit of exchange through law. For example, 'to make land as easily transferable as stock, would be one of the greatest economical improvements which could be bestowed on a country' (Mill, 1985: 246).

It would be quite wrong, however, to believe that Mill is a vulgar defender of *laissez-faire* (see Mill, 1985: 317 ff.). The important point to make is that Mill does not so much leave us with a defence of free speech but, rather, develops an abstract aesthetic ideal of thought and discussion that complements the liberal state form. This is because Mill separates a public aesthetic sphere of cultivated higher pleasures from society as a whole and then exacts a normative principle for the state as a mode for conflict resolution between different social spheres. Mill therefore develops the general liberal idea that full inclusion in the democratic life of society is premised upon a negative freedom wherein those individuals with the necessary 'disinterested' and 'cultivated' dispositions will play a leading role. Furthermore, the culture of 'cultivation' is a separate sphere to that of 'economics' and 'politics' and provides a space in society to reflect 'rationally' upon the latter two spheres (see Lloyd and Thomas, 1998: 15). Thus the liberal public sphere is seen to be instrumental for this overall cultural phenomenon. Moreover it is a phenomenon that separates the Subject into the 'the political citizen and the economic worker, each operative in different social spaces' (Lloyd and Thomas, 1998: 135). And, for Mill, this liberal form of the bourgeois public sphere is founded upon the monologic themes of thought and discussion, cultivation, rationality, education and intelligence, and the pursuit of higher pleasures.

Conclusion

In this chapter I have argued that the meaning of free speech constructed by John Stuart Mill is somewhat ambiguous. To begin with, Mill does not use the sign free speech. Rather he consistently applies the sign of 'the liberty of thought and discussion'. This sign has a number of multiaccentual themes that seek to demarcate the ideological boundaries of a specific mode of bourgeois public sphere. Liberal in both form and content, this public sphere represents the *determining* ideology of the *capitalist* public sphere because it is the form most applicable to the reproduction of the determining form of advanced capitalism constituted by the abstract dominance of the rule of law and money. Following on from this is a more general point that, as in the case of contemporary definitions of free speech, the words of right-claims matter. For, as I have tried to show, right-claims have specific ideological meanings depending upon how their different themes operate in both space and time. This may be an obvious point to make, but all too often it is easy to take at face value the words used to signify a right-claim. We should be aware that, as Voloshinov (1973) says, words are ideological units of life which both reflect and refract particular social relations and their associated power relations. As a result words contain their own unique conflicting accents, sounds and heroic struggles. Although similar, the liberty of thought and discussion is not free speech.

Acknowledgements

This chapter is based upon revised material written by the author and published elsewhere. The author would like to thank the following for their permission to use this copyright material. Blackwell Publishers for 'Spatial Governance and Working Class Public Spheres: The Case of a Chartist Demonstration at Hyde Park', *Journal of Historical Sociology* 14(3) (2001): 308–36 and Palgrave, Macmillan Publishers for *The Aesthetics of Free Speech: Rethinking the Public Sphere* (2003).

Bibliography

Bakhtin, M. (1981) *The Dialogic Imagination*, translated by C. Emerson and M. Holquist, edited by M. Holquist. Austin, Texas: University of Texas Press.

Bakhtin, M. M. (1984) *Problems of Dostoevsky's Poetics*, edited and translated by C. Emerson. Minneapolis: University of Minnesota Press.

Bakhtin, M. M. (1987) Speech Genres and other Late Essays, translated by V. W. McGee. Austin, Texas: University of Texas Press.

Bakhtin, M. and Medevedev, P. N. (1978) *The Formal Method in Literary Scholarship: A Critical Introduction to Sociological Poetics*, translated by A. J. Wehrle. Baltimore: John Hopkins University Press.

Baum, B. (2001) 'Freedom, Power and Public Opinion: J. S. Mill on the Public Sphere', *History of Political Thought* 22(3): 501–524.

Behagg, C. (1990) *Politics and Production in the Early Nineteenth*. London: Routledge.

Clarke, S. (1988) *Keynesianism, Monetariam and the Crisis of the State*. Aldershot, Hants: Edward Arnold.

Eley, G. (1990) 'Edward Thompson, Social History and Political Culture: The Making of a Working Class Public' in H. J. Kaye and K. McCelland, K. (eds), *E. P. Thompson: Critical Perspectives*. Cambridge: Polity Press.

Epstein, J. A. (1976) 'Feargus O'Connor and the Northern Star', International Review of Social History, 21(1): 51–97.

Hollis, P. (1970) *The Pauper Press: A Study in Working-Class Radicalism of the 1830s*. London: Oxford University Press.

Howarth, A. (1998) *Free Speech*. London: Routledge.

Howell, P. (1993) 'Public Space and the Public Sphere: Political Theory and the Historical Geography of Modernity', *Society and Space* 11: 303–322.

Howell, P. (1995) ''Diffusing the Light of Liberty': The Geography of Political Lecturing in the Chartist Movement', *Journal of Historical Geography*, 21(1): 23–38.

Kirk, N. (1987) 'In Defence of Class: A Critique of Recent Revisionist Writing upon the Nineteenth-Century Working Class', *International Review of Social History*, 32: 2–47.

Lloyd, D. and Thomas, P. (1998) *Culture and the State*. London: Routledge.

McNally, D. (1993) *Against the Market*. London: Verso.

Mather, F. C. (1959) *Public Order in the Age of the Chartists*. Manchester: Manchester University Press.

Mill, J. S. (1985) *Principles of Political Economy*, Books 4 and 5. London: Penguin.

Mill, J. S. (1998a) 'On Liberty', in *John Stuart Mill on Liberty and other Essays*, edited by J. Gray. Oxford: Oxford University Press.

Mill, J. S. (1998b) *Utilitarianism*, in *John Stuart Mill on Liberty and other Essays*, edited by J. Gray. Oxford: Oxford University Press.

Mill, J. S. (1998c) *Considerations on Representative Government*, in *John Stuart Mill on Liberty and other Essays*, edited by J. Gray. Oxford: Oxford University Press.

O'Rourke, K. C. (2001) *John Stuart Mill and Freedom of Expression*. London: Routledge.

Parssinen, T. M. (1973) 'Association, Convention and Anti-Parliament in British Radical Politics, 1771–1848', *The English Historical Review* 88: 504–33.

Prothero, I. (1979) *Artisans and Politics in Early Nineteenth-Century London: John Gast and his Times*. London: Dawson.

Radzinowicz, L. (1960) 'New Departures in Maintaining Public Order in the Face of Chartist Disturbances', *The Cambridge Law Journal*: 51–80.

Reid, D. A. (1976) 'The Decline of Saint Monday 1766–1876', *Past and Present* 71 (May): 76–101.

Richter, D. C. (1981) *Riotous Victorians*. Athens and London: Ohio University Press.

Roberts, J. M (2002) 'From Reflection to Refraction: Opening up Open Marxism'. *Capital and Class Capital and Class* 78 Autumn: 87–116.

Shoemaker, R. B. (1987) 'The London 'Mob' in the Early Eighteenth Century', *Journal of British Studies*, 26, July: 273–304.

Southall, H. (1996) 'Agitate! Agitate! Organize! Political Travellers and the Construction of National Politics, 1839–1880', *Transactions of the Institute of British Geographers* 21: 177–193.

Thompson, D. (1984) *The Chartists*. Middlesex: Maurice Temporal Smith Ltd.

Thompson, N. (1984) *The People's Science: The Popular Political Economy of Exploitation and Crisis 1816–34*. Cambridge: Cambridge University Press.

Thompson, N. (1998) *The Real Rights of Man: Political Economies for the Working Class 1775–1850*. London: Pluto.

Voloshinov, V. N. (1973) *Marxism and the Philosophy of Language*, translated by L. Matejka. and I. R. Titunik. London: Menthuen.

Wood, E. M. (1998) *The Retreat from Class: Towards a New 'True' Socialism*. London: Verso.

Wright, D. G. (1988) *Popular Radicalism: The Working Class Experience, 1780–1880*. London: Longman,

Yeo, E. (1971) 'Robert Owen and Radical Culture', pp. 84–114 in S. Pollard and J. Salt (eds), *Robert Owen: Prophet of the Poor*. London: Macmillan.

Yeo, E. (1982) 'Some Practices and Problems of Chartist Democracy', in J. Epstein and D. Thompson (eds), *The Chartist Experience: Studies in Working-Class Radicalism and Culture, 1830–60*. London: Macmillan.

Yeo, E. J. (1997) 'Language and Contestation: The Case of 'the People', 1832 to the Present' in J. Belchem and N. Kirk (eds), *Languages of Labour*. Aldershot: Ashgate.

On systematically distorted communication: Bourdieu and the socio-analysis of publics

Nick Crossley

In this chapter I consider the potential of the work of Pierre Bourdieu as a means of extending and deepening Habermas' critique of the public sphere. Bourdieu is not widely recognized as a theorist of the public sphere, perhaps because he does not often name the public sphere as such in his analyses. Nevertheless, much of his work on the media, artistic, educational and political fields involves a powerful analysis of the publics constituted therein. Publics, if we read Bourdieu in this way, are plural. They are differentiated across a range of sites of discursive production. But they are no less important for that. In recent work, for example, he has spoken out in defence of various fields of public discourse which, he argues, are being undermined by increasing economic encroachment (Bourdieu, 1998a; Bourdieu and Haacke, 1995). Like Habermas, but with more of an eye on the economy than on the state, he invokes an image of a process of colonization which compromises the autonomy of fields and thereby the rational debate and critique they might otherwise generate. This form of critique rejoins another which we find much earlier in Bourdieu's work, however, a form focused upon the manner in which the artistic and political fields in particular are shaped by social inequalities which they, in turn, help to perpetuate. Thus, again like Habermas, Bourdieu's defence of the public sphere against its colonisation is a defence of fields which he takes to be flawed proto-types of the communicative forms and channels adequate to a properly demo-cratic society.

The importance of Bourdieu's work is not restricted to this considerable research output, however. It offers an important framework or problematic for further research. More specifically, it effects a framework in which we can realise, both empirically and theoretically, an analysis of 'systematically distorted communication', such as was deemed central to critical theory by Habermas (1970a,b) in his earlier work. This latter point must be briefly unpacked.

'Systematically distorted communication' is central to Habermas' early defi-nition of critical theory (Habermas, 1972). The epistemology of critical theory, he suggests, should be akin to that of psychoanalysis. And the epistemology of psychoanalysis centres upon 'systematically distorted communication'. The psychoanalyst identifies distortions in the speech of the analysand, in the form of omissions, slips, defences etc, and traces them back to their root cause in the history of the individual, with a view to working through them with the analysand such that the analysand can master and overcome them. Critical theory, taking public discourse as its analysand, he continues, can and should do the same. We should seek to identify distortions in public discourse and their causes, and we should communicate our interpretations back to the public in an effort to rid them (and us too as we form part of the public) of these distortions. The relevance of this to our concern with the public sphere is obvious. The public sphere is one place where we can make a strong claim for the necessity of undistorted communication. Thus identification and critique of distorted communication therein is essential to the project of critical theory, as Habermas continues to maintain as recently as *Between Facts and Norms* (Habermas, 1993). Habermas, however, fails to consider how the concept of 'distorted communication' might be implemented in empirical analyses of actually existing publics. Indeed, his work positively hinders such implementation on at least two counts. First, the concept of 'systematically distorted communication' is never properly established and remains overly dependent upon a psychological frame of reference. In *Knowledge and Human Interests* Habermas claims that he wishes to extract the form of psychoanalytic criticism for his critical theory but not its content. He wants to establish a form of social analysis and criticism which can achieve a similar type of critique at the social level, as psychoanalysis, in his opinion, achieves at the psychological level; a process which would involve removing the psycho-biological baggage of psychoanalysis and replacing it with sociological equivalents. His account of systematically distorted communication, however, particularly in the seminal paper of that name, remains tied to the content of psychoanalysis, portraying systematically distorted communication as psychopathology. There is therefore a theoretical gap to be filled before we can implement an analysis of distorted communication. Secondly, although his later work on discourse ethics could be said to further establish the importance of 'undistorted communication', since Habermas here makes a strong case for suggesting that a defensible definition of the right can only be established through open communication between (all) interested parties, the shift in his work from the epistemological concerns of *Knowledge and Human Interests* towards the theory of communication, paradoxically, erects further obstacles to the proper analysis of systematically distorted communication. It does this because the conceptual tools that Habermas develops in his later work are ideal types which analytically distinguish aspects of the social world which the concept of systematically distorted communication suggests are entangled: eg. communication and power; understanding and strategic manoeuvring/success. This analytic separation is essential to critique. A position which refused to acknowledge, in principle, a distinction between the force of good reasons and the effect of power, bribery or trickery would have no basis for critique, as Habermas' (1990) own reflections upon post-structuralism and early critical theory suggest. Furthermore, it would have no basis from which to speak of communicative distortion. Having effected this necessary distinction, however, Habermas does not put the elements of actually-existing communication back together, thus leaving himself without a means, conceptually or empirically, of addressing the entangled communicative knots suggested by the concept of 'systematically distorted communication'. Indeed, the implication of Habermas' work sometimes seems to be that these analytically distinct categories are in fact empirically distinct. Communicatively rational interaction belongs to the lifeworld, strategic action to the system, and though system may colonize lifeworld and lifeworld may resist system, the two action types remain mutually exclusive. Where the one advances the other recedes, without overlap.

The importance of Bourdieu is that his work allows us to put the pieces of actually existing communication back together, in its 'contaminated' form. Furthermore, he implements just the sociologized psychoanalytic epistemology that Habermas envisages in *Knowledge and Human Interests*. In contrast to Habermas, Bourdieu conceives of his project as 'science'. However, Bourdieu's conception of science is similar to what Habermas calls 'critical theory'—and by implication different to what the early Habermas calls 'science'. Science, for Bourdieu, 'makes trouble' (Bourdieu, 1993). And it can do so in ways conducive to human emancipation. It explodes myths and turns conventional wisdom on its head, providing the possibility for a more liberated and enlightened way of living. From Copernicus and Galileo, through Darwin and Einstein, the 'epistemological breaks' constitutive of science have challenged conventional wisdom and the power structures based upon it. Sociology, as a science of society, can and must continue this project. More importantly than this, however, many of Bourdieu's empirically engaged projects have quite explicitly constructed a mode of critique, sometimes referred to as 'socio-analysis', which self-consciously parallels, in the social domain, the epistemological model of psychoanalysis. Echoing Bachelard (2002), whose own epistemology draws upon a psychoanalytic model, Bourdieu frequently likens his task to that of the psychoanalyst and uses the key concepts he has formulated (habitus, capital, field, doxa, illusio) to generate sociologically re-cast versions of key psychoanalytic concepts. He talks of an 'unconscious', for example, of 'repression', 'sublimations' and 'compromise formations'. And in doing so he effects a powerful critique of the place of systematic distortions in public discourse.

Much of this chapter will be devoted to an exploration of the various avenues of socio-analytic critique that Bourdieu's work opens up. In successive sections I will show how he: 1) explores the unconscious adaptation of public discourse to contaminating influences, 2) outlines a method for a 'suspicious' reading of texts, 3) identifies the role of the historical/cultural unconscious in the process of political legitimation, and 4) identifies a variety of unconscious factors which both exclude certain parties from public debate and pose obstacles to the possibility of understanding and just discussion between parties. Before I do this, however, it is necessary to reflect briefly upon some of the differences between Habermas and Bourdieu's respective conceptions of public reason.

Communicative rationality

It is my opening contention that Bourdieu adopts, albeit without naming it as such, a communicative conception of rationality. By this I mean three things. Firstly, he understands rationality to be a property and indeed an effect of human interactions rather than a property of isolated individuals or a transcendental ego. Rationality manifests as a pattern of communicative interaction and is an effect of the discipline imposed by interaction (see below). If individuals manifest this rationality in their own private deliberations it is because those deliberations are fashioned after public interactions, the thinking subject being formed through an internalization of interaction patterns and social relations (on this see also Mead, 1967). Secondly, I mean that rationality, for Bourdieu, involves an exchange of views which relies upon appeals to logic, evidence and shared beliefs or assumptions, rather than bribery, violence or threats. Interlocuters attempt to persuade one another of their views by force of argument and they mutually recognize their duty to meet and anticipate objections, concede criticisms that they cannot answer etc. What counts as logic or evidence may vary and Bourdieu is clear that the definition and enforcement of them is a social process but they are integral to his account. He nowhere explicitly defines reason as such but his discussion of it implies a definition akin to this. In a quotation cited and discussed below, for example, we find him arguing that reason is constituted both through an exclusion of what he calls economic and political 'weapons' and by way of norms which insist upon discussion, proof and the extension of 'charity' to the other (ie, norms which insist that one attempt to understand the point of view of the other and treat their claims as potentially intelligible and viable). Rational debate, as we will see, is 'regulated conflict' for Bourdieu, but integral to its regulation is the condition that interlocuters answer 'a demonstration with a refutation, one scientific fact with another' (Bourdieu, 2000, 112). The paradigm case of reason, in this respect, involves two or more persons in debate. However, to reiterate my point above, insofar as the perspective of the other (particular or generalized) can be incorporated within the habitus, it might equally apply to the self-dialogues to which writers such as Mead (1967) and Vygotsky (1986) make reference. Self-dialogues are derivative upon the social situation of dialogue with others—we learn to think by first talking with others—but no less important for that. Thirdly, one particularly pertinent feature that Bourdieu recognizes in such situations is the possibility of individual and particular perspectives being transcended and giving way to a viewpoint which is thereby *more* universal than those of which it composed. As corporeally, historically and socially situated beings we each have and indeed are a point of view but through dialogue it is possible for us to transcend the particularity of our individual points of view, moving in the direction of a universal view. And this movement is, in part, what we mean by 'reason' or 'rationality'. Bourdieu's subscription to this point of view is evidenced in a rather roundabout fashion. It emerges most clearly in those contexts where he is criticizing Kant and Habermas for assuming that agents will by nature engage in such activity (Bourdieu, 1998, 2000). Against this, to anticipate a later point, he argues that 'submission to the universal' presupposes that the rewards, punishments and controls in any given social field are configured so as to constitute an 'interest in disinterest', a 'particular interest in the universal'. In arguing his case, however, he strongly commits himself to a conception of reason as the transcendence of particularity by way of dialogue. In marking his difference from Kant and Habermas he brings an area of common ground into focus too. His disagreement with Kant and Habermas is not about the possibility or the desirability of moving from particularity to universality, nor is it about the fact that this move is of the essence of rationality. Rather, it concerns the preconditions of this movement. Where Kant views the tendency towards universalization as inherent in the subject and Habermas in the pragmatic structures of language, Bourdieu sees it as an effect of social constraint and power.

It is also important to note here that much of Bourdieu's critique of 'doxa' (see below) and of the process whereby bourgeois hegemony is legitimated is based upon what he sees as the false universalization of the particular. He argues that the middle classes represent as universal values and judgements which are, in fact, particular. Furthermore he claims that their symbolic power, as effected through, for example, their privileged position in a variety of cultural fields, allows them to secure widespread acceptance of this definition. At one level this line of criticism is clearly criticism of those liberal, enlightenment philosophies which appear to corroborate and validate particular claims to universality. In contrast to the postmodernists, however, Bourdieu is not rejecting the idea of universality altogether. On the contrary, his is an imminent critique which calls for a genuine striving towards universality and which seeks to show how earlier generations of universalizing philosophers fail in terms of their own criteria.

Habermas' transcendental arguments regarding communicative reason are one very clear target for such critique. Habermas, though he makes interesting observations on the history of public reason in *Structural Transformation* and in his account of 'rationalization' in the *Theory of Communicative Action*, seeks to ground the concept of rationality transcendentally, by way of an investigation of the 'universal pragmatics' of language. The ideals of rational communication and of his much criticized 'ideal speech situation', he maintains, are inherent in universal pragmatic structures of language use which can be uncovered through transcendental analysis and argument. Furthermore, he tends to limit his focus to a relatively singular account of practical reason (as opposed to pure reason or judgement, in the Kantian sense). In contrast to this, Bourdieu is thoroughly historical in his account, is opposed to transcendental arguments, at least of the sort Habermas is making, and offers a more pluralistic account of a variety of forms of reason (scientific, practical, aesthetic etc.). Transcendental arguments, he claims, rest upon a misrecognition of intuitions and sentiments which are, in fact, historical and social in origin; a forgetting or repression of history: 'The necesssity and self-evidence of these transcendental beings only impress themselves on those who have acquired the necessary apti-tudes to "receive" them, through a long learning process.' (Bourdieu, 2000, 114, his emphasis). This is a mistake Kant makes with respect to aesthetic judgement. His transcendental arguments overlook the socio-historical conditions of pos-sibility of aesthetic judgments (as he defines them) and the manner in which the dispositions necessary to such judgements are socially communicated (Bourdieu, 1984, 1990). And Habermas repeats this mistake in his account of public, practical reason. Furthermore, to seek to ground rationality *in this way*, for Bourdieu, is to succumb to *scholasticism*; that is, to a form of discourse founded upon false abstractions, decontextualization and abstract models which have little bearing upon the messiness of everyday praxis and cannot be used to explain them. In terms of linguistic theory, Bourdieu continues, Habermas falls into the same trap as Saussure and Chomsky. The model of communication upon which he bases his analysis is an abstraction which dehistoricizes and decontextualizes its object, overlooking the socio-historical conditions which have given rise to national languages in their current form, the heterogeneity of actually existing language games and the considerable social differences in patterns of language use.

The ideals and norms or rules of rational communicative engagement do not issue forth from invariate structures of communicative pragmatics, any more than from a transcendental ego or the heavens, Bourdieu continues. They emerge out of the dynamics and interactions of human history (as *Structural Transfor-mation* sometimes seems to suggest)[1]. Moreover, as such, they have emerged in differentiated forms. At the very least, for example, different scientific commu-nities have emerged with their own respective ideals and norms regarding evi-dence and evaluation, their own 'rules of engagement', and these contrast with those that have developed in literary and artistic circles, and in fields of politi-cal discourse. The history of each of these fields is, at one level, a history of the establishment and evolution of distinct rational forms. And, of course, Bourdieu himself writes from a vantage point within history. Historicization does not imply relativity for Bourdieu, however. What emerges out of history, as a product of historical dynamics, can have a transhistorical significance and validity, and it is possible to speak of contemporary forms of rationality (eg, contemporary science) as better than prior forms. Quite how he would reply to the objection, levelled at other defenders of Modern reason (see Wilson, 1974), that such comparative judgements are illegitimate because they are always rooted in the paradigm of rationality they deem superior, is not clear. Assumedly, however, his answer, like that of Habermas (1991), would have to rely upon the claim that modern forms of reasoning have grown out of an over-coming of limits of previous forms of reasoning; limits which become apparent within the framework of those previous forms. Like Bachelard (2002), he can maintain that the breaks and disjunctures which punctuate the history of spe-cific modes of discourse arise out of (historically emergent) recognition of the limits of earlier modes of reason and discourse, but also carry forward what was useful from those earlier modes[2]. Unlike Bachelard, however, he is much more aware of the social conditions of these dynamics and breaks[3].

The rationality of fields, Bourdieu continues, presupposes their relative autonomy. The scientific field, for example, having established its own criteria of good argument, must enjoy sufficient autonomy from other fields (such as the economic field) to allow those criteria to constitute the guiding force of scientific endeavours. If external factors compromise the criteria which shape and motivate activity in the scientific field then the rationality of the field is jeopardized, or rather the extent to which external factors compromise criteria determines the extent to which rationality can be effectively achieved. As Bourdieu puts it:

> The anarchic confrontation of individual investments and interests is transformed into rational dialogue only to the extent that the field is sufficiently autonomous (and therefore equipped with sufficiently high entry barriers) to exclude the importantion of non-specific weapons, especially political or economic ones, into the internal struggles—to the extent that the participants are constrained to use only instruments of discussion or proof corresponding to the scientific demands in the matter (such as the principle of charity), and are therefore obliged to sublimate their *libido dominandi* into a *libido sciendi* that can only triumph by answering a demonstration with a refutation, one scientific fact with another scientific fact. (Bourdieu, 2000: 112)

This passage calls for a close reading, as it reveals much that is central to Bourdieu's conception. In contrast to the position generally attributed (perhaps unfairly) to Habermas, Bourdieu's 'ideal speech situation' does not involve a suspension of power relations, strategic manoeuvring or egoistic interests. As noted above, it entails a configuring of those factors which is generative of rational debate. Power is essential since agents must be constrained to play by the rules of the game (the rules of rationality). And self-interested strategic action is necessary as long as the situation is such that individuals are best able to realize their interests by way of conformity to the game. Agents must find themselves in a situation where, paradoxically, their best interests are served by abandoning themselves to a disinterested pursuit of truth; that is, the aforementioned 'interest in disinterest'. There must be incentives for them to abandon the particularity of their point of view in the pursuit of a more objective, because more widely (and perhaps universally) agreeable, view. Not that agents involved in such games necessarily recognize this. To the contrary, involvement in the game can generate an internalization of its rules and purpose, to the point whereby the agent feels them as his or her own. They 'believe in the game' and find themselves attuned to it. They unconsciously censor and sublimate their expressions to conform to the requirements of the field, assuming its values and ideals, and their action is attuned to its structure to the degree that those structures feel natural, inevitable and correct. Even in these cases, however, this disposition towards truth is an effect of the field and of the forms of power in the field which re-mould the agent.

In this respect Bourdieu subverts the Habermasian distinction between strategic and communicative action by seeking out the structural conditions of fields which make 'communicative rationality' strategically viable. At the same time, however, he challenges the naïve and insufficiently sociological conception of strategic action posited by rational action and game theories. His strategic agent acts on the basis of deep seated and socially shaped sentiments, tastes, perceptions. Their egoism is necessarily filtered through a process of cultivation and socialization which, as Durkheim (1974) emphasized, is irreducibly collective in nature.

How this plays out in relation to different fields is variable. Bourdieu (2000) argues that the scientific field comes closest to the realization of his ideal. He also notes particular problems associated with the political field. On the one hand, for example, echoing Durkheim (1982) and Halbwachs (1960), he refers to 'morphological obstacles that the size of political units and the number of citizens put in the way of any form of direct government' (Bourdieu, 1992, 172). In other words, compared to very small and highly specialized scientific communities, the numbers and spread of individuals involved in any political community poses immense obstacles to effective rational deliberation. We are forced into representative democracy, rather than direct democracy, and even representative democracy is dogged by the size of the territory and populations it services. Secondly, political debate is particularly prone to the obstacles posed by deep-rooted dispositions which resist the force of good argument. Nationalism is one example Bourdieu (2000) gives of this. From the sociological point of view, national boundaries are arbitrary but they are deeply and passionately felt, not least because of the ways in which agents' lives are bound up in them. Agents invest, economically and psychologically, directly and indirectly, in these culturally arbitrary divisions and the deep (corporeally) rooted resistance to change these investments effect is not easily dislodged by force of 'reasons'. The precariousness of 'peace talks' addressing disputes over national boundaries around the globe, at present, is only the most obvious example of this. This is not to deny that other fields, such as science, have a variety of obstacles to contend with. The tradition of the history and philosophy of science which Bourdieu is drawing upon here is emphatic in that respect (Bachelard, 2002). Our concern here, however, is with political debate.

One might be inclined to question the necessity that different viewpoints do indeed come together, rationally, in an effort to overcome their particularity. Why should the nationalist or slave seek rapprochement with the perspective of their other? Isn't Bourdieu being a little too 'rationalist' here? I do not think so. In the first instance, he is not implying any necessity here (although the fact of our co-occupation of the world, the fact that our actions mutually interfere, generates a degree of necessity that we arrive at 'agreed' norms). His claim is that, as a matter of fact, publics of various sorts have formed around issues and striven to thrash out issues. He is not saying that they should. He is observing that they have. Furthermore, as noted above, he argues that agents will only strive for 'universality' and 'disinterest' in conditions which effect a particular interest for them doing so. Finally, I believe that his argument is that, notwithstanding many situations wherein there is no good reason to reconcile different viewpoints, in situations where the alternative is between violence and dialogue individuals of a civilized disposition will prefer the latter. 'Civilization' is, of course, a socio-historical construction (Elias, 1984) but that is no reason to abandon the moral sensibilities it entails.

Whatever its problems, this understanding of communicative rationality lends itself well to an investigation of the systematic distortions that can affect rational deliberation. As a first illustration of this point we can consider the issue of 'colonization' which, like Habermas, Bourdieu identifies as a central impediment of public discourse in the current era.

Colonization

The key precondition of the rationality of fields, for Bourdieu, as noted above, is their relative autonomy. Fields have to be allowed to develop by the logic of their own internal development and to operate according to that logic and the emergent criteria it gives rise to. What Bourdieu has in mind here, in particular, is the relative autonomy of such fields as the media and artistic fields in relation to the economic field. To the extent that artists and journalists are dependent upon the patronage and blessing of rich benefactors and press barrons, and those benefactors, in turn, are interested in the field for commercial or other external reasons, rather than by virtue of the *illusio* of the field itself, the field is potentially distorted. The agent's action is always, at best, a *compromise formation* straddling the demands of the field itself and those generated by the alien commercial interests of the benefactor. In his analysis of the journalistic and media field, for example, Bourdieu (1998a) effectively offers an account of 'dumbing down', steered by commercial imperatives. The economic demand to expand markets and sell advertising space forces journalists, perhaps unconsciously and unfortunately increasingly habitually, to compromise in relationship to norms and procedures which would otherwise preserve a necessary standard of critical interrogation. To win readers quickly journalists aim for the 'lowest common denominator'. Similarly, in his discussion with the artist Hans Haacke, he notes how private patronage of artistic production steers much art away from the innovative and critical trajectory demanded internally by the artistic field, in a more commercial direction (Bourdieu and Haacke, 1995). In both cases, he suggests, this may happen gradually, in a stepwise and almost imperceptible manner. And in both cases the steps are covered because commercial compromise, unrecognized as such, acquires a habitual basis and a natural feel. The 'slippery slope' is slippery because at each step the standards and practices of the past are not merely abandoned but forgotten, as the new (reduced) standards become established and acquire a feel of naturalness and inevitability; that is, as they take root in the habitus.

There is much in this account that Habermas anticipates in *Structural Transformation*. Bourdieu's conceptual framework goes much further, however, in explaining the dynamics of distortion. By refusing the distinction between strategic and communicative action, and looking to the strategic configuration of communicatively rational situations, Bourdieu is well placed to explain the way in which a shift in the structure of incentives and constraints, effected by an intrusion of economic powers into a field, can detract actions from their reasonable course. Action is neither communicatively nor strategically rational but always balanced between the two, or rather communicative action is always, in the final instance, strategically secured. And the degree to which the balance shifts, undermining the strategic supports of communicative action, determines the degree of systematic distortion in communication at any point in time. Putting that another way, journalists and artists are only rational and critical, in Bourdieu's view, to the extent that they are constrained and have incentives to be so. Thus, when the balance of incentives and constraints are changed by such factors as market forces, rationality and critique are inclined to suffer. Furthermore, the notion of the habitus explains both how agents prereflectively adapt to their new situations, actively distorting their own discourses and rational forms without being fully aware of doing so, and how such distorted communicative practices, in turn, attain a more durable and instituted presence in the field. Insofar as habituation naturalizes present practice it 'covers the tracks' of adaptive communicative distortion. It renders them 'unconscious'.

Suspicious hermeneutics

Another direct implication of the field model of rationality is that we can read distortions, at least in the form of sublimations, in even those communications produced in fields characterized by a high degree of autonomy. As Bourdieu (1991) shows in *The Political Ontology of Martin Heidegger*, his method lends itself to a new way of reading texts, a variety of what Ricoeur (1977), referring to psychoanalysis, called the 'hermeneutics of suspicion'.

In his reading of Heidegger and his approach to the question of Heidegger's nazi affiliation, Bourdieu strives to find a balance between closed hermeneutic readings, which focus exclusively and closely upon the text, denying that factors outside of the text have any significance for our interpretation of it, and overly sociologistic readings which seek to explain Heidegger's philosophy by reference to his social class, relationship to historical events etc, without much reference to his texts, or which simply dismiss his texts as the works of a nazi/conservative. As a field of rational discourse, he argues, philosophy constrains, censors and shapes the utterances of its participants in various ways; namely, the ways which give it its distinctly philosophical character and which distinguish it both from other forms of rational discourse, such as sociology or physics, and from fields in which the communicative rationality of discourse is less important. These restraints clearly impose a degree of rationality and rigour upon

Heidegger's philosophical works, which may not have been in evidence in other contexts in which he formulated his views. Furthermore, they very clearly prohibited him from engaging, under the pre-text of philosophy, in any straightforward nazi/conservative propagandizing, had he wanted to do this. Propaganda is not philosophy. It does not conform to the rules and standards which philosophers expect of one another and which define the 'entrance requirement' to participation in their field. On the other hand, however, Heidegger 'the man' was shaped by his social world and experiences. Like others of his generation he was swayed by nazism and the broader current of history it belonged to. And it is unrealistic to suppose that this aspect of his life is completely separate from his philosophy. To accommodate both of these points, Bourdieu argues that Heidegger's philosophy can be read as a 'compromise formation' or 'sublimation'. That is to say, we can read Heidegger's work as a compromise between the exacting standards of philosophical discourse and an 'expressive drive' shaped by social conditions and historical trends. Just as Freud claimed to read latent meaning in dreams, we can read a latent political content in Heidegger's work. And Bourdieu does precisely this. Heidegger, he argues, effects a 'conservative revolution' in philosophy homologous to that achieved in political circles by nazi propagandists. The homology can be explained by reference to structures of the habitus which Heidegger and the political conservatives share in common and the wider social and historical contexts which generated these common structures. That there is only a homology, and not an identity, however, is explained by the censorship effect of the philosophical field and specifically the difference between this effect and the censorial conditions of the political field (as it was in Germany at the time).

This does not detract from the value of Heidegger's philosophy *qua* philosophy, nor does it mean that contemporary apologists of Heidegger or those influenced by him (amongst whom we must include Bourdieu himself) are sympathetic to nazism. On the other hand, it does offer a new way to read Heidegger and anybody else for that matter; a manner of reading which can enquire into implicit social and political influences/implications of works which might claim to be free such of influences/implications on the grounds of, for example, their philosophical (or scientific) nature. Furthermore, in this way it potentially contributes to (in this case) philosophical discourse, much as psychoanalysis does in the personal lives of analysands, by bringing repressed material into view, where they can be subject to rational interrogation, analysis and control. Socioanalysis reveals what Bachelard (2000) refers to as 'epistemological obstacles' thereby allowing those obstacles to be addressed and progress achieved.

What Bourdieu implies here is that the relative autonomy of acts of expression and their fields is only ever 'relative'. This gives us all the more reason to insist upon preserving and bolstering the autonomy of fields, in order that inappropriate interests are kept in check by them, but it also requires of us that we look beyond the claims to total autonomy that practitioners, whether philosophers, scientists, journalists or artists, might make for their craft. To reiterate, it calls for a suspicious hermeneutics.

Pushing this analysis one step further, Bourdieu also explores some of the political and social dynamics which shape the community of Heidegger scholarship—an analysis which, by implication, might be applied in other cases. Heidegger's work is open to relatively crude critique if taken at face value, he notes. A literal reading of his work would find much to disagree with. The Heideggarian community protects the work of the master from 'profane' critiques, however. The words of the master are afforded a sacred status, in Durkheim's (1915) sense, and thus exempted from having to deal with *prima facie* objections. Heidegger's use of everyday language is elevated such that the everyday meaning of what he says is refused. His analysis of being-in-the-world, for example, at his own instigation, is distinguished from 'ontic' empirical analyses and is thereby closed off to the contributions and critiques which empirical social scientists might otherwise make of it. It is 'ontological'—and even then in an ancient sense which Heidegger claims modern philosophy has forgotten and lost touch with—and is only open to legitimate comment by those who are willing and know-how to treat it as such; that is, those who are disposed to recognize, respect, revere and reproduce its sacred status.

This is a fascinating but also potentially problematic element of Bourdieu's approach. He is alerting us to important psycho-social dynamics of group formation which affect public debate and the rhetorical and reading strategies which these groups use to sustain their collective identity and distinction. Furthermore, he is sensitizing us to the social function of intellectual distinctions and categories. We can see the ontic/ontological distinction advocated by Heidegger, and perhaps also Husserl's empirical/transcendental distinction, as social barriers used to demarcate and protect specific intellectual fields and monopolies. The danger of the approach, however, and what we must avoid, is the tendency to suggest that all distinctions and rules are 'merely' strategies. They may be strategies and they are most certainly rooted in human social history but, as Bourdieu himself insists, that does not mean that they are 'merely' this. The discussion of reason in *Pascalian Meditations* is as much opposed to nihilism and relativism as to Habermasian transcendentalism. Bourdieu argues that some historically emergent practices, and specifically those constitutive of various forms of reason, have a transhistorical significance and validity. There is a very fine line to tread here, however, and a constant danger that suspicious hermeneutics will degenerate into nihilistic relativism. We must tread the line carefully and it is not clear that Bourdieu always does.

Doxa and the discursive unconscious

As my discussion of 'colonization' suggests, debate in the media, parliamentary, literary and artistic fields is very important for Bourdieu. It provides an important check upon the power of the state and it provides an obvious potential source of emancipatory change. However, he argues throughout his work that we need to be mindful of the limited role that discourse plays in securing the necessary conditions of social-political reproduction, including the reproduction of the many varieties of domination evident in contemporary societies. Discourse is the tip of an iceberg in terms of the reproduction and steering of the social world. Contrary to the claims of liberal political thinkers and certain more naïve schools of ideology-critique, he argues, political order is not the product of a reflective or conscious agreement over values, norms, opinions and beliefs (or 'ideologies'). At most it entails what Wittgenstein (1953) referred to as an 'agreement in forms of life'. More concretely, however, his claim is that political order is achieved at the level of assumptions and pre-reflective corporeal dispositions, which he labels 'doxa':

> . . . in order to fully understand the immediate submission that the state order elicits, it is necessary to break with the intellectualism of the neo-Kantian tradition to acknowledge that cognitive structures are not forms of consciousness but *dispositions of the body*. That the obedience we grant to the injunctions of the state cannot be understood either as a mechanical submission to an external force or as a conscious consent to an order (in the double sense of the term). The social world is riddled with *calls to order* that function as such only to those who are predisposed to heeding them as they *awaken* deeply buried corporeal dispositions, outside the channels of consciousness and consent. (Bourdieu, 1998: 54–5, his emphasis)

He continues:

> Submission to the established order is the product of the agreement between, on the one hand, cognitive structures inscribed in bodies by both collective history (phylogenesis) and individual history (ontogenesis) and, on the other, the objective structures of the world to which these cognitive structures are applied. State injunctions owe their obviousness, and thus their potency, to the fact that the state has imposed the very cognitive structures through which it is perceived . . . (ibid.)

This claim should not be read in an overly mechanistic fashion. Like Merleau-Ponty (1962), Bourdieu is attempting to tease out the complex nature of embodied human being, as a third term between *en-soir* and *pour-soir*. Doxa consists of embodied and practical understandings and know-how, not mechanical reflexes. But it is *practical* and *embodied* and, at least insofar as it remains doxic, it is neither reflective or conscious. The doxic is what we know without knowing that we know it; what we abide by and adhere to with, at best, only a vague and inarticulate sense of doing so.

As long as this unspoken and doxic level of discipline, this unconscious submission to the demands of social order, remains in place, so too does that order. Society can tolerate freedom of expression and argument because, and only because, so little of what is essential to the securing of social order crosses the threshold of discursive articulation. Thus, however 'rational' public debate may be, its efficacy is always limited by the range of issues and topics that are raised within it.

Doxa is historically and politically contingent. What is doxic now may previously have been a subject of discursive struggle, only having become doxic in the course of conflict and the acts of repression imposed by the victors in this struggle:

> What appears to us today as self-evident, as beneath consciousness and choice, has quite often been the stake of struggles and instituted only as the result of dogged confrontations between dominant and dominated groups. The major effect of historical evolution is to abolish history by relegating to the past, that is, to the unconscious, the lateral possibles that it eliminated. (Bourdieu, 1998a: 56–7)

As such, doxa is not neutral. It reflects the interests of dominant groups, whose rise to dominance has enabled their views and interests to achieve a taken-for-granted status, beyond opinion and beyond question. This, moreover, allows these groups to adopt an apparently 'disinterested' and rational stance in debates. It is easier for them to be or at least appear disinterested because their interests are secured at a level of assumption and habit, below the threshold of discourse.

By the same token, anything which is currently doxic could become or revert to the level of discursive argument if conditions of political crisis disturb their taken-for-granted nature (se Crossley, 2002a,b, 2003). In these instances, Bourdieu argues, dominant groups, whose interests are served by doxic assumptions, will typically seek to defend them. They will cease to be doxic but, being supported by dominant groups, will remain 'orthodox', at least unless or until engaged opponents manage to successfully challenge them. This is the exception for Bourdieu, however. Most of what is essential to the preservation of the status quo remains, most of the time, below the threshold of discourse and opinion. It is doxic.

Much of this resonates with what Habermas writes, admittedly in a less 'corporeal' vain, in his various discussions of the lifeworld. Bourdieu, however, develops these observations in a way which illuminates the systematically distorted nature of public communication and opens up a socio-analytic epistemology. The doxic level of culture is society's 'unconscious' for Bourdieu, born not only of habituation and the forms of forgetfulness it entails but equally of conflict and repression. This is not simply a matter of history being written and told by the winners—although that is an aspect of it. It is equally a matter of practices, once contested and resisted, becoming instituted as an unquestioned and habituated norm. History is recorded on two registers, the discursive and the corporeal-habitual. The unconscious of history consists in the gap between the two. And we can explore this unconscious. Just as the psychoanalyst delves into the repressed history of the individual subject, so the sociologist can and should delve into the repressed history of contemporary societies, bringing previously doxic assumptions, which serve the interests of élites, to the level of reflective argument. Any form of discourse will, of course, presuppose a range of assumptions, habits, traditions, prejudices etc. There can be no discourse free of doxa. This applies to the discourse of the sociologist as much as anybody else and generates a very real need for the reflexive vigilance of sociological practice recommended by Bourdieu. As he says in a later paper,

> In the work of objectifying the historical unconscious, the researcher (historian, anthropologist or sociologist) faces two unconsciouses, the unconscious which s/he takes for his/her object and his/her own educational unconscious (which is shaped by national and disciplinary traditions), which she must also take as an object or risk unknowingly investing it in his/her analysis of the historical unconscious of others. The work of double objectification . . . (Bourdieu, 2002: 4, my translation)

This will not free the sociologist of unconscious influence. At the very least every act of self-clarification will always stand in need of its own clarification. The 'limits' of sociological reflexivity, given that they are the limits of all discourse, should not, however, detract from the importance and possible contribution of a socio-analysis of publics. The sociologist can unearth the systematic distortions of public communication in such a way as to bring those distortions under greater control by the public.

The means of participation

Through the concept of doxa and his understanding of the social-political conditions of its formation, Bourdieu is able to identify systematic distortions in public discourse at a general level; that is to say, he identifies distortions which affect the reasoning and discourse of all members of society equally, even if those distortions are more beneficial to dominant than to dominated groups. Not all distortions have this general character, however. Some are more probable in some groups than others and, in particular, in some classes rather than others. We see this in Bourdieu's work on the class composition of literary, artistic and academic publics. These publics claim to be open to all, Bourdieu argues, or at least to be restricted only in accordance with ability and interest. Anybody with a 'love of art' and a talent for appreciating and discussing it, for example, is welcome to participate in artistic publics. This is a misrepresentation, however. In essence, setting aside complexities, he argues that the offspring of the educated middle class are more likely to be introduced to such publics in their childhood, with the consequence that they will develop the competence, confidence and taste for participation in later life (Bourdieu *et al.*, 1990). They acquire the cultural capital which constitutes the effective 'entry requirement' for participation in those publics and the habitus that predisposes them to do so.

These studies are, as many commentators have pointed out, somewhat dated by now and possibly reflect specificities of French society. Recent data from the UK, however, at least with regard to some of the activities Bourdieu refers to (eg, reading books, visiting museums/galleries, and going to the theatre, opera and ballet), bear his analysis out (see Graph One). It is evident that, with the exception of reading books, these activities are far from being 'popular' in any social class. We are thus forced to say, as Bourdieu and his colleagues say of camera club membership, that these forms of participation in public culture are 'deviant'. Nevertheless, it is also clear that social class plays a considerable role

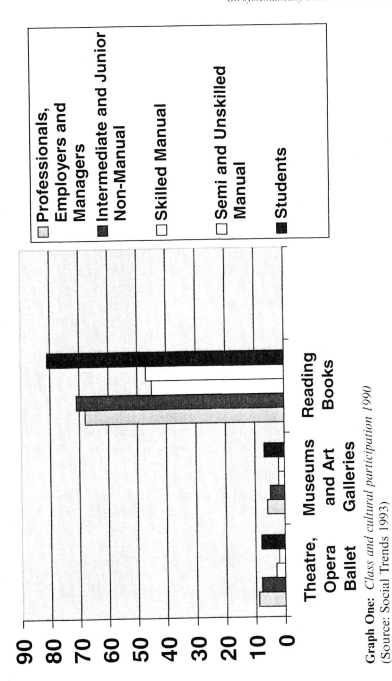

Graph One: *Class and cultural participation 1990*
(Source: Social Trends 1993)

in the shaping of these deviant subcultures, with manual workers being considerably less likely to become involved in them.

Insofar as artistic publics form a part of what, for convenience, we call *the* public sphere, these subtle exclusions can be said to constitute politically significant communicative distortions. Public discourse is not as open as those involved in it might, in good faith, believe it to be. Furthermore, there is at least an implication here that we should be wary in assessing the broader political meaning of the various symbolic challenges levelled within artistic fields. The symbolic challenges posed by avant garde artists presuppose, for their meaning and thus their challenge, a form and level of cultural capital which is effectively concentrated into the hands of a small elite. Duchamp's *Fountain*[4] to take an example, may constitute a defining and subversive moment for publics who are privy (excuse the pun) to and at home within the Western artistic tradition, but to the wider public it may just be an autographed toilet—which is precisely what it is when stripped of the sedimented meanings and sacred status which shape the 'cultured' perception of it. Worse still, it is a humiliating indication that they are excluded from high culture by the limits of their own understanding. As such this 'radical' gesture may serve to put culturally dominated groups 'in their place' far more effectively than a conventional landscape painting or portrait, which most people can recognize and make a claim to understand and evaluate (even if only 'in their own way').

Bourdieu also applies this analysis directly to political publics (see esp. 1984, 397–465). His point of departure is a reflection upon the social distribution of 'don't know' answers on political polls conducted in France in the late 1960s and early 1970s. It is commonly acknowledged, he notes, that 'don't knows' are not randomly distributed. Women, at this time, were more likely to 'not know', as were the lower paid and less well-educated. This, Bourdieu argues, reveals the social preconditions of political deliberation and opinion formation. More to the point, closer examination of the data reveals that the discrepancies only reach significant proportions as the questions asked move in the direction of issues which are more abstract or distant from the immediate lived experiences and interests of the groups in question, questions which presuppose an understanding of political and economic games not immediately given to direct experience: eg, the state of the economy and international affairs. This points to the role of acquired competence or cultural capital in political discourse and opinion formation. Abstract political debate is a (language) game, like aesthetic criticism, and like the competence entailed in aesthetic criticism, its requisite competence must be acquired. It presupposes immersion, experience and perhaps some formal instruction. But as with aesthetic competence, these formative experiences manifest a structured and unequal social distribution. They are, for the most part, the preserve of the educated middle classes. Furthermore, like aesthetic criticism, reflection upon abstract political issues presupposes the luxury of being able to stand back from immediate experiences, responses and impulses, in order to play a formal game. It is thus, in Bourdieu's view, more suited to the habitus of those groups whose immediate needs are secure, whose interests are doxic, and who enjoy the luxury to indulge in abstraction and asceticism.

This is not simply a matter of competence. It is equally about barriers set up at the level of agents' feelings of where they belong; their lived sense of social position. For as long as women felt that 'the economy' or 'international affairs' were not for them, they did not develop the 'feel for the game' required for effective participation in debates about these issues. Likewise with class. The status of the middle classes, as experienced from within, entails a felt sense of entitlement to 'views', a sense of both the right and the duty to have and express opinions on general issues. This, Bourdieu (1984) argues, is related to the 'individualism' which belongs to their class ethos. The ethos of the working class is different, however, and less conducive to the development of such 'disinterested' debates. Thus, as with museum visiting, the habitus of some groups inclines them to participate in political debate, whilst the habitus of others disinclines them. These debates, as a consequence, are systematically distorted.

As with his arguments concerning artistic publics, it is possible, on the basis of already existing data, to offer a partial transposition of this argument to the UK in the present. A series of studies conducted between the 1960s and the 1990s, for example, have pointed to the overrepresentation of the educated middle classes within the so-called new social movements (for an overview see Rootes, 1995). The details of this overrepresentation and its possible causes (eg, family socialisation, higher education experiences, occupational experiences, post-material values, material resources and time) are hotly debated (Bagguley, 1995) but the basic fact of overrepresentation is not, and it can be interpreted both in term of Bourdieu's conception of class habitus (Eder, 1982, 1983, 1993; Crossley, 2002a), and as proof of his contention regarding the role of the habitus in political participation. The working classes are not averse to social movement participation, of course, as the labour movement demonstrates. In relation, however, to the issues raised by the new social movements, which are more removed from immediate everyday material interests (eg, the state of the environment, the ethics of nuclear proliferation and the rights of other species), they are less likely to be directly involved.

A similar pattern is evident in relation to the media field, particularly regarding newspaper consumption. Bourdieu notes quite specific class differences in both patterns of newspaper consumption and the meanings which consumers and producers attach to newspapers. Different social groups tend to buy different newspapers, if they buy them at all. And they buy newspapers for different reasons, using their paper in different ways. The educated middle classes are more likely to buy 'quality' daily papers and thereby find themselves addressed as one might expect in a political public sphere: ie, as an astute and critical reader who will want to make up their own mind about issues. This contrasts with working-class consumers, who more often buy papers for entertainment, gossip, sport results or perhaps simply to hear the personal opinions of others (whom may they agree with or enjoy disagreeing with):

Like 'difficult' art as opposed to facile art, or eroticism as opposed to pornography, the so-called quality newspapers call for a relation to the object implying the affirmation of a distance from the object which is the affirmation of a power over the object and also a dignity of the subject. They give the reader much more than the 'personal' opinions he needs; they acknowledge his dignity as a political subject capable of being, if not a subject of history, then at least the subject of a discourse on history. (Bourdieu, 1984: 446)

Just as the aesthetic subject constitutes their-self as such by establishing a distance from their immediate visceral reaction to images, so too the political subject stands back from the fray and, to the extent that they can, from their own immediate interests and prejudices. They strive to work through different points of view in search of a more universal view. But again this presupposes a process of learning, a specific habitus and a form of cultural capital. Those who do not have this capital effectively exclude themselves from the political process and thereby contribute to their own continued subordination.

I cannot hope to bridge the gap between the French media studied by Bourdieu in *Distinction* and the contemporary British press. However, as graphs two and three indicate, the class bias in newspaper consumption is strong in the current British context. This data is drawn from the British Readership Survey and reflects their class groupings.[5] What is important, for our purposes, is that

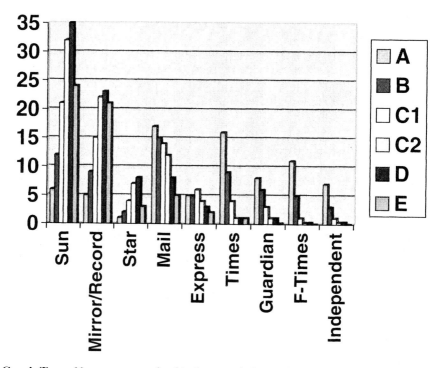

Graph Two: *Newspaper readership by social class (the Dailies)*
(Source: National Readership Survey 2001)

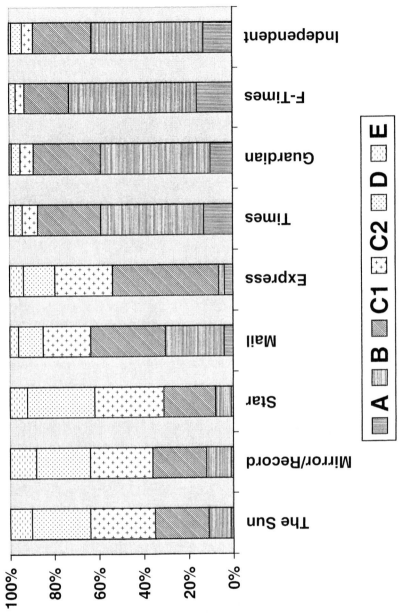

Graph Three: *Class base of newspaper readership (Dailies)*
(Source: National Readership Survey 2001)

the higher classes (a and b) constitute the majority of readers of those newspapers generally deemed 'quality' papers (*The Times, The Guardian, The Financial Times* and *The Independent*) and are more likely to read these papers than any of the others. The lower class groupings (d and e) are extremely unlikely to read the quality papers and much more likely to read those papers generally deemed 'scandal rags' (*The Sun, The Mirror, The Star*). The middle grouping (c1 and c2) make up the majority readership of these scandal sheets, as of the 'middle brow' papers (*The Express, The Mail*) but they are also much less likely to read the qualities. These trends, which the same survey also discerns for the Sunday papers and a variety of magazines, invites far greater analysis than I have the space to offer here. It is clear, however, that participation in the media field, at the level of newspaper reading at least, remains a class divided phenomenon. Given the same 'free' choice of newspapers, members of different social classes, by force of their class specific habitus, select differently and thereby position themselves differently in relation to both the public sphere and, by means of it, the political field (qua parliamentary field).

Habitus, misunderstanding and symbolic power

The relationship of the habitus to political debate cannot be reduced to a question of inclusion and exclusion, however. From his earliest studies of misunderstanding in educational communication, Bourdieu has emphasized the importance of the habitus in communicative encounters. The perceptual and linguistic schemas of the habitus shape the ways in which agents make sense or fail to make sense of each other's communications. This may mean that they find different meanings in communications to those which the authors of those communications identify in them. It may mean that they 'miss the point' or just fail to make any sense of what is communicated. Whatever the details, however, communication is always a meeting of habitus and the chances of a consensual meaning being arrived at are always less likely if interlocuters are more distant in social space. This is not simply a matter of vocabulary, 'linguistic code'[6] or the hexis of communication qua embodied act. These are important but it is equally a matter of the 'common sense' or rather not so common sensibilities, assumptions, connotations and background knowledge which are drawn upon in communication and which give shape and meaning to what is said. For example, as I know to my cost, an off-hand ironic remark about 'Mrs Thatcher's belief in the importance of trade unions' may be completed misread by a young person who did not live through the Thatcher era, and who is thus not disposed to hear the irony. When individuals meet to talk they bring their social position (class, gender, race, generation etc.) with them. Indeed, their social position constitutes, via the habitus, the schemas of transmission and reception generative of the communicative process. In this respect communication is always systematically distorted since the possibility of undistorted communication, if that means communication not structured through socially shaped habitus, is nil. But there are degrees of systematic distortion relative to the distance in social space of interlocuters and the inclusion/exclusion of all affected parties or their representatives. As such the critique of distortion is meaningful and necessary.

The communicative distortions potentiated by social distance are more than matters of misunderstanding, however. As Bourdieu's educational studies amply illustrate, when social distance reduces the level of comprehension achieved in a communicative encounter, 'symbolic power' determines which party is attributed the blame (see esp. Bourdieu *et al.*, 1994). For example, when the students in Bourdieu's study were unable to comprehend the lectures of their professors, this was interpreted in terms of their own lack of ability. When the professors were unable to understand the essays of their students, however, it was the competence of the communicator which was called into question. This is a formal institutional context wherein powers are clearly demarcated. The words of the teacher are invested with institutional power like those of the politician, the judge and the psychiatrist. It does not take too great a leap of the imagination, however, to recognize that similar effects, attached to a range of social statuses, can take effect in less formal and apparently 'democratic' communicative encounters. We are disposed to be more charitable, even deferential, in interpreting the utterances of the highly educated than we are the less highly educated, however silly or incomprehensible the claims of the former may sometimes be. Furthermore, as Bourdieu has shown, social position, whether officially marked or not, is communicated in interaction situations by way of bodily hexis: eg, accent, demeanour, 'linguistic code', dress etc. As such it can have subtle effects upon both the meaning and the authority of what is said. Actually existing communication is never a meeting between abstract interlocuters, always a meeting of social positions, and always a relationship of power.

Conclusion

The largest part of this chapter has been devoted to a consideration of some of the ways in which public communication is systematically distorted, according to the work of Pierre Bourdieu. Bourdieu considers how an individual's social position, which they carry both in the form of embodied dispositions (habitus) and effective resources (capital), shapes the forms of public participation they opt for, the nature of their communications and the (socially sanctioned) authority with which they speak. He considers the cultural unconscious (doxa) which underlies all forms of communication and the manner in which the relative autonomy of fields, which is the ultimate guarantee of rationality within them, can be undermined by the introduction of a variety of forms of colonization and contamination. In these respects Bourdieu makes bold steps towards the definition of critical theory posited by the early Habermas; that is, critical theory as the investigation of 'systematically distorted communication' and, more particularly, of systematic communicative distortions in the public sphere. More to the point, to the degree that Bourdieu's work conveys, in addition to findings, a set of theoretical and methodological tools which we can take up and use, he imparts a framework for the continuation of this work.

Bourdieu also forces us to shift the gestalt in our apprehension of these matters, however. Because Habermas' conception of the 'ideal speech situation' is based upon transcendental deductions from abstract and decontextualized models of communicative engagement, these ideals seem impossible to realize in actual social contexts. They are asocial models; that is, models based upon a bracketing out of 'real world' conditions. For this reason the inevitable real-world conditions of discourse, including power, constraint and strategic action, appear necessarily as contaminants. The logic and consequence is very similar to that of Rawls' (1973) 'veil of ignorance'; justice is deemed feasible only in a social vacuum. Bourdieu has a very different view. He advises us to seek out those social conditions which enable, encourage and constrain interlocuters to engage rationally with one another. The implication of this is that rather than devising ways of minimizing the impact of the social environment upon debating citizens, a fruitless task, we should be looking for the best ways to secure such an impact. How can we restrain politicians, journalists, academics and artists in such a way that they best further their ends by way of furthering the ends of us all? And how can we ensure that all citizens have equal access to this 'regulated conflict'? These are not easy questions but they are more realistic than the Habermasian alternative.

Notes

1 Bourdieu does not recognize this historical element in Habermas. He portrays Habermas almost exclusively as a transcendental and 'scholastic' thinker.
2 Garry Gutting (1990) offers an interesting contrast of the work of Bachelard and Thomas Kuhn along these lines. Although Bachelard was a key precursor of the theorists of discontinuity, such as Foucault, he observes, there is careful attention to questions of both continuity and progress in his work.
3 These social dynamics may be those of a specific, evolving discursive community but they might equally be those of the wider historical society to which this community belongs.
4 *Fountain* consisted of an old, standard toilet bowl upon which Duchamp had signed the name 'R Mutt'. The purpose of the exercise, seemingly, was to question ideas of individual artistic creativity and to raise the question of what art itself is and whether it is isn't simply what is sanctioned as art by the art world (eg. by placing it in a museum).
5 Which are: A = Higher managerial, administrative of professional ('Upper Middle Class'), B = Intermediate managerial, administrative or professional ('Middle Class'), C1 = Supervisory or clerical and junior managerial, administrative or professional ('Lower Middle Class), C2 Skilled manual workers ('Skilled Working Class'), D = Semi and unskilled manual workers ('Working Class'), E = State pensioners or widows (no other earner), casual or lowest grade workers ('Those at lowest levels of subsistence').
6 The idea of linguistic codes dates back to the work of Bernstein (1975) and Labov (1969). It is not my intention here to take sides in this (now quite old) debate. Suffice it to say that Middle and working class speakers manifest different patterns of speech which can make each relatively difficult to understand to the other.
7 This article is published in Japanese translation. The English language original is available from the author on request.

110

Bibliography

Bachelard, G. (2002) *The Formation of the Scientific Mind*. Manchester: Clinamen.

Bagguley, P. (1995) Middle Class Radicalism Revisited, in T. Butler and M. Savage, (1995), *Social Change and the Middle Classes*. London: UCL.

Bernstein, B. (1975) *Class, Codes and Control* (3 Vols). London: RKP.

Bourdieu, P. (1977) *Outline of a Theory of Practice*. Cambridge: Cambridge University Press.

Bourdieu, P. (1984) *Distinction*. London: Routledge.

Bourdieu, P. (1986) *Homo Academicus*. Cambridge: Polity.

Bourdieu, P. (1990) *Photography: A Middle Brow Art*. Cambridge: Polity.

Boudieu, P. (1991) *The Political Ontology of Martin Heidegger*. Cambridge: Polity.

Bourdieu, P. (1992a) *The Logic of Practice*. Cambridge: Polity.

Bourdieu, P. (1992b) *Language and Symbolic Power*. Cambridge: Polity.

Bourdieu, P. (1998a) *Practical Reason*. Cambridge: Polity.

Bourdieu, P. (1998b) *On Television and Journalism*. London: Pluto.

Bourdieu, P. (2000a) *Pascalian Meditations*. Cambridge: Polity.

Bourdieu, P. (2000b) L'inconscient d'école, *Actes de la Recherche en Sciences Sociales*, 35, 3–5.

Bourdieu, P. Darbel, A. and Schnapper, D. (1991) *The Love of Art*. Cambridge: Polity.

Bourdieu, P. and Haakce, H. (1995) *Free Exchange*. Cambridge: Polity.

Bourdieu, P., Passeron, J.-C. and Martin, M. (1994) *Academic Discourse*. Cambridge: Polity.

Bourdieu, P. and Passeron, J.-C. (1996) *Reproduction*. London: Sage.

Crossley, N. (2002a) *Making Sense of Social Movements*. Buckinghamshire: Open University Press.

Crossley, N. (2002b) 'Habitus, Agency and Change: Engaging With Bourdieu' *Gendai Shakai-Riron Kenku* (Journal of Studies in Contemporary Social Theory) 12, 329–577.

Crossley, N. (2003) From Reproduction to Transformation: Social Movement Fields and the Radical Habitus. *Theory, Culture and Society* 20(6), 43–68.

Durkheim, E. (1915) *The Elementary Forms of Religious Life*. New York: Free Press.

Durkheim, E. (1965) *The Rules of Sociological Method*. New York: Free Press.

Durkheim, E. (1974) *Sociology and Philosophy*. New York: Free Press.

Eder, K. (1982) A New Social Movement? *Telos* 52, 5–20.

Eder, K. (1985) The New Social Movements: Moral Crusades, Political Pressure Groups, or Social Movments, *Social Research* 52(4) 869–90.

Eder, K. (1993) *The New Politics of Class*. London: Sage.

Elias, N. (1984) *The Civilising Process*. Oxford: Blackwell.

Gutting, G. (1989) *Michel Foucault's Archaeology of Scientific Knowledge*. Cambridge: Cambridge University Press.

Habermas, J. (1970a) On Systematically Distorted Communication, *Inquiry* 13(3), 205–18.

Habermas, J. (1970b) Towards a Theory of Communicative Competence, *Inquiry* 13(4), 360–75.

Habermas, J. (1972) *Knowledge and Human Interests*. London: Heinemann.

Habermas, J. (1987) *The Theory of Communicative Action Vol II: System and Lifeworld*. Cambridge: Polity.

Habermas, J. (1989a) *The Structural Transformation of the Public Sphere*. Cambridge: Polity

Habermas, J. (1990) *The Philophical Discourse of Modernity*. Cambridge: Polity.

Habermas, J. (1991) *The Theory of Communicative Action: Reason and the Rationalisation of Society* (Vol 1). Cambridge: Polity.

Habermas, J. (1992) *Moral Consciousness and Communicative Action*. Cambridge: Polity.

Habermas, J. (1993) *Justification and Application*. Cambridge: Polity.

Halbwachs, M. (1960) *Population and Society*. Glencoe: Free Press.

Labov, W. (1969) The Logic of Nonstandard English, in P. Giglioli (1972) *Language and Social Context*. Harmondsworth: Penguin, 283–308.

Mead, G. (1967) *Mind, Self and Society*. Chicago: Chicago University Press.

Merleau-Ponty, M. (1962) *The Phenomenology of Perception*. London: Routledge.

111

Rawls, J. (1973) *A Theory of Justice*. Oxford: Oxford University Press.

Ricoeur, P. (1977) *Freud and Philosophy*. New York: Yale University Press.

Rootes, C. (1995) A New Class? The Higher Educated and the New Politics, in L. Maheu. (1995) *Social Movements and Social Classes*. London, Sage.

Vygotsky, L. (1986) *Thought and Language*. Cambridge: MIT.

Wilson, B. (ed.) (1974) *Rationality*. Oxford: Blackwell.

Wittgenstein, L. (1953) *Philosophical Investigations*. Oxford: Blackwell.

Habermas and social movements: what's 'new'?

Gemma Edwards

In this chapter I consider the contemporary relevance of Habermas' 'New Social Movement' theory (Habermas, 1981, 1987). This is an important point of contemplation when thinking about the 'public sphere' and the movements that may generate it in the present context. For Habermas, it is the 'new' movements of the post-1960s era (such as the Women's, Youth, Alternative and Ecology Movements) that form the raw materials of the public sphere. In their struggles over lifestyle and identity, new social movements respond to questions about the legitimacy and accountability of governments, and in-turn, raise them[1]. What is 'new' about these movements, Habermas argues, is the conflict around which they organize. The central conflicts of advanced capitalist societies have shifted away from the 'capital-labour' struggles of the Labour Movement (now seen as 'old' politics), and towards grievances surrounding the 'colonization of the lifeworld'. In rejecting 'colonization' the new social movements reassert communicatively rational action against the imposing agendas of the state and economy. They contain, therefore, the ideal possibility of constructing a relatively autonomous space for public debate. The shift from 'old' to 'new' politics therefore compounds the potential in new social movements for generating a genuine public sphere.

This argument suggests two things. Firstly, conflicts located at the 'seam between the system and lifeworld' (Habermas, 1981: 36), provoke public-sphere generating social movements. Secondly, that these conflicts are divorced from capital-labour conflicts and can be considered as something 'new'. I question here whether these assumptions remain valid in the present context of struggle. The chapter is comprised of three sections. In section one, after a brief exposition of Habermas' general argument, I refer to recent work on the Anti-Corporate Movement, which suggests that in part they do (Crossley, 2003). Anti-corporatism generates public debate through a struggle against the 'colonization of the lifeworld' by an expanding global economic system. On the other hand, the 'old' politics of labour are still very much a part of anti-corporate activity, begging the question of what exactly is 'new' for Habermas?

This question is tackled in section two by reconsidering Habermas' general theory. Avoiding the debate over the relative mix of old, new (and even newer?)[2]

political issues within today's social movements, I argue that 'newness' lies in Habermas' perception of a *conflict-shift* from capital-labour to the 'seam between system-lifeworld' (Habermas, 1981: 36). The question I pose here (in line with Widmann, 1981) is not whether conflicts lie at this seam, but whether this can be considered anything specifically different or 'new'. When we look at Habermas' general theorizing with the help of more recent generations of critical theorists (Honneth, 1981), we can see that the essence of the 'system-lifeworld' dynamic is the changing relationship between the state and the economy in the process of capitalist modernization, and the effects that this has at the level of social integration (the lifeworld). This is a powerful explanation of 'new' social movements because it is a powerful explanation of social movements *per se*. What is 'new' in Habermas' theory in these terms, therefore, is nothing much at all.

In line with this revision, I argue that whilst system-lifeworld conflicts may spark public-sphere generating social movements, these movements do not have to be distinct from capital-labour struggles. In denoting the tensions between state, economy and everyday-life in the process of capitalist modernization, system-lifeworld conflicts fail to mark a shift from capital-labour conflicts; on the contrary, they encompass them. The battle against the colonization of the lifeworld and the reassertion of communicative rationality against the functional agendas of the state and economy need not therefore be confined to Habermas' 'new' social movements. Instead, it is a battle taken up by social movements in capitalist societies *per se*. If this is true, then the Labour Movement retains a key role in generating a relatively autonomous space for public debate in advanced capitalist societies. It is my intention, in section three of the chapter, to support this suggestion by drawing upon two cases from the present context of struggle: Community Unionism (Wills *et al*, 2002a, 2002b) and the British Firefighters' Dispute (2002/3).

Section one: the relevance of Habermas' 'New Social Movement theory'

Habermas and 'New Social Movements': the thesis of internal colonization

Habermas' theory of 'New Social Movements' is outlined in a paper appearing in the Journal *Telos* (1981), extracted from *The Theory of Communicative Action Volume II* (1987). Here he introduces the idea of a shift in the key agents of social change and the key battles of modern society in which they engage. The essential battle is no longer fought through the 'old' politics of the Labour Movement but through the 'new' politics of the new social movements. For Habermas, the Labour Movement has ceased to be a radical source of change because it is integrated into the political system by way of labour parties and trade unions. This integration marks the containment of labour struggles for two main reasons. Firstly, the growth of trade unionism means that conflicts around capital and labour become increasingly formulated in terms of the legal rights of workers and fought through legal channels. Habermas argues that this process of 'juridification' leads to containment because it brings capital-labour conflicts under the instrumental-rational procedure of the system (Habermas, 1987: 356).

The second point is that trade union and labour party organisations work with a narrowed set of instrumental demands, usually distributive in nature (such as wage increases). Once posed, these demands are easily placated by monetary compensation. The welfare state has a part to play here by giving material compensation to workers calling for redistribution. Whatever the grievance of the worker, the welfare state is on hand to reduce the possibility of a radical threat by offering a material compromise. Considering this, the source of more radical change must come from outside the institutional framework and from conflicts that escape being contained by it. Movements inhabiting the peripheral ground have battle-lines drawn far beyond the distributive concerns of the modern Labour Movement, reaching into the cultural realms of identity and lifestyle. The agents now crucial for generating a public sphere of debate, for Habermas, are not those asking about *what we should get* but those asking about *who we are, how we live*, and *who is accountable*. They are the Feminists, the non-conformist Students, the Environmentalists, and people living alternative lifestyles. These groups form Habermas' new social movements and mark the shift from old to new politics in the post-1960s era. The 'new' movements are rooted in a different dynamic from the Marxist model of capital and labour, however. The conflicts they organize around are located instead 'at the seam between the system and lifeworld' (Habermas, 1981: 36).

The 'system-lifeworld' distinction is the hallmark of Habermas' general theory, and it is no less crucial for understanding his theory of 'New Social Movements' and their ability to generate a public sphere (Habermas, 1987). Indeed, Habermas' new movements are to be understood in terms of his 'thesis of internal colonization'. Essentially, they are a reaction to the tendency in advanced capitalist societies for the lifeworld to be engulfed by the growing 'economic-administrative complex' of the system (Habermas, 1981: 33). In basic terms, the system, made up of institutions of the state and economy, is impinging negatively upon the lifeworld, made up of the public and private spheres of everyday life (eg, family, work, leisure, education). This is set in motion through the extension of state bureaucracy, legal regulation, political socialization and economic privatization. Habermas (1987) sums these processes up in his umbrella terms: 'juridification' and 'commodification'.

It is crucial to note that the destructive capacities of these processes are contained within the different forms of rationality that interaction takes in the system and lifeworld. The institutions of the state and the economy run on the basis of instrumental rationality, or as Habermas later and more accurately termed it; *functional rationality* (Habermas, 1991: 258). Political and economic institutions must act strategically and purposively, to achieve specified ends, and are steered by the media of money and power. Interaction in system realms is therefore 'functional', short-circuiting the morals and values of the lifeworld to fulfil system imperatives. This piece of Parsonian systems-theory is corrected by the notion of a 'lifeworld' (the everyday) in which interaction is based instead upon *communicative rationality*. Interaction in private areas of life (like the family) and public areas (like work, education and leisure) for example, is rational, but not in a 'functional' sense. Instead it is orientated to moral, aesthetic, practical and political considerations (Habermas, 1987: 304–5). Action is mediated not by the money and power of the system, but by G.H Mead's symbolic mutual understandings.

The key issue in Habermas' 'colonization thesis' is that everyday realms of action are increasingly organized, not on the basis of the norms we have mutually agreed ('principles of social integration') but on the basis of the money and power that already drive our political and economic system ('principles of system integration') (Habermas, 1987). The concern is that the 'system' in this respect, is growing in advanced capitalist societies through the extension of state administration and legal bureaucracy into everyday life. This imposes functional rationality on lifeworld interactions (Habermas, 1981), distorting them with system-steering money and power, and creating 'new' conflicts and tensions surrounding culture, identity and lifestyle. Not only does colonization threaten the traditions and the moral fabric of the lifeworld (leading to movements that defend existing lifestyles) but also the extension of rationality into new areas of life raises the possibilities for a critical re-evaluation of them (leading to more progressive movements like Feminism and non-conformist Youth Groups). Equally, the extension of money and power as principles affecting the physical environment of the lifeworld itself, supplies the fuel for environmental conflicts (Habermas, 1981: 35).

Colonization processes, therefore, provide new sources of struggle and change in agents seeking to defend traditional lifestyles or institute new ones on their own terms (Habermas, 1981: 33). The theoretical cornerstone of the argument is the assertion that system-level changes generate effects at the level of social integration (Habermas, 1987: 305). As the relationship between the state and economy changes in the course of capitalist development, contradictions and tensions arise that create financial and 'rationality' crises for the system (Habermas, 1988). Measures to solve these crises, such as the legal intrusions of a welfare state, impact upon areas of everyday life, like the family (Habermas, 1981, 33). The system therefore becomes increasingly complex as economic-administrative processes are specialized and differentiated (Habermas, 1987). What follows is not only a wealth of bureaucracy but, also, a kind of post-fordist fragmentation writ large that leads to 'cultural impoverishment' and a 'loss of meaning' in the lifeworld, much like Weber's image of the 'iron cage' (Habermas, 1987: 302).

Habermas, however, is careful to correct Weber's rationale for its existence. For him it is not caused by a unidirectional rationalization (the emphasis shared by the earlier generation of critical theorists, Adorno and Horkheimer), but 'internal colonization' (Habermas, 1987: 303). This is Habermas' key to the 'pathologies' of advanced capitalist societies. Problems and crises in the system are thus merely transferred to the lifeworld, where interactions become distorted by the imposition of money (eg, the market) and power (eg, state administration, law) as principles organizing interaction in its different realms. This raises both legitimation and motivation crises (Habermas, 1988) that cannot be solved in system terms and act to perpetuate the lifestyle and identity woes of the new protestors. Habermas states:

> ... the new conflicts arise in areas of cultural reproduction, social integration and socialisation. They are manifested in the sub-institutional, extra-parliamentary forms of protest. The underlying deficits reflect a reification of communicative spheres of action; the media of money and power are not sufficient to circumvent this reification. The question is not one of compensations that the welfare state can provide. Rather, the question is how to defend or reinstate endangered lifestyles, or how to put reformed lifestyles into practice. In short, the new conflicts are not sparked by *problems of distribution*, but concern *the grammar of forms of life*. (Habermas, 1981: 33).

New social movements are thus united in a 'critique of growth' (Habermas, 1981: 34), and through this they can reassert communicatively rational action against the distortions of an increasingly intrusive system. They do so by constructing a space (anchored in a relatively autonomous lifeworld) in which they can openly debate and pose questions about the legitimacy and accountability of the system. In the process, new social movements, ideally, keep the vision of democracy and freedom alive within the modernist project (Habermas, 1981: 37). Habermas presents these strong claims, however, in the context of 1980s social movements. The question in need of attention now is how far they are relevant to the struggles of twenty-first century social movements.

A Habermasian approach to the Anti-Corporate Movement

Attempts to explain the emerging phenomena of anti-corporatism have sparked a renewed interest in Habermas' 'New Social Movement' theory. Here I take up Crossley's (2003) argument that anti-corporate activity (marked by protests in Seattle 1999, Washington 2000, and Prague 2000) can be usefully viewed as a reaction against the 'colonization of the lifeworld'. The emphasis in this specific case is upon 'economic colonization', rather than Habermas' preoccupation with 'political colonization' (Habermas, 1981). Anti-corporate concern is not so much over a bureaucratically expanding welfare state, as the growth of corporate power and international institutions (like the IMF and World Bank). This is not to suggest that all social movements today should be understood as reactions to economic, rather than political, colonization but that anti-corporatism has been best understood in these terms. For example, Crossley (2003) suggests that a theory of 'economic colonization' strikes a chord with several 'anti-corporate'[3] texts (eg, Klein, 2000; Hardt and Negri, 2000; Monbiot, 2000; Hertz, 2001).

Despite its controversial standing amongst today's anti-corporate activists, Naomi Klein's *No Logo* (2000) illustrates this point clearly when it stresses the ways in which our culture, identity, education, employment and citizenship are being attacked by the branding and profiteering of multinationals. For example, public space becomes organized on the basis of corporate money and power rather than public discussion. As such it is colonized by corporate advertising and billboards, whilst city centres give way to malls and shopping outlets that ensure our leisure is confined to 'more and more spaces where commercial messages are the only ones permitted' (Klein, 2000: 280). Even our ways of communicating are becoming colonized, trademarked and censored by the language of the 'brand', marking what Klein calls a 'climate of cultural and linguistic privatization' (Klein, 2000: 177). It is not hard to see why Habermas has been usefully applied in this context. Economic colonization can be seen to extend the 'functional rationality' of a global capitalist market into areas of everyday life, like leisure and cultural discourse, by establishing the money and power of corporate rule as action-mediating principles there. The result is the distortion (or 'reification' in Habermas' terms) of communicatively rational action that would otherwise prevail.

Attempts to prevent this from happening come in the form of various struggles defending areas of the lifeworld, like education, from the imposition of a corporate agenda. For example, campus protests in Britain and America have criticized the link between education and private business/commercial interests. Monbiot refers to this as the 'silent takeover of the universities', arguing that corporate influence (in the way of funding and personnel) distorts educational agendas, research questions and findings (Monbiot, 2000). In place of debate, discussion and critical thinking, 'Britain's universities have swiftly and silently been colonized by corporations' (Monbiot, 2000: 283):

> In both universities and schools, corporate teaching materials, advertisements and even, in some cases, educational programmes appear designed subtly to influence the way in which the student views the world. Business now stands as a guard dog at the gates of perception. Only enquiries which suit its needs are allowed to pass (Monbiot, 2000: 301).

In raising these sorts of issues, anti-corporate protests substantially (although by no means exclusively), question the legitimacy and moral validity of global capitalist processes and defend areas of the lifeworld (whether it be public space, leisure, culture or education) from the distortions created by a corporate takeover. It is exactly in this context that Habermas' ideas on the 'colonization of the lifeworld' seem to have supplied social scientists with the tools to explore and predict.

Alongside this optimism however is the proverbial 'double-edged sword'. The existence of anti-corporatism also poses a challenge to the relevance of Habermas' 'New Social Movement' theory (Crossley, 2003). The shift from political to economic colonization, perhaps unsurprisingly, triggers a resurfacing of issues like working conditions, wage disputes, distribution and military concerns, which Habermas attaches to the 'old' politics of labour and condemns to the past (Habermas, 1981: 33). In this sense, anti-corporatism perhaps fits the model of 'old' politics as well as it fits the 'new'. In fact, Crossley (2003) suggests that it marks the onset of an 'even newer' breed of social movements in a newer 'global' era.

After promising initial insight, Habermas' theory seems to falter. Whilst the thesis of colonization has proved insightful, the Anti-Corporate Movement cannot be manipulated into the mould required of a 'new' movement. Instead, issues of production and distribution are wrapped up with culture, identity and lifestyle and placed at its very core (Crossley, 2003: 300). This begs the question of what is 'new' in Habermas' theory? The answer, I suggest, does not require that we enter the fairly rudimentary debate over the relative mix of old and new issues in today's social movements. Instead, it requires that we challenge the idea of 'newness' on a theoretical level, in terms of the perceived *conflict-shift* from capital-labour to the 'seam' between system and lifeworld.

Section two: rethinking the theory: what is 'new'?

In this section of the chapter, I argue that Habermas' perception of a *conflict-shift* from capital-labour to system-lifeworld is the result of theoretical assumptions that can be challenged. In order to do this, however, I initiate the help of a newer generation of critical theorists and in particular the New Left cultural turn in Marxism (Honneth, Knodler-Bunte and Widmann, 1981). Looking at Habermas' general theorizing through this lens can posit revisions to his movement theory that suggest that what is 'new', is ultimately, nothing much at all.

Firstly, by looking at Habermas' (1987) general theory, we can see that the role played by rationalization processes in the course of historical development is crucial to the idea of 'new social movements'. This requires a brief re-cap of Habermas' argument in terms of rationalization processes. As capitalism develops, a 'rational-instrumental' logic differentiates out the state and economy as subsystems in their own right, functionally steered by the system-media of money and power. As we discussed earlier, Habermas highlights the role of an expanding welfare state (run by this instrumental logic), in marking the shift from capital-labour struggles to struggles against the colonization of the lifeworld (Habermas, 1987: 361). Here, this 'system' logic subverts the communicatively rational action on which social integration (or 'sociation') is based, by introducing money and power. The social movements that take up the struggle against colonization are 'new' for Habermas, essentially because he sees this struggle as 'new'. He is able to see it as such because it is initiated by the *historical development of rationalization*. This development is progressive in its course, and so the conflict between social and system logic can be identified as *replacing* that between capital and labour in the great historical scheme of things.

As societal rationalization develops therefore, we see historical shifts in the type of conflicts that can generate genuine public debate. The 'new' movements are key in the post-1960s era for Habermas because, as discussed earlier, they raise issues outside the parameters of the institutional framework (Habermas, 1981: 33). In this respect, they form the vanguard of communicatively rational action and can generate public debates free from the reification effects of intrusive system media. In doing so, they would ideally, for Habermas, create the space in which we can decide by means of mutual co-operation and agreement, the norms upon which our social relations are to be based (Habermas, 1987). This somewhat utopian vision accounts for Habermas' claim that new social movements contain the potential for creating radical social change. Even as movements of 'resistance and retreat', they retain the capacity to reassert communicative rationality and 'promote the revitalization of buried possibilities for expression and communication' (Habermas, 1981, 36). This claim is perhaps the result of Habermas' (1987) work on linguistic community and the importance of an 'ideal-speech situation' for freedom and democracy. Here, the idea that truth is contained in 'speech acts' shapes his interpretation of the public sphere as an essential component of democracy, and subsequently, his view of new social movements as an essential component of the public sphere.

Rationalization processes are therefore central to Habermas' assertion that there is a *conflict-shift* to the system-lifeworld seam, addressed by the 'new' movements. Pushing aside the historical development of rationalization and concentrating instead upon the historical development of capitalism, however, can challenge this view. In this endeavour I follow a suggestion put to Habermas by Honneth (1981); that history could just as validly be looked at in terms of a process of 'capitalization' as it could 'rationalization'. Honneth (1981) suggests that the choice made by Habermas is somewhat arbitrary. I suggest further that it can be traced back to both his linear view of history and his utopian visions of linguistically based democracy that I have just flagged up.

For our purposes, we can take 'capitalization' to mean the historical process of capitalist modernization and, it should be noted, this theme is not one Habermas disregards. Whilst he asserts the priority of rationalization processes, these are inherently related to the development of capitalism and, 'one can demonstrate a functional connection between the central conflicts of the lifeworld and the requirements of capitalist modernization' (Habermas, 1981b: 19). What Habermas does not adequately consider, however, is that it is not rationalization processes *per se*, but the use to which they are put, which generates destructive tendencies towards colonization.

Habermas takes time to correct Weber's vision of rationalization as the unidirectional assault of instrumental rationality on the lifeworld, arguing instead that it is the reification of communicative rationality by instrumental (or functional) rationality in that is to blame (Habermas 1987: 303–5). A dip into Marcuse (1955) however, may have lifted the blame from the shoulders of reason altogether. It is not instrumental reason itself, but the ends to which it is put in a particular social, economic and political system, which is problematic for Marcuse. Similarly, it is not the battle between competing forms of rationality, but between the competing goals within capitalist society that is, perhaps, the real issue for Habermas. The state and the economy are not simply endowed with potential to be an 'intrusive system' because they run on instrumental rationality, but because they are mutually adapting in the wake of capitalist modernization. It is this process of mutual adaptation that is ridden with the potential crises outlined by Habermas (1987), and necessitates changes in the relationship between the state and economy as capitalism develops.

The changing relationship between the state and economy is, for all intents and purposes, Habermas' 'system'. It is the multifarious effects of this dynamic, set within a global context, which can be extremely useful in exploring the conflicts that generate social movements today. In these terms, what the system-lifeworld approach looks for is not primarily the historical evolution of spheres of instrumental and communicative rationality, but the changing relationship between the state and the economy (and its effects on the lifeworld) due to dynamics unleashed by capitalist modernization. Although the idea of *distinct spheres of rationality* may be crucial to understanding the nature of colonization (for example in terms of the displacement of action based upon principles of mutual co-operation and understanding), it is secondary to the relationship between *distinct spheres of activity*.

Such a modification begs the suggestion made by Widmann: that the conflicts sparking social movements have always been situated, in this sense, at that seam between system and lifeworld because they have always entailed a 'defensive reaction against the capitalist penetration of the lifeworld and the destruction caused by capitalist modernization' (Widmann, 1981). Indeed, system-lifeworld conflicts can now be seen as encasing capital-labour conflicts and both are subsumed within the wider dynamic of 'capitalization'. Crucially, this move enables us to rediscover the materialist concerns submerged within Habermas's system-lifeworld approach by his over-emphasis on normative-linguistic factors. This means that the system-lifeworld approach to social movements, in its revised format, is compatible with the New Left's cultural turn in Marxism, rather that at odds with it (a point of much debate in the interview between Habermas, Honneth, Knodler-Bunte and Widmann, 1981). This also allows a revised Habermasian approach to pick up Gramscian-style concepts, such as 'cultural hegemony' and 'cultural visibility', which would help analysis move away from normative-linguistic concerns by underlining the 'old' *materialist* core of lifestyle politics (as Honneth, Knodler-Bunte and Widmann, 1981, point out to Habermas). Equally, it allows the approach to converge with historical critiques of new social movements, which have stressed the 'old' *lifestyle* core of labour politics (Calhoun, 1995; Tucker, 1991), but without having to discard the system-lifeworld approach to social movements, which is too often the result.

Habermas' weakness then is not in pointing to the conflicts that generate movements in terms of the seam between system and lifeworld. It lies instead in failing to see the wider applicability of his analysis to movements beyond his own historical specificity. He does so by failing to underline the essence of that analysis in terms of a state-economy-lifeworld dynamic. Returning then, to our initial question of what is 'new' in Habermas' theory, we can posit the answer, 'nothing much at all'. Ironically, it is in this conclusion that we discover Habermas' overlooked novelty: a highly useful framework for the analysis of contemporary protests as reactions against the negative (and colonizing) effects that capitalist modernization has on everyday life. The present context shows that this is something that is far from confined to the 'new' movements Habermas writes about in the 1980s.

Section three: the Labour Movement and the battle against colonization

Community unionism and the living wage campaigns

In this section of the chapter, I illustrate how the revised Habermasian approach to social movements, freed from the confines of 'newness', can be of value in analysing contemporary social protest, including that of the Labour Movement. My first example is the case of Community Unionism (Wills and Simms, 2002a; Wills, 2002b). The idea of Community Unionism originates from 1990s North America, in the form of AFL-CIO's Union Cities Programme, Jobs for Justice and Living Wage Campaigns (Wills and Simms, 2002a). Issues such as a minimum wage are campaigned for outside the usual realm of the workplace and in connection with wider struggles for social justice in the community (Fine, 2000). Wills explores recent attempts in the UK to set up community-based trade unionism, notably Battersea and Wandsworth Trades Union Council's Organising Centre (BWTUC) (Wills and Simms, 2002a), and the Living Wage Campaign run by East London based TELCO (Wills and Simms, 2002a; Wills, 2002b).

The existence of Community Unionism and the assertion from Wills *et al.* (2002a) that it is to become an avenue for effective trade union organising in the present context, reinforces the weaknesses associated with Habermas' 'New Social Movement' theory as it stood at the beginning of the chapter. The problems come from the distinct nature of Community Unionism as a mix of Habermas' 'old' and 'new' politics. Interestingly, as a movement it also has the flavour of Crossley's 'even newer' politics of anti-corporatism (Crossley, 2003). In Living Wage Campaigns we see the 'old' concerns of material distribution, minimum wages and rights at work encased within language and action more easily identifiable as Habermas' 'new' politics. Work-related demands are couched in community-based claims surrounding the quality of life, basic human rights, inclusivity and participation. Here, however, they are not new political conflicts *per se*, but rather new spaces and new ways of communicating 'old' struggles. Habermas' (1987) idea that the Labour Movement becomes subject to containment in welfare state societies looks rapidly outdated in this context. It is testament to the underestimation of the power of agency within Habermas' 'thesis of internal colonization' (Cohen, 1981). Agency however, is the key to understanding the direction of change in the Labour Movement. Trade unions do not lie down and die as the inevitable march of Habermasian history stampedes towards its goal of colonization. On the contrary, agents change the way they organize in order to combat decline. In the process the 'old' politics of the Labour Movement has adapted to converge with the characteristics of Habermas' new social movements. This resistance and adaptation by agents in the course of struggle is something that is overlooked in the original Habermasian scheme, lost under the rubric of decisive conflict shifts.

It is re-found however when we accept the futility of debating the relative mix of 'old' and 'new' politics in the social movements of today and accept instead an ever-changing landscape of movements adapting to the protest opportunities and constraints offered by processes of capitalist modernization. For this adaptation is driven by agents themselves seeking to find more effective points of struggle. The move away from workplace based organizing to community based social justice campaigns can be seen as a reaction to the changing relationship between the state and economy as capitalism develops globally[4]. In a global era resistance is more effectively couched by agents in the 'new language of capitalism' that such a situation supplies (Wills, 2002b). This is a moral language of corporate responsibility. A moral attack on global capitalist processes is therefore not the exclusive domain of 'new' or 'newer' movements like anticorporatism. It follows then that new social movements, identified with lifestyle and identity concerns, are not the exclusive generators of public debate and moral rejuvenation. Living Wage Campaigns generate debate firmly rooted in working practices and distributive issues like wages, linking them to the wider network of local social movements campaigning for the ethical responsibility of corporations, the environment and local structures of participation (Wills, 2002b). This is exactly the type of debate that contributes to a Habermasian public sphere in advanced capitalist societies. The campaigns of the Living Wage show that the potential for this does not lie in a break from 'old' to 'new' social movements, but is contained within the Labour Movement itself. To see it as anything other is a misinterpretation, not only of history but also of the present context of struggle.

A 'burning issue': the British Firefighters' Dispute 2002/3

A more in-depth example of the utility of a revised Habermasian approach is found in the British Firefighters' Dispute 2002/3. On 13 November 2002, British firefighters commenced strike action (for the first time since the 1977–8 dispute) after the breakdown of negotiations over pay. The Fire Brigades Union put forward a demand for a 40 per cent[5] wage increase following suggestions made in an independent report into the Fire Service by the Department of Transport, Local Government and the Regions (surfacing May 2002). This report suggested that British firefighters were relatively underpaid for the type of work they performed[6]. Under the pressure of strike threats the Government set up an 'independent' inquiry into the Fire Service under Sir George Bain, which formed their grounds for insisting that any wage increase (finally settled at 16 per cent in the overall wage bill), would have to be offset by a programme of 'modernization' (The Bain Report, December 2002).

The terms of a 'modernization' policy for the Fire Service remain ambiguous, however it has been packaged as the biggest change to present working conditions firefighters have seen (Maguire, *Guardian*, 12/11/02). Commentators in the FBU camp have suggested that if implemented from above, modernization could involve potentially negative alterations to the organization and management of the Fire Service (as argued in the document, *Modernization: the Facts from the FBU*). This includes less favourable working practices (like changes to the shift system) and cuts in resources, fire stations and workers. Critics and the FBU relate these changes to a government agenda of public sector financial savings. For example, Roger Seifert argues that the Bain Report seeks an 'economically efficient' Fire Service (i.e., one that costs less to run), rather than a service efficient at saving lives (Seifert, 2003). Changes arising from financial considerations, it is argued, could produce a Fire Service that is ultimately less attuned to the needs of the public and the workers (Gilchrist, *Guardian*, 27/11/02).

The protest of firefighters was therefore a dual affair shifting over the course of the dispute: *for* wage increases on the one hand and *against* a government-led agenda of modernization on the other. It took the form of a series of strikes in which the provision of the Fire Service became the responsibility of the British Army 'Green Goddesses' and a small number of 'retained firefighters'. The battle-lines were clearly drawn by the Labour Government, any wage increase must be offset by Bain's 'modernization' plans in order to protect the British economy and defend against further strike chaos across the public sector.

To call the firefighters' strike a 'burning issue' is not primarily to invoke a pun. For the nature of the dispute fits what Habermas himself calls a 'burning issue' when discussing new social movements (Habermas, 1987: 350). Here, he is referring to a type of conflict that sits somewhat uneasily with his idea that the 'old' capital-labour wars between workers and the state are a redundant source of major upset in welfare state societies. This type of conflict is labelled by Habermas a 'burning issue' because it becomes the exception to the rule. It is relevant when despite the fact that 'conflicts over distribution . . . *(have lost)* their explosive power' they 'in dramatic, exceptional cases . . . go beyond the institutional boundaries of collective bargaining and become a burning issue' (Habermas, 1987: 350). In Habermas's terms then, the British firefighters' dispute is a prime example of a 'burning issue'. It is the exception to the rule that says industrial disputes are contained in welfare state societies. For despite the fact that this dispute remained within the legal institutional framework, it was still reported to 'rock the Government' and became one of the most important labour battles in Britain since the 1980s (Toynbee, *Guardian*, 27/11/02). Revolution may not have ensued, but in relative terms the overwhelming vote by firefighters in favour of strike action, and the subsequent walkouts leaving Britain devoid of adequate fire cover, do not amount to the effective containment of labour conflicts. They suggest instead that there is life in the workers yet, and that conflicts over distribution may still be central to movements creating the kind of public-sphere generating debates we experience today.

In order to look beyond these problems created for Habermas, however, I posit another account of the firefighters' dispute, which does not rely upon the handy, one-size fits all, theoretical hole-filler of 'exceptions and rules'. Instead, it rests upon the revised Habermasian model developed in section two of the chapter, and in turn, demonstrates the power of analysis it harbours in the present context. To recall, this revised model proposed that social conflicts *per se* could be analysed in terms of Habermas' system-lifeworld distinction because the essence of that distinction is the changing relationship between the state and economy in the process of capitalist modernization. Subsequently, the effects this generates in the lifeworld are as much 'old' as 'new' to the point that we can abandon the concept of 'newness' as meaning a fundamental conflict-shift. We can start to analyse present labour conflicts like the firefighters' dispute then, using Habermasian tools of analysis gleaned for probing the 'new' social movements. On this note, a more profound insight and understanding of the dispute can be achieved by looking at it in terms of the 'thesis of internal colonization' (Habermas, 1987). We are no longer left out in the cold, armed with only rules and exceptions, but have managed to sneak back into the Habermasian framework through the side door. Once in, the conceptual advantages won make the task of analysing this dispute a prime example of the mutual benefit to theory and research gained by setting up a dialogue between Habermas and the present context of struggle.

Firstly, it is significant to note that the issue of modernization, rather than pay, became the main driving force of the British Firefighters' Dispute. FBU General Secretary, Andy Gilchrist, states that, 'what began as a Campaign for Professional Pay has developed into a wide ranging debate about "modernization" and the Fire Service' (Gilchrist, 2003). The question of 'lifestyle', albeit at work, was therefore central. The Fire Service is perhaps unique in the extent to which negotiation and mutual agreement (seen in shift work arrangements and daily routines) are the basis of working practices as they currently stand (Pounder, 2002). The picture from the ground is one of communicatively geared teams working to provide quality public service (Seifert, *Guardian*, 19/12/02[7]). The concern was that government-led modernization would change this balance, putting the functional concerns of the state and economy first through increasing administration of the workplace. A prime example of this is the proposal to abolish Section 19 of the 1947 Fire Services Act, making it possible for the Government to impose the closure of local fire stations without consulting the community, as is required at present.

Using a Habermasian approach helps us to see beyond the distributive aspect of conflict, represented by the 40 per cent pay demand, and to the kind of struggles over lifestyle and identity typical of 'new' movements. Sources of conflict for protesting firefighters were changes to the way they work, like the abolition of 'home stations', and challenges to their work identity, such as the use of firefighters as paramedics. Such changes were interpreted by firefighters as the result of the Government imposing an economic agenda of cuts and closures, which undermines the camaraderie of the teams they work in and their ability to fulfil what is seen as an ethical responsibility to the community to save lives[8]. It is this imposition that I argue can be seen as akin to the 'colonization' of ways of life by the 'functional' actions of the system, which bypass firefighters' moral and communicative lifeworlds for its own ends of financial crisis management.

Using the idea of colonization, therefore, cuts straight to the issue of resistance to modernization as a struggle to retain the autonomy of communicative spheres of work (the lifeworld) from the growing complex of politico-administrative and economic control (the system). In fact, Roger Seifert argues further that modernization from above was set to erode workers' knowledge and increase the control of managers (Seifert, *Guardian*, 19/12/02). The struggle to assert the communicative logic of social integration over the functional logic of the system cannot be fully divorced from workplace struggles and the distributive issues of wages; and, as the firefighters' dispute shows, the Labour Movement engages with both. The following statement by Habermas refers to the 'new' social movements, but still manages to express very clearly a major concern of firefighters:

> . . . to protect areas of life that are functionally dependent on social integration through values, norms and consensus formation, to preserve them from falling prey to the systemic imperatives of economic and administrative subsystems growing with dynamics of their own, and to defend them from becoming converted over, through the steering media of the law to a principle of sociation that is, for them, dysfunctional. (Habermas, 1987: 372–3).

The struggle between social and system logic is also translated into one over the definition of the employee role. As Habermas argues, employed, citizen, client and consumer roles are institutionalized versions of the destructive exchanges between system and lifeworld (Habermas, 1981: 36). The British firefighters were rejecting not only colonization but also the re-definition of their roles as employees that might have followed it. Instead they wished to reassert communicatively rational action, and through it the priority of the lifeworld over the system in deciding the norms that regulate the workplace. It is a case of fighting for the principles of social integration over system integration and achieving a form of sociation that they themselves determine together. In this sense they are the same as Habermas' (1981) new 'alternative lifestylers'. As Knodler-Bunte (1981) has suggested, young trade unionists and alternative lifestylers share a common aim in attempting to live and work differently. Rather than old class conflicts being divorced from the new postmaterialist concern to reassert communicatively rational action, they are fundamentally implicated in it.

This is not to say that Habermas' speculation on the nature of trade union politics does not have any validity here. Leftist commentators have pointed out that New Labour's unreceptive manner towards the FBU was tantamount to a desire to defeat one of Britain's most powerful remaining trade unions (*S darity*, 14/11/02). This might complete that process of integration and thereby containment that Habermas points to with the 'juridification' of class struggle (Habermas, 1987). This was reflected in the proposals to make strike action by firefighters illegal on the grounds of public safety. Habermas' error is, therefore, not in the processes he identifies with regard to changing class politics but in the conclusion that these processes were somehow completed and that the agents involved passively accepted them. The strike action of British firefighters shows the contrary; agents do not accept the historical inevitability of these attempts, but resist them, and resisting colonization in the workplace is a key point of struggle.

This dispute suggests that colonization (both inside union politics and out) has become a key focus of conflict in advanced capitalist societies (although this is not to claim of course that it is anything fundamentally 'new'). The power initiated by control over private and public spheres of everyday life is recognized by a government willing to trade wage concessions for increasing regulation of working practices by instrumentally rational concerns. Colonization then, could not be more of an old class issue and it certainly is not the domain of the post-material. This indicates that Habermas' claim that 'the reification of communicatively structured areas of action, whilst conditioned by capitalist relations, works itself out in ways that are less and less class specific' (Habermas, 1987: 302) is misplaced. The British Firefighters' Dispute and Community Unionism show that it only does so, if like Habermas, you look less and less class-specifically at social conflicts.

Summary

Habermas is central to discussions about a public sphere in modern democratic societies. But below this is a layer of theory that relates to the 'new' social movements responsible for generating it. When this layer itself is studied, we find not only grave problems with Habermas' understanding but also untapped strengths. A dialogue between theory and the present context of political struggle enables us to pinpoint both. The existence of the Anti-Corporate Movement has once again unleashed Habermas' potential for analytic insight into the realms of contemporary social theorizing. His reception, however, is also met with caution, as the real world sheds light on problems in Habermas as much as Habermas sheds light on problems in the real world. The issue, it seems, comes down to this model of 'newness' Habermas insists upon attaching to his analyses of social movements in terms of the 'system-lifeworld' distinction. It is an attachment that is down to false theoretical assumptions that I have challenged by reaching again into the repertoire of critical theory and looking anew at Habermas' general theorizing.

When assessed, the challenge to Habermas should not however be its downfall. Indeed, it would be a mistake for theorists to limit or abandon the use of a Habermasian approach to social conflicts because of these problems. Anti-corporatists, British Firefighters and Community Unionists show that Habermas has put his finger on something that looks likely to become only more relevant to the political struggles of today. The value of the insight gleaned from ideas of 'internal colonization' should not be overlooked or understated. The task with Habermas is therefore one of revision not abandonment. The revised model attacks the idea of 'newness' not by joining the debates over the relative mix of old and new politics, but by challenging the idea of a *conflict-shift* to the seam between system and lifeworld. The challenge is not over whether conflicts lie at this seam, but over whether this is anything that can be considered 'new' (Widmann, 1981). When we push rationalization processes aside we see that the essence of Habermas' 'system-lifeworld' distinction is that changing relationship between the state and the economy in the process of capitalist modernization (for the state and the economy *are the system*). Teamed with the idea that changes at the system-level generate conflicts at the level of social integration (the lifeworld), this forms a powerful explanation of 'new' social movements because it forms a powerful explanation of social movements *per se*. What is 'new' is nothing much at all. It is in fact the 'red herring' of Habermas' theory. What it masks is not failure, but a highly useful framework for the analysis of present day social conflicts and the protests and movements that they generate.

In closing, I return to the question of the processes that generate a Habermasian public sphere in the present context. From my discussions of Community Unionism and the British Firefigters' Dispute it can be said with some certainty that Habermas overemphasizes the role played by the 'new' social movements by unjustly omitting the 'old' politics of the labour movement from the lifeworld battle against colonization. Contemporary struggles suggest that the Labour Movement is not fully subject to containment by the welfare state, but also engages in conflicts at the seam between system and lifeworld, and possibly always has (Widmann, 1981). In doing so, it raises public debate not just about *what we get* (wage demands), but also about *how we work* and *what it means to be an employee* (modernization). Identity and lifestyle *at work* are just as much sites of contention, colonization and moral defence, as they are outside of it. The 'old' politics, then, is not only about the compensations that the welfare state can provide but also about defending the communicative logic of sociation against the functional agendas of an imposing system. In short, it is also about the 'grammar of forms of life' (Habermas, 1981: 33) and the struggle to hold on to a rapidly fragmenting meaning. By engaging with these issues, along with the distributive angles they incur, these Labour Movements are a major source of debate and moral rejuvenation in the present British context, showing how the generation of a public sphere is as much down to the wrongly termed 'old' politics as the 'new'. In fact, both are part and parcel of the same story. A story that is predictable only in the historical certainty that it will keep on changing.

Notes

1 The World Social Forum offers a topical example of this.
2 This relates to Crossley's suggestion that anti-corporatism could be seen as an 'even newer' social movement in Habermas' terms (Crossley, 2003: 18).
3 It should be noted that 'anti-corporatism' consists of eclectic groups with different referents and different agendas (eg. anti-capitalist, anti-globalization, anti-neo-liberalism), which perceive and relate to the tensions of economic colonization in different ways. The discussion here is thus meant to be suggestive rather than definitive.
4 Wills (2002b) argues in line with Castells that 'networked trade unionism' is the response to global 'networked capitalism'.
5 This figure represented an increase in a whole-time firefighter's pay from £21,531 to £30,000 p/a, alongside parity for retained firefighters and Emergency Control Room staff currently paid at 92% of firefighters' pay (www.fbu.org.uk).
6 FBU state that a police constable after 5 years of service earns £23,323 p/a rising to £29,062 at 14 years, whereas a firefighter earns £21,531 after 5 years and £22,491 at 15 years (2001 salary levels) (*Modernization: the Facts from the FBU*, 30).
7 Seifert's article appears in full in *Red Pepper Magazine*, January 2003.
8 This observation is drawn from my own empirical (interview based) research on the firefighters' strike.

Bibliography

Agreed Proposal—Fire Service Pay and Conditions Agreement, 2003. Downloaded from www.fbu.org.uk

Bain Report, December 2002. Excerpts, downloaded from www.fbu.org.uk

Calhoun. C. (1995) 'New social movements of the early nineteenth century', in Traugott. M. (ed.) *Repertoires and Cycles of Contention*, pp. 173–216. Durham, NC: Duke University Press.

Cohen, J. (1981) 'Why more Political Theory?' *Telos*, 49.

Crossley, N. (2003) 'Even Newer Social Movements? Anti-corporate Protests, Capitalist Crises and Rationalisation of Society'. *Organisation*, 10(2): 287–305.

Fine, J. (2000) 'Community Unionism in Baltimore and Stamford'. *Working USA*, Winter, 4: 59–85.

Gilchrist, A. (2002) in *The Guardian*, 27 November.

Gilchrist, A. (2003) 'Introduction', in *Modernization: the Facts from the Fire Brigades Union*, 2003. Downloaded from www.fbu.org.uk February 2003, pp. 3.

Habermas, J. (1981). 'New Social Movements'. *Telos*, 49: 33–37.

Habermas, J. (1981b) 'The Dialectics of Rationalization: An Interview with Jürgen Habermas by Axel Honneth, Ederhard Knodler-Bunte and Arno Widmann', *Telos*, 49: 5–31.

Habermas, J. (1987) *The Theory of Communicative Action Volume II: System and Lifeworld*. Cambridge: Polity.

Habermas, J. (1988) *Legitimation Crisis*. Cambridge: Polity.

Habermas, J. (1991) 'A Reply', in Honneth, A. and Joas, H. (1991). (eds). *Communicative Action: Essays on Jürgen Habermas's The Theory of Communicative Action*. Cambridge: Polity. Pp. 214–265.

Honneth, A. (1981) 'The Dialectics of Rationalization: An Interview with Jürgen Habermas by Axel Honneth, Ederhard Knodler-Bunte and Arno Widmann', *Telos*, 49: 5–31.

Klein, N. (2000) *No Logo*. London: HarperCollins.

Knodler-Bunte, E. (1981) 'The Dialectics of Rationalization: An Interview with Jürgen Habermas by Axel Honneth, Ederhard Knodler-Bunte and Arno Widmann', *Telos*, 49: 5–31.

Maguire, K. (2002) 'Union Anger at 11% Fire Pay Offer', *The Guardian*, 12 November, pp. 1.

Maguire, K. (2003) 'Fire Union Chiefs Back New Offer', *The Guardian*, March 19, pp. 12.

Marcuse, H. (1955) *1898–1979: Reason and Revolution: Hegel and the rise of social theory*. London: Routledge & Kegan Paul. 2nd edition.

Modernization: the Facts from the Fire Brigades Union, 2003. Downloaded from www.fbu.org.uk

Monbiot, G. (2000) 'Silent Science—The Corporate Takeover of the Universities', Chap. 9 in, *Captive State: The Corporate Takeover of Britain*. London: Macmillan.

Pounder, B. (2002) Interview with FBU Representative, led by Sheila Rowbotham and Hilary Wainwright. *British Trade Unionism Today Conference*, University of Manchester, 2 December.

Seifert, R. (2002) 'The Real Modernisers', *The Guardian*, 19 December, pp. 19.

Seifert, R. (2003) 'Comments on the Full Bain Report', January 2003, www.fbu.org.uk/pay2002/rogerseibain.html

Solidarity (2002). 'Blair puts lives at risk to bash Unions', Headline, 14 November.

The Fire Brigades Union Position Statement on the True Modernization of the UK Fire Service, Executive Council, FBU, 19 November 2002.

Toynbee, P. (2002), in *The Guardian*, 27 November.

Tucker, K. (1991) 'How new are the new social movements?' *Theory, Culture and Society*, 8(2): 75–98.

Widmann, A. (1981) 'The Dialectics of Rationalization: An Interview with Jürgen Habermas by Axel Honneth, Eberhard Knodler-Bunte and Arno Widmann', *Telos*, 49: 5–31.

Wills, J. and Simms, M. (2002a) 'Building reciprocal Community Unionism in the UK'. *Working Paper Four*.

Wills, J. (2002b) 'Networked Trade Unionism'. Paper presented at *British Trade Unionism Today Conference*, University of Manchester, 2 December.

Expanding dialogue: The Internet, the public sphere and prospects for transnational democracy

James Bohman

New technologies are often greeted with political optimism. The Internet was thought to herald new possibilities for political participation, if not direct democracy, even in large and complex societies, as 'electronic democracy' might replace the mass media democracy of sound-bite television. The high hopes for electronic democracy seem to have faded, however, as critics such as Sunstein (2001) and Shapiro (1999) have come to argue that central features of the Internet and computer-mediated communication generally undermine the sort of public sphere and political interaction that is required for genuine democratic deliberation. Whatever the empirical merits of such criticisms, they do point to an, as yet, unclarified problem in discussions of 'electronic democracy': we still lack a clear understanding of how the Internet and other forms of electronic communication might contribute to a *new* kind of public sphere and thus to a new form of democracy. Certainly, globalization and other features of contemporary societies make it at least possible to consider whether democracy is undergoing another great transformation, of the order of the invention of representative democracy and its institutions of voting and parliamentary assemblies in early modern European cities.

Both the optimistic and pessimistic positions in the debate suffer from clear conceptual problems. Optimists take for granted that the mode of communication or technological mediation itself is constitutive of new possibilities. As examples such as the Chinese discovery of gunpowder show, however, technology is embedded in social contexts that may make its various potentials unrealizable. Pessimists make the opposite error of holding institutions fixed, here the institutions of the sovereign nation state. If we ask the question of whether or not electronic communication contributes to deliberation in representative institutions and to national public spheres, the answer is that more than likely it contributes little or even undermines them. Indeed, there has been much discussion concerning whether or not the Internet undermines sovereignty, much in the way that states previously considered the telegraph's capacity to cross borders as a direct threat to its sovereignty (see Held, 1995; Poster, 2001 and *Indiana Journal of*

Global Legal Studies, 1998). But when the political context is shifted and a broader array of institutional alternatives are opened up to include a possible transnational public sphere, it seems likely that electronic and computer-mediated network communication may well expand the scope of certain features of communicative interaction across space and time, solving some of the problems of scale inherent in the literary public sphere and the limitations on deliberation in the institutions of representative democracy. A proper assessment, then, will not only have to consider new possibilities; it will also have to take more fully into consideration the fact that public spheres and democratic institutions do not exist separately but only in an ongoing historical relation to each other.

Why should these technologies lead to such opposing assessments? One reaction to such debates would be to show that many of the structural features of computer-mediated communication could just as well speak against the very idea of an electronic public sphere, including its anonymity, limitation of access and thus restricted audience, its network form, and so on. Although such empirical facts need to be considered, such an approach needs first to ask prior conceptual and normative questions concerning cyberspace as a public sphere, without which it is impossible to judge whether such facts close off possibilities or open up new ones. If the public sphere and democracy exhibit historical and institutional variation that elude the attempt to construct fixed standards, some of its supposed defects in one historical setting may well prove to be virtues in another. However successful, the sovereign nation state provides no democratic baseline for such judgments.

Such an open-ended and pragmatic approach, with its emphasis on possibilities, seems inevitably to lead to more optimistic conclusions about the public sphere and democracy under conditions of computer-mediated communication, although not unreservedly so. My argument has four steps. First, I undertake the conceptual clarification of the necessary conditions for a public sphere, with the requirements of deliberative democracy in mind. This conception of democracy and of the public sphere is dialogical, where dialogue is public only if it is able to expand and transform the conditions of communicative interaction. Second, I then consider the potentials of computer-mediated communication on the Internet in light of these necessary conditions. Since it is software rather than hardware that constructs how communication occurs over the network, the Internet's capacity to support a public sphere cannot be judged in terms of intrinsic features. If this is true, then the Internet is a public sphere only if agents make it so, if agents introduce institutional 'software' that constructs the context of communication. This context is transnational rather than national, distributive rather than unified in form. Here the role that the Internet could play in specific institutions is examined through the experiences of governance in the European Union. Finally, I consider whether the novel public sphere that is created in transnational politics might itself feed back upon democratic institutions and help to promote new institutional forms that address the problems of space and time inherent in considering global democracy, including issues of collective identity. Participants in transnational public spheres become citizens of the world not merely because they form a 'community of fate' via complex interdependence but, also, because they may now have the means and public sphere at their disposal to make normative claims upon each other in a properly dialogical and deliberative fashion. The first step is to unhook the conception of the public sphere from its first modern realization through the print medium and the institutions of the state.

Dialogue, technology and the public sphere

Two normatively significant but potentially misleading assumptions guide most concepts of the public sphere and complicate any discussion of electronic democracy. These assumptions are normatively significant precisely because they directly establish the connection between the public sphere and the democratic ideal of deliberation among free and equal citizens. They are misleading, more often than not, because the connection that is made is overly specific and leaves out an essential condition for the existence of a public sphere in large and highly differentiated modern societies: the technological mediation of public communication. In this section I argue that if we consider this technological condition of possibility for any modern public sphere, we must relax the requirements of the public sphere as a forum for face-to-face communication. There are other ways to realize the public forum and its dialogical exchange in a more indirect and mediated manner, even while preserving and rearticulating the connection to democratic self-rule.

The public sphere (or *Öffentlichkeit* in the broad sense) is for these reasons not a univocal concept, even if it does have necessary conditions. First, a public sphere that has democratic significance must be a forum, that is, a social space in which speakers may express their views to others and who in turn respond to them and raise their own opinions and concerns. The specific ideal forum is too often taken to be a town meeting or perhaps a discussion in a salon, coffee shop or union hall, in which participants are physically present to each other in face-to-face interaction. Second, a democratic public sphere must manifest commitments to freedom and equality in the communicative interaction in the forum. Such interaction takes the specific form of a conversation or dialogue, in which speakers and hearers treat each other with equal respect and freely exchange their roles in their responses to each other. What makes dialogue so crucial is that it not only proceeds as a communicative exchange, in the form of turn-taking, but also that it is guided by the mutual expectation of uptake; that is, speakers offer reasons to each other and expect that others will consider their reasons or concerns at least to the extent that their speech acts contribute to shaping the ongoing course of the interaction, without anyone exerting control over it or having special status. What is potentially misleading is the assumption that dialogue must be modelled on one-to-one communication, perhaps counterfactually to the extent that each speaker addresses any other, demands a response, and so on. Instead, the other's response can be understood in a quite expansive spatial and temporal sense, in that someone in the indefinite future could give a response, without the speaker even conceivably having intended to address that hearer.

When modelled on the ideal process of face-to-face communication, such an interpretation of these features imposes severe spatial and temporal restrictions on public and political interaction. This leads to a third necessary feature for any public sphere, one that corrects for the limits of face-to-face interaction: communication must address an indefinite audience. In this sense, any social exclusion undermines the existence of a public sphere. This indefiniteness is required even of face-to-face interaction, since a conversation is public not simply because it could be heard by others but to the extent that it could be taken to address anyone. We might call this feature the 'publicness' or 'publicity' of communication, the necessary feature of its being 'public.' Communication is 'public', then, if it is directed at an indefinite audience with the expectation of a response. In this way, it constitutes a common, open space for such interactions that is realized in iterated responses through similar acts of communication. In this way, a public sphere depends upon the opening up of a social space for a particular kind of repeated and open-ended interaction and, as such, requires technologies and institutions to secure its continued existence and regularize opportunities and access to it.

If this account of the necessary features of public communicative action is correct, then the scope of the ideal model of the face-to-face interaction needs to be revised. Such a forum is a special, rather than a general and ideal case. Furthermore, if the very existence of the public sphere is thus always dependent on some form of communications technology, then actors use that technology to create a space for social interaction that mediates and extends dialogue beyond the limits of face-to-face encounters. Historically, writing first served to open up this sort of indefinite social space of possibilities with the spatial extension of the audience and the temporal extension of uptake or response. Taking the potentials of writing further, the printed word produced a new form of communication based on a one-to-many form of interaction. With the mass literacy of the national public sphere that emerged in modernity it also produced the sort of mass audience that acquires the indefinite features proper to the public sphere. Nonetheless, it is only one such mediated public sphere that is constituted by interaction mediated through the print medium. Television and radio did not essentially alter this one-to-many extension of communicative interaction, even as they reduced entry requirements for hearers and raised the costs of adopting the speaker's role to a mass audience.

Computer-mediated communication also extends the forum, by providing a new unbounded space for communicative interaction. But its innovative potential lies not just in its speed and scale but also with in new form of address or interaction: as a many-to-many mode of communication, it has radically lowered the costs of interaction with an indefinite and potentially large audience, especially with regard to adopting the speaker role without the costs of the mass media. Moreover, such many-to-many communication with newly increased interactivity holds out the promise of capturing the features of dialogue and communication more robustly than the print medium. At the very least, computer-mediated communication offers a potentially new solution to the problem of the extension of communicative interactions across space and time and thus, perhaps, signals the emergence of a public sphere that is not subject to the specific linguistic, cultural and spatial limitations of the bounded national public spheres that have up to now supported representative democratic institutions. This network-based extension of dialogue suggests the possibility of re-embedding the public sphere in a new and potentially larger set of institutions. At present, there is a lack of congruity between existing political institutions and the wider potential for public communicative interaction. Hence, the nature of the public or publics is changing.

Before leaping from innovative possibilities to an unwarranted optimism about the Internet's contribution to global democracy, it is first necessary to look more closely at the requirements of publicity and how the Internet might fulfill them. The sheer potential of the Internet to become a public sphere is insufficient to establish democracy at this scale for two reasons. This mediated many-to-many communication may increase interactivity without preserving the essential features of dialogue, such as responsive uptake. Further, the Internet may be embedded in institutions that do not help in transforming its communicative space into a public sphere. Even if it is a free and open space, the Internet could simply be a marketplace or a commons as Lessing and others have argued (Lessing, 1999: 141). Even if this were so, actors could still transform such communicative resources and embed them in institutions that seek to extend dialogue and sustain deliberation. What would make it a 'public sphere'?

Consider first the normative features of communicative public interaction. Publicity at the level of social action is most basic, in the sense that all other forms of publicity presuppose it. Social acts are public only if they meet two basic requirements. First, they are not only directed to an indefinite audience but also offered with some expectation of a response, especially with regard to interpretability and justifiability. The description of the second general feature of publicity is dominated by spatial metaphors: public actions constitute a common and open 'space' for interaction with indefinite others. Or, as Habermas puts it, publicity in this broadest sense is simply 'the social space generated by communicative action' (Habermas, 1996: 360). Electronic communication is similarly dominated by such metaphors, now of 'virtual' 'cyberspace.' However, we may here speak only of a 'public space' (rather than a public sphere), which can be broader or narrower in comparison with others in terms of topics, available social roles, forms of expression, requirements of equal standing, and so on.

Entering into any such social space may be more or less difficult, depending on the requirements of background knowledge or the presence or absence of egalitarian norms and styles of social interaction. This difficulty gives rise to debates about a 'digital divide.' More than mere accessibility, some argue for the need for a 'public culture,' which might include a wide variety of practices, from performances to demonstrations and writing, in which participation is open to those who have mastered some basic conventions.[1] In this respect, we may see spaces on the Internet as gendered or culturally specific, even if indefinite in the communicative extension of its underlying social action. This is because the 'space' for publicity must also be normatively structured and these norms open to challenge and revision.

Beyond this general and elementary level of publicity as a feature of some social actions and the space generated by them, higher levels of publicity are also possible. By higher I mean not higher on some normative scale but, rather, higher in the sense of levels of reflexivity. Higher order publicity introduces talk about talk, 'second-order' deliberation and dialogue, that is, dialogue about the norms of publicity and the normative contours of the social space that is opened up by communicative interaction. Such second-order publicity requires two further nested and institutionalized features: first, not just the expectation of a response but expectations about the nature of responsiveness and accountability to others; and, second, the context of a more socially structured setting and forms of interaction than is available by means of communicative action alone. With respect to responsiveness, a higher level of publicity requires more than that speakers merely presuppose that they are addressing a potentially indefinite audience. It requires a normative concern for publicity itself.

The space of mutual accountability that is thereby opened up has a more egalitarian structure than simply being addressed by a speaker: in a public sphere, these communicative exchanges suspend the sharp distinction between audience and participants, thereby allowing exchange of speaker and hearer roles across all social positions and identities. This reciprocity of roles introduces further egalitarian features to audience-oriented communication: participation in the public sphere now means that one must be responsive to others and that they may have expectations about the appropriateness of a reason in a public context; besides speaking to an indefinite audience, one is now accountable to their objections and answerable to demands to recognize their concerns.[2] The recognition of equal standing as citizens in a political community is one, potentially self-transformative form that egalitarian publicity has taken.

Introducing second order levels does not necessarily narrow the public sphere, since second order questions are themselves open to challenge. Expanding and structuring such a social space for communication requires embedding it in a wider social context. A specifically egalitarian expansion of the public sphere requires a more elaborated institutional structure to support it (such as that achieved by the modern democratic state but not identical with it), as the social contexts of communication are enlarged with the number of relevant speakers and audience. When such contexts increase the scale of public interaction and include more participants, communicative action alone cannot fully constitute or control the contours of the social space that it generates. In societies characterized by social differentiation, the political space for publicity is delimited in relation to other social domains and institutions. It is with the differentiation of society that we begin to see the emergence of what is specifically 'the public sphere.'

Continuing the spatial metaphor that dominates thinking about publicity, the public sphere becomes a space 'in-between' the formal political institutions and civil society. Thus, the very existence of a distinct public sphere requires a certain degree of social complexity, typically in the internal differentiation of social spheres such as centralized administrative institutions (the state) on the one hand, and a separate sphere of autonomous associations and economic activity (or civil society) on the other. Not all public spheres relate to the state. There may, then, be many publics and overlapping public spheres. A city's institutions may create a local public sphere but that public overlaps with and interacts with other publics. In this sense, it is indeterminate to whom a claim is addressed or who is expected to respond, given the indefiniteness of the audience. When a public sphere interacts with a set of institutions, the set of participants is potentially extended beyond the restrictions of membership or constituency, whenever a claim or utterance is given uptake and considered relevant. By using norms as a resource, actors in higher order public spheres cannot limit to whom they are answerable.

In differentiated societies (in whatever institutional form), one role of the distinctive communication that goes on in the public sphere is to raise topics or express concerns that cut across social spheres: it not only circulates information about the state and the economy, but also establishes a forum for criticism in which the boundaries of these spheres are crossed, primarily in citizens' demands for mutual accountability. But the other side of this generalization is a requirement for communication that crosses social domains: such a generalization is necessary, precisely because the public sphere has become less socially and culturally homogeneous and more internally differentiated into diverse normative perspectives and social positions. It is certainly the case that the relative absence of state regulation in cyberspace means that censorship is no longer the primary means of inhibiting the formation of public spheres. Those powerful social institutions that may now inhibit the formation of a public sphere in electronic space are no longer states but, rather, corporations and other market actors who increasingly design and control its architecture. Publics now develop in new and politically unbounded social contexts, some of which may even be global in scope, as civil society and the supporting institutions of the public sphere become more transnational.

While the mass and electronic media form the basis for global networks for the production and distribution of information, they produce a different kind of public space and hence develop a form of publicity different from a 'cosmopolitan' or global public sphere. Certainly the costs of exchanging information across space go down considerably. In comparison with the past, the epistemic requirements for participating in large scale and potentially transnational communication are lessened, to such an extent that it is widely available beyond élites in wealthy societies. By employing new technological means for lower cost distribution and by lowering epistemic entry requirements, electronic media can create a mass audience of such a size as to be conceivably global in scope. But the type of audience so created has certain characteristics: the larger an unstructured and undifferentiated audience is, the less likely it is that the public and reflexive use of reason is required to be part of it. The audience is therefore more likely to be 'anonymous,' both to each other and to the producers of its publicly conveyed messages. The addressees of such anonymous communication are an indefinite audience in a purely *aggregative* sense: it is not an idealized audience that is addressed, but the aggregate audience of all those who can potentially gain access to the material and interpret it as they wish. In the print public sphere, anonymous authorship had a particular purpose, especially in resisting the institutions of the state in which it was embedded (as when Locke published his *Second Treatise* anonymously). Anonymity is employed to maintain the freedom and diversity of speech, as human rights groups, who report abuses of various governments around the world, use it on the Internet. The anonymity of such political communication is a form that, even on the Internet, continues the resistance to censorship and state power in the public sphere.

It is easy to mistake the communicative function of anonymity. Anonymity does not fully strip away the identity of the speaker, for Locke could publish his treatise with the full knowledge that the author of the *Second Treatise* would be taken to have a particular political identity, even if that identity was not that of John Locke, and thus provokes responses as such. Rather than subjective or authorial, Internet anonymity is structural. Who is speaking is not in principle independently knowable by others. For this reason, participants in networks cannot have the full range of normative expectation of face-to-face publics or even print publics in which authorship may become a textual designator. In a serial public of publics, participants may address themselves to a segment of the public rather than the whole public of publics. In a network mediated by a computer interface, we do not know who is actually speaking; we also do not know whom we expect to respond, if they will respond or if the response will be sustained. Thus, while anonymity promotes freedom of expression under certain circumstances, it changes the expectation of communication by making speaker and audience not only indefinite but also indeterminate in its many-to-many form.

In this sort of public sphere, how would actors exhibit their concern for publicity or employ the self-referentiality of the public sphere to criticize others? Instead of appealing to an assumed common norm of 'publicity' or a set of culturally specific practices of communication, a *transnational* public sphere is created when at least two culturally rooted public spheres begin to overlap and intersect, as when translations and conferences create a cosmopolitan public sphere in various academic disciplines. Such culturally expansive, yet socially structured rather than anarchic, public spheres emerge as political institutions and civic associations and come to include previously excluded groups. Instead of relying on the intrinsic features of the medium to expand communicative interaction, networks that are global in scope become publics only with the development and expansion of transnational civil society. The creation of such a civil society is a slow and difficult process that requires the highly reflexive forms of communication, boundary crossing and accountability typical of developed public spheres. Thus, we can expect that under proper conditions and with the support of the proper institutions, existing vibrant global publics will expand as they become open to and connected with other public spheres. On the basis of their common knowledge of violations of publicity, their members will develop the capacities of public reason to cross and negotiate boundaries and differences between persons, groups and cultures.

In such boundary-crossing publics, the speed, scale and intensity of communicative interaction facilitated by the Internet provides that open social space that is a positive and enabling condition for democratic and perhaps even cosmopolitan deliberation. Contrary to misleading analogies to the national public sphere, such a development hardly demands that the public sphere be 'integrated with media systems of matching scale that occupy the same social space as that over which economic and political decision will have an impact' (Garnham, 1995: 265). But if the way to do this is through multiple communicative networks rather than the mass media, then the global public sphere should not be expected to mirror the cultural unity and spatial congruence of the national public sphere; as a public of publics, it permits a decentred public sphere with many different levels. This fact also distinguishes it from the idealizations of an implied universal audience typical of the print-mediated public sphere. Disaggregated networks must always be embedded in some other set of social institutions rather than in an assumed unified national public sphere. This suggests that they will be embedded in different, disaggregated political institutions, if they are to be the institutions that transform the deliberation of such public spheres in the communicative power of collective action. Once we examine the potential ways in which the Internet can expand the features of communicative interaction, the issue of whether or not the Internet can support public spheres changes in character. It depends not only on which institutions shape its framework but also on how participants contest and change these institutions and on how they interpret the Internet as a public space. It depends on the mediation of agency, not on technology.

The Internet as a network and as a space of publics

The main lesson that I wanted to draw at the end of the last section is that discussions of the democratic potential of the Internet cannot be satisfied with listing its positive or intrinsic features, as for example its speed, its scale, its 'anarchic' nature, its ability to facilitate resistance to centralized control as a network of networks, and so on. The same is true for its negative effects or consequences, such as its disaggregative character or its anonymity. Taken together, both these considerations tell against regarding the Internet as a variation of existing print and national public spheres. Rather, the space opened up by computer-mediated communication supports a new sort of 'distributive' rather than unified public sphere with new forms of interaction. By 'distributive,' I mean that computer mediation in the form of the Internet 'decentres' the public sphere; it is a public of publics rather than a distinctively unified and encompassing public sphere in which all communicators participate. Rather than simply entering into an existing public sphere, [the Internet becomes a public sphere only through agents who engage in reflexive and democratic activity.] For the Internet to create a new form of publicity beyond the mere aggregate of all its users, it must first be constituted as a public sphere by those people whose interactions exhibit the features of dialogue and are concerned with its publicity. In order to support a public sphere and technologically mediate the appropriate norms, the network form must become a viable means for the expansion of the possibilities of dialogue and of the deliberative, second order features of communicative interaction. These features may not be the same as manifested in previous political public spheres, such as the bourgeois public sphere of private persons; what it must be is, at least, a space for publics but not itself a public sphere. It can, however, enable such a public of publics to emerge, given the emergence of democratic actors and the proper supporting transnational institutionalization.

If the Internet has no intrinsic features, it is because, like writing, it holds out many different possibilities in its transformation of the public sphere. Here it is useful to distinguish between hardware and software. As hardware, the World Wide Web is a network of networks with technical properties that enable the conveyance of information over great distances with near simultaneity. This hardware can be used for different purposes, as embodied in software that configures participants as 'users.' Indeed, as Lessing notes, 'an extraordinary amount of control can be built in the environment that people know in cyberspace,' perhaps even without their knowledge (Lessing, 1999: 217).[3] Such computer programmes depend on 'software' in a much broader sense: software includes not only the variety of programmes available but also the ways in which people improvise and collaborate to create new possibilities for interaction. Software in this sense includes both the modes of social organization mediated through the Net and the institutions in which the Net is embedded. For example, the indeterminacy of the addressees of an anonymous message can be settled by reconfiguring the Internet into an intranet, creating a private space that excludes others and defines the audience. This is indeed how most corporations use the Web today, creating inaccessible and commercial spaces within the networks, by the use of firewalls and other devices for commercial and monetary interactions among corporations and anonymous consumers. Such actions show the variety of ways in which power and control may be manifested in the Web. Certainly, the Web enables the power to be distributed in civil society but it also permits power to be manifested, less in the capacity to interfere with others than in the capacity to exclude them and alter the freedom and openness of its public space. This same power may alter other public spaces, as when the *New York Times* offers to deliver a 'personalized' paper that is not identical with the one that other citizens in the political public sphere are reading. In this way, the Internet can be controlled so that it may be used for the privatization of information as a commodity.

   The fact of social power reveals the importance of institution₅
and maintaining public space, and the Internet is no exception
shows how the Internet has historically reflected the institutions ɪɴ
been embedded and configured. Its 'anarchist' phase reflected the ways in w.
it was created in universities and for scientific purposes. While the Web still bears
the marks of this phase as possibilities of distributed power, it is arguably entering a different phase, in which corporations increasingly privatize this common
space as a kind of *terra nullia* for their specific purposes, such as financial transactions. 'We are at a particular historical moment in the history of electronic
space when powerful corporate actors and high performance networks are
strengthening the role of private electronic space and altering the structure of
public electronic space' (Sassen, 1998: 194). At the same time, it is also clear that
civil society groups, especially transnational groups, are using the web for their
own political and public purposes, where freedom and interconnectivity are
what is valued.

   The broader point here is not merely to show the effects of privatization and
the particular ideology of neoliberalism that supports it, but to show how the
Internet develops in interaction with the larger social structures, 'offline' problems and conflicts that it internalizes and refracts. This particular conjuncture
of forces opens the potential not only for conflicting interpretations of cyberspace but also for newly reflexive activity of civil society actors over the public
character of the Internet, much as the eighteenth-century public sphere strug-
gled with the state over censorship of the print medium that created a public
concerned with its own publicity. Those concerned with the publicity, freedom
and openness of the Internet as a public space may see those of its features that
extend dialogical interaction threatened by its annexation by large scale economic enterprises. Such a concern requires that civil society actors not only
contest the alterations of public space but, also, that these actors place themselves between the corporations, software makers, access providers and other
powerful institutions that often enjoy an immediate and highly asymmetrical
relation to individuals as 'users' who enter into public spaces as they configure
them in the literal and institutional software they create for those who enter their
private cyberspaces. We are now in a period of the development of the software
and hardware of the Internet in which the nature of the Web is at issue, with
similar processes of political decentralization and social contestation that characterize the problems, struggles and contradictions found in many areas of
social life. The process of development here is hardly unprecedented or *sui
generis*.

   This suggests a particular analysis of threats to public space. It is now com-
monplace to say that the Internet rids communication of intermediaries, of
those various professional communicators whose mass-mediated communication is the focus of much of public debate and discussion and political information. Dewey lauded such a division of labour to the extent to which it can
improve deliberation, not merely in creating a common public sphere but also
in 'the subtle, delicate, vivid and responsive art of communication.' This task is,

at least in part, best fulfilled by professional communicators who disseminate the best available information and technologies to large audiences of citizens. Even with this dependence on such art and techniques of communication, the public need not simply be the object of techniques of persuasion. Rather than a 'mass' of cultural dopes, mediated communication makes a 'rational public' possible, in the sense that 'the public as a whole can generally form policy preferences that reflect the best available information' (Page, 1995). If we focus upon the totality of political information available and a surprising tendency for the public to correct media biases and distortions, as stories and opinions develop and change over time, it is possible to see how mediated communication can enhance the communication presupposed in public deliberation. In a complex, large-scale and pluralistic society, mediated communication is unavoidable if there are to be channels of communication broad enough to address the highly heterogeneous audience of all of its members and to treat issues that vary with regard to the epistemic demands on speakers in diverse locales who can discuss them intelligently.

For all of these reasons, proponents of deliberation often claim there is a net normative loss in the shift to networked communication, further amplified by 'the control revolution' in which various corporations and providers give individuals the capacity to control who addresses them and whom they may respond to (Shapiro, 1999: 23).[4] Or, to put this criticism in the terms that I have been using here, the mass public sphere is not replaced by any public sphere at all; rather, communicative mediation is replaced by forms of control that make dialogue and the expansion of the deliberative features of communication impossible. In the terms of economic theory, agents whose purpose it is to facilitate individual control over the communicative environment replace intermediaries. Such a relation though inevitably leads to 'the reversal of agency,' where the direction of control shifts from principals to the agents they delegate. It is false to say that individuals possess immediate control; they have control only through assenting to an asymmetrical relationship to various agents who structure the choices in the communicative environment of cyberspace.

There is more than a grain of truth in this pessimistic diagnosis of the control revolution. But this leaves out part of the story concerning how the public exercises some control over intermediaries, at least those concerned with publicity. As with the relation of agent and principal, the problem here is to develop democratic modes of interaction between expert communicators and their audience in the public sphere. Citizens must now resist the 'mediaization of politics' on a par with its technization by experts. The challenge is twofold. First of all, the public must challenge the credibility of expert communicators, especially in their capacities to set agendas and frames for discussing issues. And, second, as in the case of cooperating with experts the public must challenge the reception of their own public communication by the media themselves, especially insofar as they must also report, represent and even define the 'public opinion' of citizens who are strangers to each other. This self-referential aspect of public communication can only be fulfilled by interactions between the media and the public, who challenge both the ways in which the public is addressed and its opinion is represented.

Mass-mediated communication inhibits deliberation in cases when experts, especially in the tight communicative circle of the media and officials, define both the nature of the public and its opinions. In the American context, it is 'when officials of both parties and the mainstream media take a position similar to each other and opposed to the public' (Page, 1995: 119). This tight linkage is not merely a contingent affair. It is part of the interaction between media, government and audience that is typical of mediated political communication. Media outlets are dependent on government agencies for much of their information; and officials and candidates must use the media as their main channel for communication to the widest possible audience. Such problems are exacerbated as the mediated interaction becomes predominant in modern political and public spheres, creating new forms of social interaction and political relationships that reorder in space and time and become structured in ways less and less like mutually responsive dialogue (Thompson, 1995). The same is true for computer mediation, which always includes the constructive mediation of institutions as software that shape and maintain the space for interaction and may set up this interaction asymmetrically.

Analogous considerations of agency and asymmetries of access to the norms that shape communicative interaction are relevant to the Internet. It is clear t hat corporations could function as the main institutional actors in developing electronic space and exert an influence that would restrict communication in ways even more impervious to corporate media and political parties. Just as all public spheres have technological mediation of features of communicative interaction, all public spheres require counter-intermediaries and counter-public spaces of some kind or another to maintain their publicness; that is, their sustainability over time depends precisely upon those members of the public concerned with the public sphere and public opinion and, thus, concerned to have a say in the construction of the public space in whatever technical means of communication is available. The Internet and its governance now lacks the means to institutionalize the public sphere, especially since there are no functional equivalents to the roles played by journalists, judges and other intermediaries who regulated and protected the publicity of political communication in the mass media.

Who are their replacements once the technology of mediation changes? The Internet has not yet achieved a settled form in which intermediaries have been established and professionalized. As in the emerging public spheres of early modernity, the potential intermediary roles must emerge from those who organize themselves in cyberspace as a public sphere. This role falls to those organizations in civil society that have become concerned with the publicity of electronic space and seek to create, institutionalize, expand and protect it. Such organizations can achieve their goals only if they act self-referentially and insist that they may exercise communicative power over the shape and appropriation of electronic public space. Thus, contrary to Shapiro and Sunstein, it is not that the Internet gets rid of intermediaries as such; rather it operates in a public space in which the particular *democratic* intermediaries have lost their influence. This is not a necessary structural consequence of its form of communication.

With the development of the Internet as a public sphere, we may expect its 'reintermediarization,' that is, the emergence of new intermediaries who counter its privatization and individualization, brought about by access and content providers for commercial purposes, and who construct the user as a private person. Actors can play the role of 'counterintermediaries' when they attempt to bypass these narrow social roles on the Internet; more specifically, the role of a 'user' in relation to a 'provider' who sets the terms of how the Internet may be employed. The first area in which this has already occurred is in Internet self-governance organizations and their interest in countering trends to annexation and privatization. Here institutions such as ICANN have attempted to institute public deliberation on the legal and technological standards that govern the Internet (Froomkin, 2003). The other is more issue-specific, as when the Internet is used deliberatively to contest the lack of information or public debate on important issues, such as the recent successful attempt to create opposition to the 'multilateral agreement on investment' in the absence of any significant print media discussion. Such actors are concerned with the public sphere itself and use the Internet as the social space in which to construct counterpublics and new forms of access to deliberation and decision making. Here it is civil society that provides counterintermediaries, that is, they transform passive 'users' in a social space, into democratic agents who are concerned with the quality of the Internet as a public sphere. This and other examples of a deliberative process through multiple intermediaries bears further examination.

Given that what is needed are alternatives to the current set of intermediaries rather than the absence of them, civil society organizations have distinct advantages in taking on such a responsibility for publicity in cyberspace. They have organizational identities they are not anonymous; they also take over the responsibility for responsiveness that remains indeterminate in many-to-many communication. Most of all, they employ the Internet, but not as Users; they create their own spaces, promote interactions, conduct deliberation, make available information, and so on. For example, a variety of organization created a forum for the debate on the Agreement on Investment, an issue that hardly registered in the national press. Not only did they make the Agreement widely available, they held detailed on-line discussions of the merits of its various provisions (Smith and Smythe, 2001: 183). As a tool for various forms of activism, the Internet promotes a vibrant civil society; it extends the public sphere of civil society but does not necessarily transform it. Even in this regard, the point is not simply to create a web site or to convey information at low cost. It becomes something more when sites interact as a public space in which free, open and responsive dialogical interaction takes place. This sort of project is not uncommon and includes experiments among neighbourhood groups, non-governmental organizations, and others. Hence, the organization acts as an intermediary in a different way: not as an expert communicator but, rather, as the creator and facilitator of institutional 'software' that socializes the commons and makes it a public space.

This role for civil society organizations, in periods in which public spaces are contested, is not unprecedented. Nor does it require purity from economic motives or the disinterestedness of the press journalist; it was, after all, the various trade associations that sought to establish free and open public spheres in which information about distant locales could be available, through newsletters to all, with the emergence of global trade in England. This new sort of public role, however, does change how many NGOs and civil society organizations understand themselves; they would have to understand themselves as responsible for transnational structures of communication and not simply for the particular issue at hand. They can only achieve their goals if democracy is extended in the appropriate ways, and it can be extended only if electronic space becomes a public sphere, a place in which publics of various sorts can emerge and communicate with other publics.

So long as there are cosmopolitan actors who will create and maintain such transnational communication, this sort of serial and distributed public sphere is potentially global in scope. Its unity is to be found in the general conditions for the formation of publics themselves, and in the actions of those who see themselves as constituting a public against this background. Membership in these shifting publics is to be found in civil society, in formal and informal organizations that emerge to discuss and deliberate on the issues of the day. But while the creation of publics is a matter of the agency of citizens, the sustaining of general conditions that make such a process possible is a matter for formal institutionalization, just as sustaining the conditions for the national public sphere was a central concern of the democratic nation state. In the case of such shifting and potentially transnational publics, the institutions that sustain publicity and become the focus of the self-referential activity of civil society must also be innovative, if they are to have their communicative basis in dispersed and decentred forms of publicity. At the same time, these institutions must be deliberative and democratic. Because they become the location for second order reflexive political deliberation and activity, these institutions are part of the public sphere, as its higher order and self-governing form of publicity that transforms the Internet from a commons to an institutionally organized and embedded democratic space.

From publics to public sphere: the institutional form of transnational democracy

In the last section, I argued that reflexive agency of actors within cyberspace was required, to create the 'software' that could transform networks into publics making use of the distributive processes of communication in order to overcome the limitations of space and time presupposed in the national public spheres and state forms. While such publics establish positive and enabling conditions for democratic deliberation, they are not themselves democratic (even if they are transnational and cosmopolitan rather than national). Transnational civil society is a further enabling condition for the transformation of networks into publics, to the extent that it is from this sphere that we can expect to find agents who will act self-referentially so as to address, create and sustain publics; but not all such actors will have explicitly democratic goals, just as in the national public sphere a vibrant civil society need not contain only democratically oriented actors as a condition of the possibility of democratic deliberation. The public must itself be embedded in an institutional context, not only if it is to secure the conditions of publicity but also in order to promote the interaction among publics that is required for deliberative democracy. Thus, both network forms of communication and the publics formed in them must be embedded in a larger institutional and political context, if they are to be transformed into public spheres in which citizens can make claims and expect a response.

There are several reasons to think that current democratic institutions are insufficient for this task. States have promoted the privatization of various media spaces for communication, including not only the Internet but also broadcast frequencies. Even if the Internet is not intrinsically anarchistic and even if states were willing to do more in the way of protecting the public character of cyberspace, it remains an open question whether this form of communication escapes the way in which state sovereignty organizes space and time, including public space and the temporality of deliberation.[5] It is precisely its potentially aterritorial character that makes it difficult to square with centralized forms of authority over a delimited territory. This sort of process, however, does not require convergence, especially since Internet use may reflect inequalities in the access to rule-making institutions as well as other older patterns of subordination at the international level. It is also true that people do not as yet identify with each other on cosmopolitan terms. Nonetheless, new possibilities that the Internet affords for deliberation and access to influence in its distributive and network forms do not require such strong preconditions to have opened up new forms of democratization.

This is only one feature of the state's constraints on the organization of space, which also includes various cultural and linguistic limitations of the unified public sphere that is formed around and is supported by the democratic state. It is not the case that states are now entirely ineffective, nor is it true that national public spheres are so culturally limited that they serve no democratic purpose. Rather, what is at stake is not so much the continued existence or specificity of either democracy or the public sphere but, rather, that the Internet escapes the particular connections and feedback relations between the national public sphere and the democratic state. Whatever institutions could promote and protect such a dispersed and disaggregated public sphere will represent a novel political possibility that does not 'merely replicate on a larger scale the typical modern political form' (Ruggie, 1996: 195). Indeed, it must be a political form for which such a dispersed public sphere does not produce negative consequences for the capacity to transform political communication into effective political influence and authorization but, rather, develops a form of democratically organized decision-making, in which such dispersal has the positive effect of creating wider opportunities for political participation. In the absence of such a public sphere, other, often private, sources of power intervene, with or without political delegation. In this case, forms of contestation concerning economic issues may emerge in transnational social movements that do not simply appeal to states and their current unwillingness to constrain market forces.

The difficulties that the globalization of political space poses for territorial sovereignty are widely discussed, particularly with regard to the effectiveness of state regulation of the economy. Because the political institutions of democracy must be congruent with the available forms of publicity, the difficulties posed by the disunity of a global public sphere cut much deeper for the idea of deliberative democracy. As Will Kymlicka has pointed out, territoriality continues to survive by other means, particularly since 'language is increasingly important in defining the boundaries of political communities and the identities of the actors' (Kymlicka, 1999: 120). For this reason, Kymlicka argues, national communities 'remain the primary forum for democratic participatory democratic debates.' Whereas international forums are dominated by élites, the national public sphere is more likely to be a space for egalitarian, mass participation in the vernacular language and is thus the only forum that guarantees 'genuine' democratic participation and influence. Moreover, since deliberation depends on common cultural assumptions, such as shared newspapers and political parties, the scope of a deliberative community must be limited to those who share a political culture. This argument is particularly challenging to the view defended here, since it employs the same idea of a dialogical public sphere within a democracy oriented to deliberation in order to reach the opposite conclusion. Can the argument about mediated communication and the extension of dialogue go beyond a territorial, self-governing linguistic community?

As Kymlicka thinks of the public sphere, print and mass media extend properties of linguistic interaction, insofar as a national politics facilitates mass egalitarian participation around a unified set of themes and concerns. If this is the requirement for democracy, then we face a dilemma of scale. The larger the linguistic community, the more likely it will be that citizens will not have access to influence or be able to participate in an egalitarian form of decision-making in a unified public sphere. Transnational democracy will not be participatory and deliberative, perhaps not even 'genuinely' democratic at all (Dahl, 1999: 19). But here the question is simply begged in favor of pessimism: the question is not whether transnational institutions are more or less democratic by the standards of a monolinguistic national community but, rather, whether they are adequately democratic under the circumstances. The criticism holds only if democratic agents in the transnational public sphere seek to approximate the assumptions of the national variant. To look only at the constraints of size in relation to a particular form of political community begs the question of whether or not there are alternative linkages between democracy and the public sphere that are not simply scaled up. Such linkages might be more decentralized and polycentric than the national community requires. The issue here is the standard of evaluation, not whether some other public sphere or form of community 'is totally or completely democratic, but whether it is adequately democratic given the kind of entity we take it to be' (MacCormick, 1997: 345). For a nation state to be democratic, it requires a certain sort of public sphere sufficient to create a strong public via its connections to parliamentary debate. A transnational and thus polycentric and pluralist community, such as the European Union, requires a different sort of public sphere in order to promote sufficient democratic deliberation. Once a transnational and post-territorial polity rejects the assumption that it must be what Rawls calls 'a single cooperative scheme in perpetuity', a more fluid and negotiable order might emerge, with plural authority structures along a number of different dimensions rather than a single location for public authority and power. In this case, linguistic differences do not loom as large an impediment to egalitarian interactions as Kymlicka thinks.

Without a single location of public power, a unified public sphere becomes an impediment to democracy rather than an enabling condition for mass participation in decisions at a single location of authority. The minimal criteria of adequacy would be that, even with the diffusion of authority, participants in the public sphere would have to be sufficiently empowered to create opportunities and access to influence over transnational decision-making. This access will not be attained once and for all, as in the unified public sphere of nation sates in which citizens gain influence through the complex of parliamentary or representative institutions. These distributive publics have to gain access to influence over the deliberation of governmental and non-governmental actors. Currently they are 'weak' publics, who exert such influence through public opinion generally. But they may become 'strong publics' when they are able to exercise influence through institutionalized decision procedures with regularized opportunities for *ex ante* input.[6] Thus, transnational institutions are adequately democratic if they permit such access to influence distributively, across various domains and levels, rather than merely aggregatively in the summative public sphere of citizens as a whole. But because there is no single institution to which strong publics are connected, the contrast between weak and strong publics is much more fluid than the current usage presupposes. That is because strong publics are assumed to be connected to a particular sort of legislatively empowered collective will. In the transnational case, strong publics may be required to seek more direct forms of deliberative influence given the dispersal of authority and the variety of its institutional locations.

Rather than look for a single axis on which to judge the democratic deficit of transnational and international and transnational institutions, it will be more useful to consider a variety of possible forms, given various ways in which publicity might be institutionalized. While the full range of such cases cannot be considered fully here, the European Union provides an interesting case study for a transnational polity, precisely because it obviously lacks the unitary and linguistic features of previous public spheres. I will consider only one aspect of the debate here: proposals that are suggestive of how a polycentric form of publicity would permit a more rather than a less directly deliberative form of governance, once we abandon the assumption that there is a unified public sphere connected to a single set of state-like authority structures that seem to impose uniform policies over its entire territory. As Charles Sabel has argued, a 'directly deliberative' design in many ways incorporates epistemic innovations and increased capabilities of economic organizations, in the same way as the new regulatory institutions of the New Deal followed the innovations of industrial organization, in the centralized mass production they attempted to administer and regulate (Dorf and Sabel, 1996: 292). Roughly, such a form of organization uses nested and collaborative forms of decision-making based on highly collaborative processes of jointly defining problems and setting goals already typical in many large firms with dispersed sites of production.

Such a process requires a design that promotes a great deal of interaction within the organization and across sites and locations. Within the normative framework established by initial goals and benchmarks, the process of their application requires deliberation at various levels of scale. At all levels, citizens can introduce factors based on local knowledge and problems, even as they are informed by the diverse solutions and outcomes of other planning and design bodies. Local solutions can also be corrected, as these solutions can be tested by the problem-solving of other groups. Thus, while highly dispersed and distributed, various levels of deliberation permit testing and correction, even if they do not hierarchically override decisions at lower levels.

Such a collaborative process of setting goals and defining problems produces a shared body of knowledge and common goals, even if the solutions need not be uniform across or within various organizations and locations. Sabel calls this 'learning by monitoring' and proposes ways in which administrative agencies could employ such distributive processes even while evaluating performance at lower levels by systematic comparisons across sites. Innovations are not handed down from the top, since its learning does not assume that the higher levels are epistemically superior. It cannot do so, if it is to be a non-hierarchical alternative to agent/principal relationships that emerge across levels of governance and lead to the common problem of the reversal of agency. Besides problems of scale, democracy on the model of a national community writ large leads to a proliferation of such forms of agency in dealing with external problems as issues of 'foreign policy,' typically the most undemocratic component of national governance.

The European Union implements such a decentralized process of regulation in its 'Open Method of Coordination.' Such deliberative processes provide a space for on-going reflection on agendas and problems, as well as an interest in inclusiveness and diversity of perspectives. These enabling conditions for democracy can take advantage of the intensified interaction across borders that are byproducts of processes of the thickening of the communicative infrastructure across state borders. Regulatory, but still decentralized, federalism provides for modes of accountability in this process itself, even while allowing for local variations that go beyond the assumption of the uniformity of policy over a single bounded territory typical of nation state regulation. Sabel and Cohen argue that the European Union already has features of a directly deliberative polyarchy in the implementation of the OMC in its economic, industrial and educational standards (Sabel and Cohen, 1998).[7] The advantage of such deliberative methods is that the interaction at different levels of decision making promotes robust accountability; accountability operates upwards and downwards and, in this way, cuts across the typical distinction of vertical and horizontal accountability (O'Donnell, 1994: 61). Thus, directly deliberative polyarchy describes a method of decision-making in institutions across various levels and with plural authority structures.

Unlike attempts to exert public influence upon hierarchical representative institutions, this sort of institutionalized method is directly rather than indirectly deliberative. Indirectly deliberative institutions hold out the promise of democratic legitimacy to the extent that their formal institutions are connected to the various public spheres in which all citizens participate (although not necessarily all in the same ones). Directly deliberative institutions might, at the level of fixing general goals and standards that guide such a process, require a similar sort of connection to the European public sphere at large, which in turn may be mediated through a more effective European parliament. Given various linguistic and mass media limitations, this public sphere would not be a unified one, but a public of publics in which various linguistic public spheres debate common issues and, through intermediaries, translate across linguistic and cultural boundaries the results of deliberative processes in other publics.

But what is the public at large at the level of implementation and democratic experimentation in directly deliberative processes? Sabel provides no answer to this question, asserting only that the process must be open to the public (Sabel and Cohen, 1998: 29).[8] Without a clear account of the interaction between publics and the various levels of the institutional decision-making process, it is hard to see why the process does not simply reduce to a more open form of commitology, of expert deliberation at various levels governed by various interests which attempt to influence their decisions. In this case, such deliberation may have a certain epistemic quality but its sole claim to be democratic is that committees are internally pluralistic, across national identity, and are governed by some conception of the common European good. But committees are then hardly directly deliberative, except in the sense that there is vigorous interaction among various indirectly deliberative, loosely representative bodies with different tasks and goals. Direct deliberation must be kept institutionally distinct from commitology, precisely with respect to its particular disaggregated form of publicity. What is needed here, to go beyond commitology, is not a new method but rather a Europe that is a public of publics.

The problem for institutional design of directly deliberative democracy is to create precisely the appropriate feedback relation between disaggregated publics and such a polycentric decision-making process. As my discussion of the Internet shows, there is a technology through which this form of publicity is produced and which expands and maintains the deliberative potential of dialogue.

150

Thus, the European Union, at least in some of its decision-making processes, could then seek the marriage of directly deliberative decision making and computer assisted, mediated and distributive forms of publicity. When compared to the nation state democracies that are members of the EU, such a proposal is based on two different forms of disaggregation: the disaggregation of both representative democracy and the national public sphere in order to promote a more deliberative form of transnationalism. At the European level, this would require an innovative form of a symmetrical federalism that would go beyond the hierarchy of territorial federalism along the model of the United States. Most of all, it would require experimentation in reconciling the dispersed form of many-to-many communication with the demands of the forum. Rather than merely seek to determine an institutional formula such direct and vigorous interaction among dispersed publics at various levels of decision making, it is more fruitful to say that in each case, such democratization requires the existence of a vibrant, transnational civil society in which organizations and groups create publics around which various sort of decisions are debated and discussed, similar to the sort of Internet counter-public sphere that emerged around the Agreement on Investment. Appropriately designed decision-making processes and the existence of a suitable form of publicity, to enable access to influence, speak at least in favour of the feasibility of such a proposal. This sort of procedure also suggests that familiar problem of scale that plague public deliberation when it does not consider alternative ways in which the dialogical features of the public sphere may be technologically and institutionally extended and democratically secured.

Conclusion

My argument here has been two sided. On the one hand, I have developed the innovative potential of electronic public space for democracy, especially when applied to a deliberative transnationalism. This potential transformation of democratic institutions shows the fruitfulness of thinking about cyberspace in political terms that are related to the sort of publicity that it generates. On the other hand, such a potential public sphere can be secured only through innovative institutions. In each case, new circumstances suggest rethinking both democracy and the public sphere outside the limits of its previous historical forms. Tied up with the nation state and its political culture, this framework misrepresents the potentials of new forms of mediated communication for democracy and public deliberation. Rethinking publicity allows us see that some critical diagnosis of the problems of electronic democracy are short-circuited by a failure to think beyond what is politically familiar, as when it is argued that communication over the Internet leads to a general phenomena of 'disintermediation,' when what it actually leads to new intermediaries (Shapiro, 1999: 55). The same is true of diagnoses that see the Internet as inherently democratic and dialogical. Critical analyses of the potential of the Internet and the globalization of communication are better served neither by pessimism nor by optimism, but by examing potential transformations of our understanding of both democracy and the public sphere. If my argument is correct, that the Internet preserves and extends the dialogical character of the public sphere in a potentially cosmopolitan form, then a deliberative transnational democracy can be considered a 'realistic utopia' in Rawls' sense; it extends the range of political possibilities for deliberative democracy. Even as such communication does indeed threaten some of the best realizations of political ideals of democracy that have been achieved so far in the modern era, contrary to critics such as Kymlicka, it also opens up new possibilities that are recognizably democratic and directly deliberative. Deliberative publics can be strong publics distributively, capable of exerting political influence in real decision-making processes under certain institutional conditions.

While I have rejected Kymlicka's criticism of transnational democracy as lacking an egalitarian public sphere for mass participation, he is correct to press a further point that proponents of global or cosmopolitan democracy have not taken seriously: the problem that the lack of a shared identity poses for cosmopolitan political form. In a similar vein, Habermas has also argued that solidarity at this level cannot simply be based on a shared moral conceptions of human rights but only on a shared political culture; otherwise Europe may not become a public of publics in the full democratic sense (Habermas, 2001: 126). In conclusion, I would like to suggest the ways in which these innovative forms of publicity may, when institutionally secured, themselves provide a solution to the problem of cosmopolitan identity and solidarity. It does so in light of the specific qualities of the interaction that occurs in an extended but mediated dialogical public sphere.

I have argued that the Internet and other contemporary public spaces permit a form of publicity that results in a public of publics rather than a unified public sphere based in a common culture or identity. In order for it to be an adequate extension of the dialogical public sphere for democratic purposes, a public of publics must still enable communication with an indefinite (although not unitary) audience. It cannot simply remain a fragmented series of publics but must become what I have called a serial public that is potentially connected in the proper institutional context to other publics. If this is the case, participants in the political public sphere of such publics relate to reach other in a particular way that preserves perhaps the most essential feature of dialogue for democratic citizenship, in which each is equally entitled to participate in defining the nature and course of such interaction: all participants may mutually make claims upon each other, in that they address and are addressed by each other in terms of claims that every speaker puts forth as something that others ought to accept. Thus, speakers and their audience stand in the essential normative relation of dialogical interaction: they address each other in the normative attitude in which all may propose and incur mutual obligations.

This relation of mutual obligation is the core of the political relationship of citizenship: persons become citizens when they participate in an institutionalized public sphere backed by institutions that make it possible for them to make claims upon each other only if they stand as equals to those who may make the same claims upon them. To have the standing to make claims and incur obligations within an institutional framework is to have a political identity. To participate in a cosmopolitan public sphere is precisely to be open to the claims of any participant in any public, to be the addressee of claims that are made to the human community as such. Similarly, it may open up a particular community and its public sphere to the claims made by other communities in their public sphere, whether that is a claim to justice made on behalf of those who have suffered past wrongs or by those who suffer real harms in the present. Once such claims are taken up and responded to in the present or in our community, we see ourselves as standing toward others whose standing is our concern and for whom we act to constitute a larger public sphere in taking up their claims upon us.

If this obligation-constituting element of dialogue is preserved and extended and finds a new form of a deliberative public sphere, then a further essential democratic element is also possible: that the public sphere is a source of social criticism, of those whose critical claims open up the public sphere and expose its limitations. Either in adopting the role of the critic or in taking up such criticism in the public sphere, speakers adopt the standpoint of the 'generalized other,' the relevant critical perspective that opens up a future standpoint of the whole community. Democratic self-government clearly entails that it is, in some relevant sense, the whole community that is self-governing. This is usually taken to suggest that self-government entails that the various members of the self-governing 'body-politic' must adopt a common or shared perspective, if not in deliberation itself then at least in the outcome of deliberation. Certainly, Mead saw the issue of the scope of the political community as one of being responsive to others and adopting their perspectives. As he put it: 'The question whether we belong to a larger community is answered in terms of whether our own actions calls out a response in this wider community, and whether its response is reflected back into our own conduct' (Mead, 1934: 271). This sort of mutual responsiveness and interdependence is the basis for a potential democratic community, and this in turn depends on the capacity to make and respond to claims available to social actors even in cases of conflict. To the question of the applicability of such norms and institutions internationally, Mead is optimistic: 'Could a conversation be conducted internationally? The question is a question of social organization.'(ibid.) Given the clearly pluralist basis of international society, we might expect the institutional forms of a multiperspectival polity to unlink democratic authority from the exclusive and territorial form of democratic citizenship and authority tied to the nation states, as it begins to reflect the enriched possibilities of politically relevant perspectives. The value of such deliberation is that it permits precisely the sort of reflection necessary for the transformation of democracy within states into multiperspectival polities that incorporate a cosmopolitan public sphere into their political life. If the distributively strong public sphere that the Internet enables contributes to making dialogue with others who serve the role of the generalized other possible, then it may also enable the mediation of dialogue across borders and publics. But it does so only if there are agents who make it so and transnational institutions whose ideals seek to realize a transnational public sphere as the basis for a realistic utopia of citizenship in a complexly interconnected world.

Notes

1 The term 'public culture' usually denotes those aspects of cultural identity and symbols that become the subject matter for public debate and opinion; the public sphere denotes a social space that emerges out of civil society and is outside of state control. On these debates and an analysis of sports as part of public culture in China, see Brownell (1994, ch. 3). Brownell shows the odd locations for publicity even in 'state saturated societies,' such as in criticisms of the Party in Chinese sports journalism. Public culture can develop autonomously from the larger culture in which it is embedded.

2 Such mutual responsiveness or answerability to others is crucial to the justificatory force of public agreements. For an elaboration of this form of justification in relation to making one's actions 'answerable' to others, see Freeman (1991), p. 281–303.

3 The issue here is that private sources of power have the same effects as public power manifested in state censorship.

4 Shapiro ignores the way in which the process of deliberation is never under the control of anyone.

5 See, for example, Joel Trachtman, 'Cyberspace, Sovereignty, Jurisdiction, and Modernism, in *Global Legal Studies* (1998), especially on the problems of jurisdiction and territoriality. On why the term 'aterritorial' is superior to 'post-territorial' in discussing electronic space; see p. 570ff. A further advantage of the term is that it does not elide the ways in which Internet usage could reflect structural inequalities in the world economy.

6 On the distinction between strong and weak publics, see Fraser (1989), 109–142. Habermas appropriates this distinction in his 'two track model of democracy in *Between Facts and Norms* (Habermas, 1998) chapter 7. The requirements of a strong pubic sphere for both are closely tied to access to influence over national legislation, in which the collective will is transformed into the coercive power of law.

7 Charles Sabel and Joshua Cohen, 'Directly-Deliberative Polyarchy,' in *Private Governance, Democratic Constitutionalism and Supranationalism* (Florence: European Commission, 1998), 3–30. For a more direct application to the EU, see Joshua Cohen and Charles Sabel, 'Sovereignty and Solidarity: EU and US', in *Governing Work and Welfare in a New Economy: European and American Experiments*, eds J. Zeitlin and D. Trubek (Oxford: Oxford University Press, forthcoming).

8 Sabel and Cohen, p. 29.

Bibliography

Brownell, S. (1994) *Training the Body for China*. Chicago: University of Chicago Press.

Cohen, J. and Sabel, C. (2003) 'Sovereignty and Solidarity: EU and US', in J. Zeitlin and D. Trubek (2003) *Governing Work and Welfare in a New Economy: European and American Experiments*. Oxford: Oxford University Press.

Dahl, R. (1999) 'Can International Organizations Be Democratic? A Skeptic's View,' in J. Shapiro and C. Hacker-Cardan (1999) *Democracy's Edges*. Cambridge: Cambridge University Press.

Dorf, M. and Sabel, C. (1996) 'The Constitution of Democratic Experimentalism,' *Columbia Law Review* 98(2), 267–473.

Fraser, N. (1989) 'Rethinking the Public Sphere,' In *Habermas and the Public Sphere*, ed. C. Calhoun. Cambridge: MIT Press, 109–142.

Freeman, S. (1991) 'Contractualism, Moral Motivation, and Practical Reason,' *Journal of Philosophy* 88, p. 281–303.

Froomkin, M. (2003) 'Habermas@discourse.net: Towards a Critical Theory of Cyberspace,' *Harvard Law Review* 16, 751–873.

Garnham, S. (1995) 'The Mass Media, Cultural Identity, and the Public Sphere in the Modern World,' *Public Culture* 5.

Habermas, J. (1996) *Between Facts and Norms*. Cambridge: MIT Press.

Habermas, J. (2001) *The Postnational Constellation*. Cambridge: MIT Press.

Held, D. (1995) *Democracy and Global Order*. Stanford: Stanford University Press.

Kymlicka, W. (1999) 'Citizenship in an Era of Globalization,' in J. Shapiro and C. Hacker-Cardan (1999) *Democracy's Edges*. Cambridge: Cambridge University Press.

Lessing, L. (1999) *Code*. New York: Basic Books.

MacCormick, N. (1997) 'Democracy, Subsidiarity and Citizenship,' *Law and Philosophy* 16(4), 331–54.

Mead, G. H. (1934) *Mind, Self and Society*. Chicago: University of Chicago Press.

O'Donnell, G. (1994) 'Delegative Democracy,' *Journal of Democracy* 5.

Page, B. (1995) *Who Deliberates?* Chicago: University of Chicago Press.

Poster, M. (2001) *What's the Matter With the Internet?* Minneapolis: University of Minnesota Press.

Ruggie, G. (1996) *Constructing the World Polity*. London: Routledge.

Sabel, C. and Cohen, J. (1998) 'Directly-Deliberative Polyarchy,' in *Private Governance, Democratic Constitutionalism and Supranationalism*. Proceedings of the COST A 7 Seminar, Florence, 22 to 24 May 19997, Luxembourg 1998: Office for Official Publications of the European Communities.

Sassen, S. (1998) *Globalization and Its Discontents*. New York: The New Press.

Shapiro, A. (1999) *The Control Revolution*. New York: Century Foundation.

Smith, P. and Symthe, E. (2001) 'Globalization, Citizenship and Technology: the Multilateral Agreement on Investment (MAI) Meets the Internet,' in F. Webster (2001) *Culture and Politics in the Information Age*. London: Routledge.

Sunstein, C. (2001) *Republic.com*. Princeton: Princeton University Press.

Thompson, J. (1995) *Media and Modernity*. Stanford: Stanford University Press.

Trachtman, J. (1998) 'Cyberspace, Sovereignty, Jurisdiction, and Modernism, in *Indiana Journal of Global Legal Studies* 5(2), 561–81.

Feminism and the political economy of transnational public space

Lisa McLaughlin

Introduction

Despite the richness of the various contributions to public sphere theory, one deficit has become increasingly conspicuous over the past fifteen years: the overall failure to confront adequately a contemporary scenario in which a globalizing capitalist economy is restructuring the public sphere and reshaping its modes of exclusion. The majority of scholars have remained so tied to a notion of the public sphere as a nation-centered arena that they have not been able to offer a significant contribution to our understanding of the current status of, or the democratic prospects for, transnational public spaces. In addressing the fixation of Habermas' critics on the stage of capitalism that provides the background for the conclusion of *The Structural Transformation of the Public Sphere*, Postone (1992: 176) surmises that 'any critical theory that, like the French General Staff, prepares for future battles by planning to win the previous war may all too easily find itself outwitted by what apparently can still be characterized as the cunning of history.' Viewed from another angle, current critiques of Habermas appear to have been outmaneuvered by the cunning of the public sphere itself, which, as Negt and Kluge (1993: 79) have pointed out, has always worked to avoid its own disintegration by reaching out into the future. At the very moment that Habermas and other critics were preparing their responses to the English translation of *The Structural Transformation*, the largely national arrangement described by 'the public sphere' was already changing its costume.

It is only in the past few years that the more prominent contributors to public sphere theory have begun to address the ways in which the contours of both the nation and its semblance of a public sphere are changing under the pressures of an ascending neoliberal economic orthodoxy. And yet, since at least the early 1990s, there has been evidence that an incipient transnational civil society is emerging as networks of activists and nongovernmental organizations (NGOs) have begun to make connections in cyberspace in an attempt to intervene in matters of global governance. In a less 'official political' sense of the public sphere, we can also see the development of a semblance of transnational public spheres in the form of web site and chat room venues for fans of music, videogames, and television programmes, along with those that summon audiences for televised media events such as the O. J. Simpson trial and the Olympic Games.

These examples point to what has become a glaring omission in most contributions to public sphere scholarship: a thorough engagement with the ways in which the public sphere has been reshaped through the globalizing, mediated forms of communication that constitute the representational infrastructure for today's public spaces. The issue is not, as some scholars would have it, that the very notion of a public sphere is hopelessly old-fashioned in a context in which the Internet has become the exemplar of public space (eg.: Dean, 2003; Poster, 1995). As I argue in this chapter, public sphere theory is capable of reasserting its relevance, but only if it ceases to ignore the impact of globalization processes on the public sphere, and, indeed, on almost every aspect of cultural, social, political, and economic life.

This chapter is focused primarily on the potential for, and obstacles to, the creation of a transnational feminist public sphere. Today, one of the most discernible indications of the development of a transnational public sphere is the emergence of transnational feminist networks that have been constituted in order to consolidate struggles against gender inequality and injustice. Although, for many scholars, these networks have become a sign of the existence of a transnational public sphere, feminist public sphere theorists have had little to say about this development. This chapter represents an initial attempt to push feminist scholarship on the public sphere toward an engagement with transnational public spaces, in a way that neither marginalizes considerations of the global political economy nor reconciles itself to this as an unassailable barrier to the achievement of economic justice for women.

From *The Structural Transformation* to the 'Linguistic Turn'

The 1989 publication of the English translation of Habermas's *The Structural Transformation of the Public Sphere* has come to serve as a reference point for current trends in public sphere theory. In this groundbreaking contribution to democratic political theory, Habermas draws the concept of a public sphere based in norms of inclusiveness and universality from a description of the emergence of an eighteenth-century Western European liberal-bourgeois public sphere, an arena for critical, rational debate that eventually deteriorates into the pseudo-publicity of the mass media. Habermas' overarching project, however, is to illuminate how changes in the economic system and the political system influence the transformation of cultural institutions and practices (Hohendahl, 1979). The bourgeois form of the public sphere is set into motion when long-distance capitalist trade makes possible a 'traffic in commodities and news' (Habermas, 1989: 15). Whereas the discussion of print materials within the salons and coffee houses of the eighteenth-century bourgeois was largely responsible for the emergence of the liberal model of the bourgeois public sphere, the rise of the mass media is, for Habermas, a key factor in its decline and eventual disintegration as, under the economic and political pressures of late capitalism, the rational-critical debate that had been motivated by news and opinion pieces becomes buried under privatized, mass-mediated forms of communication.

Habermas denounces the media as the primary site for the support of private interests and the degeneration of critically-reasoned public discourse to passive cultural consumption and apolitical sociability. In this respect, his account typifies the critique of mass culture offered by other members of the Frankfurt School, particularly Adorno and Horkheimer. Today, both Habermas and the majority of his critics tend to respond to his Frankfurt School-inspired theme regarding the public's manipulation by a corrupted mass culture by exiling it from critical reflection, as though it were an unfortunate appendix that detracts from the overall grandeur of his theory. And yet, to the extent that reactions to the 'disintegration thesis' represent a defining moment in public sphere theory, the conclusion of *The Structural Transformation* is more of a watershed event than is recognized by many critics. In Habermas' case, this is the point at which he disappointingly abandons the critique of a mass-mediated public sphere, along with any attempt to imagine an alternative to its present constitution. Although his narrative of the rise and fall of the liberal-bourgeois public sphere is often interpreted as a tragic tale (Garnham, 1992), it could just as easily, and more productively, be read as a crossroads in public sphere theory, one at which Habermas, faced with the development of 'welfare state mass democracy' and the industrial-commercial manipulation of popular opinion, gives up hope that a socialist public sphere may arise out of the conditions of late capitalism. It is at this point that he takes on an attitude of nostalgia in regard to the liberal-bourgeois public sphere and abandons the material circumstances that facilitate or obstruct the emergence of democratic form of communications.

The Structural Transformation concludes with a faint appeal for the need to bring a critical publicity to life and to democratize the institutions of civil society, including the media (1989: 232). Although Habermas has produced an impressive amount of scholarship throughout the 1980s and 1990s, none of this offers a systematic analysis of the nature, social functions, and structures of mediated communications, the role of contemporary media in democratic processes, or the potential for democratization of the media (Kellner, 2000). Instead, he refocuses his attention to the philosophical dimensions of language and communication, taking a 'linguistic turn' and focusing on 'communicative action,' or the capacity of language to generate norms that might allow rational discursive will-formation and consensus-building (Kellner, 2000).

With the 'linguistic turn,' we are introduced to a categorical opposition that appears consistent with the rise and fall scenario, one that he refers to as 'lifeworld' and 'system.' This is the juncture at which Habermas develops the notion of an 'ideal speech situation' to be applied to the interpersonal relations of the lifeworld in order to ensure its distance from the systemic resources of money and power. His distinction between 'system' and 'lifeworld,' with 'system' denoting the state (power) and the economy (money), and 'lifeworld' designating the public sphere and the intimate sphere, is an attempt to refine his four-quadrant schema describing the private and the public (Habermas, 1987). The opposition between lifeworld and system, he suggests, is a way of acknowledging the complexity of modern societies, which must be systemically differentiated in ways that were not necessary for pre-modern societies. The separation of lifeworld from system also becomes an occasion for shielding the interpersonal relations of the lifeworld from the systemic resources of monetary and administrative power. However, the problem is that only one celebrated category—in this case, the lifeworld—remains in Habermas' sights. All spheres become unavailable for empirical analysis, the lifeworld because it is idealized and the economic and political spheres because, as that from which the lifeworld must be shielded, they fall outside Habermas' lens. The requirement that undistorted communication take place in the lifeworld creates unease toward the media: they are either sources for degradation of the lifeworld or mere instruments for the transmission of information within civil society (Kellner, 2000).

Rather than to offer a more productive approach to questions of mass culture, in which even less-than-praiseworthy forms of communication might be considered worthwhile for analysis, the majority of Habermas' critics have joined him in evading the question of the role of the mass media in society, particularly in its political-economic dimensions. In the context of the 'linguistic turn,' what seems to have been forgotten is that, in the most fundamental sense, the concept of the public sphere invokes a symbiotic relationship between the state of well-being of a democratic society and the condition of its communication environment (Dahlgren, 2001: 35). The public sphere describes a social imaginary that is created and reproduced through discourse, but, at the same time, it denotes a collection of historically-specific institutions that structure the possibilities for communicative access (Negt and Kluge, 1993). As Garnham (1992: 360) has written, one virtue of Habermas' early interpretation of the public sphere is its insistence on 'the indissoluble link between the institutions and practices of mass public communication and the institutions and practices of democratic politics.' Within the confines of the 'linguistic turn,' what are presumed to be advances in public sphere theory also represent a great loss to the degree that they depart from the material concerns that provided the groundwork for *The Structural Transformation*'s (however imperfect) contribution to a critical theory of communication. In this sense, Habermas' critics have not followed his lead closely enough. In another sense, however, many have followed his lead too exactly; as Calhoun (1992: x) observes, philosophers in particular have tended to treat *The Structural Transformation* as a book that merely lays the groundwork for Habermas' 'real work' focusing on communicative action (Calhoun, 1992: x). The crux of the matter is that today's public sphere theory has remained too attached to the academic moment and environment in which it has developed, and, as a result, it has drawn numerous boundaries that narrow the scope of the visible. Although it is frequently acknowledged that a vast number of injustices are rooted in the political economy, structural inequalities within late capitalism tend to be presented as a sort of faded background for debates regarding discourse and signification. Even Fraser's (1989) materially-based conception of a 'struggle over needs' has too often had the sense of serving as a vehicle for struggles over theories of discourse, arising from scholarly commitments to postmodernism, poststructuralism, pragmatism, and deliberative and participatory forms of democracy.

One might attempt to rescue the emphasis on discourse from political-economic critique by maintaining, as Fraser (1992: 185) does, that 'the concept of a discourse links the study of language to the study of society,' and that pragmatic approaches are preferable to structuralist approaches in that they 'insist on the social context and social practices of communication' (Fraser, 1992: 191). But this begins to ring very hollow when public sphere theorists speak of socially-situated agents without carefully describing their social situations. I would argue that this occurs whenever contemporary renderings of the public sphere focus on 'discursive sites and practices' (Fraser, 1992: 191) and yet fail to offer an analysis of the socio-historical context and political-economic institutional mechanisms that help to constitute the conditions under which democratic modes of communication are enabled or constrained.

In many respects, feminist scholarship on the public sphere has served as something of a countervailing force against the mainstream of the current theoretical environment. Scholars including Nancy Fraser, Mary Ryan, Joan Landes, Carole Pateman, Seyla Benhabib, and Iris Young have done a great deal to elucidate the relationship of power to material conditions and the activities of agents and institutions. Feminists have revealed the ways in which political and economic factors that have played a role in the exclusions constitutive of the normative and historical dimensions of a liberal-bourgeois public sphere, where the very meaning of 'civil society' was constructed through the significant exclusion of women, the proletariat, and popular culture (Landes, 1988; Fraser, 1990; Ryan,1992; Pateman, 1988). Feminists have underscored the extent to which the liberal-bourgeois model's abstract principle of generality acted in fact as an exclusionary mechanism, such that the discussion of 'common concerns' tended to preclude debate that was disassociated from the interests of white, male, educated property-owners. In doing so, they have helped to reinvigorate the project of immanent critique that seemed to have diminished by the conclusion of *The Structural Transformation*. Moreover, in reconceptualizing the notion of the public sphere so that it may be more relevant to a critique of the political milieu of late capitalist societies, feminist scholars have contributed significantly to the task of preserving the emancipatory possibilities of the public sphere while severing the concept from its liberal-bourgeois form. Importantly, they have introduced the concept of the counterpublic sphere, a space for the invention and circulation of counter-discourses by members of subordinated social groups. Within the context of a counterpublic, subordinated groups are able to offer interpretations of their identities, needs, and interests in opposition to a comprehensive public sphere imbued with dominant interests and ideologies (Fraser, 1997: 81; Felski, 1989).

Despite the magnitude of these contributions, one of the key failings of feminist scholarship on the public sphere is that its analyses have too often had the parochial quality that is characteristic of most public sphere theory. In making this charge of parochialism, I want to tread lightly, given that such feminist concerns as an 'ethics of care' have too often been described as such within a patriarchal academy. I am not suggesting that engagement with 'the personal' or 'the personal as political' is too insular an activity, rather that feminist public sphere theory has remained too focused on categorical distinctions embedded in Western modernism and on forms of discursive interactions that prevail within Western societies, particularly within the boundaries of the United States. Most feminist scholarship on the public sphere departs from Habermas in more fully addressing the ways in which language serves hegemonic functions, such that power is always embedded in communication, but most of this scholarship follows his lead in emphasizing discourse and treating the media as mere instruments for the dissemination of discourse. Overall, feminist critics have been far more focused on the emancipatory allure of the normative dimensions of the public sphere than on understanding the political-economic realities of the current media and information environment. Little attention is paid to how the most public modes of discourse are invariably produced, enabled, and obstructed through the hegemonic practices of the media. Even Nancy Fraser, the theorist who seems most aware that privately-owned, for-profit media constitute the material support for the circulation of views (1997), fails to offer a sustained analysis of the media's role in the framing of discourses on 'dependency' in US welfare debates or on the encounter between gender and race, in the case of her analysis of the Clarence Thomas/Anita Hill controversy.

Feminism and the Transnational Turn

In a recent commentary regarding the need to reconstruct democratic political theory so that it is capable of addressing 'the postnational constellation,' it is revealing that Fraser specifically cites the field of media studies as having newly confirmed the fact that it is possible for discursive arenas to escape the boundaries of the nation-state (Fraser, 2002). The reconstitution of the socio-spatial scale of the public sphere from a nation-centered arena to a global or transnational social space is not a recent development; indeed, this is a process that has been ongoing since the nineteenth century, with capitalist growth having motivated the development of border-crossing telecommunications and transportation systems (Herman and McChesney, 1997: 12). Neither is it the case that the field of media studies has just recently begun to address a context in which public spheres have begun to spill beyond national boundaries. Scholars concerned with the political economy of communication have been focusing on the role of electronic media in the global political economy since the 1950s.[1] This effort was stepped up during the 1970s, as an increasing number of scholars began to challenge the spread of cultural domination and imperialism through the growing global hegemony of US media industries. Media scholars' early attempts to address the need to democratize global communications came to a head during the New World Information and Communication Order (NWICO) debate that was initiated under the auspices of the United Nations Educational, Scientific and Cultural Organization (UNESCO) during the mid-1970s. Although it failed ultimately, the NWICO represents a key moment in which scholars, government leaders, and policy experts sought to institutionalize a global communications policy regime that would reorient the development of a transnational public sphere from one based on the free market flow of Western-controlled news and entertainment to one in which resource redistribution might offer developing countries the opportunity to build their own communication systems and thus to break out of a cycle of cultural dependency.

By the time that *The Structural Transformation* was published in the late-1980s, it should have been abundantly clear that public spheres are not cordoned off within the boundaries of the Westphalian nation-state. For a number of years, global restructuring has been straining the capacity of both the nation-state and its semblance of a public sphere to represent the needs and interests of citizens. Neoliberal orthodoxies have worked to intensify the cross-border expansion of transnational corporations, and, along with them, the transnational flow of people, products, and politics. It has become apparent that most nation-states are either unable or unwilling to contest a neoliberal economic framework based in liberalization, deregulation, and privatization, one which prefers to treat communication as a commodity whose worth is based on the amount for which it can be traded on the global market. The emphasis on trade within media and communications policy-making has had enormous consequences for the public sphere, as increases in commercialization, concentration in media ownership and an unprecedented growth in large media corporations have been accompanied by an erosion of community and national control over media and a collapse in public expenditures that might otherwise be used to support noncommercial forms of media (McChesney and Schiller, 2002: 7).

Public sphere theorists have been almost entirely silent on these developments. An attachment to the notion of the public sphere as a nation-centered arena is one reason for critics' delayed recognition of the importance of understanding transnational public spaces. Fraser (2002) attributes the failure of scholars to notice the emergence of transnational public spheres to a conceptual dilemma posed by the tacit assumption that a Westphalian national frame should provide the appropriate context for a critique of the public sphere. In a somewhat similar vein, Habermas (2001) has suggested that the notion of a transnational public sphere is complicated by the traditional understanding of citizenship as the achievement of a sense of collective identity within the boundaries of the nation. Without denying the sincerity or veracity of these claims, I want to argue that such diagnoses are not thorough enough. Both Fraser and Habermas suggest that the obstacles encountered in conceptualizing transnational public space are ones that inhere within the very notion of the public sphere. Given that problematizing the public sphere has become something of a cottage industry, it is difficult to accept that qualities that are intrinsic to the concept of the public sphere have been the primary roadblocks to imagining beyond the imagined community of the nation-state.

It is too easy to suggest that the main hindrance to transnationalizing the public sphere is that scholars encounter a dilemma whenever there is a challenge to the implicit assumptions that are invoked upon mention of 'the public sphere.' In these post-structuralist/deconstructionist times, it seems untenable to pose a causal relationship between a concept and the inability to imagine beyond it. While a fixation on the nation-state is provincial almost by definition, it is only one among several complicating factors that have the appearance of being inherent to the public sphere but which are in fact symptomatic reflections of the overall parochial character of current public sphere theory.

One root of the problem is that public sphere theory seems overly beholden to the use of heuristic devices that create opposed categories out of phenomena that are in fact interwoven. Such heuristic devices too often have taken on a life of their own, employing rigid categories of rise/demise, lifeworld/system, and civil society/state/economy that are able to remain so strictly differentiated only when one ignores the material circumstances that facilitate or obstruct the emergence of democratic forms of communication. As feminists have shown, opposing one category of the public to another, one realm against another, serves to mask the ways in which the professed functional differentiation of spheres associated with civil society, the state, and the economy is achieved through the workings of hegemonic forms of power. Fraser (1989), for example, has offered compelling analyses of the ways in which Habermas's four sector schema, which distinguishes among realms associated with the market economy, the administrative state, the public sphere, and the intimate sphere, works to establish the latter as the appropriate place for women. As she (1989: 127) suggests, the over-privatization of women's issues as 'personal' or 'domestic' fails to notice that 'gender identity is lived out in all arenas of life: paid work, state administration, citizenship, familial and sexual relations.' Gender helps to structure each of these areas and acts as a 'medium of exchange' among them (p. 128). Habermas, she notes, errs in his assumption that the domestic sphere is somehow removed from questions of money and power. In fact, the forms of male dominance that were intrinsic to classical capitalism were premised upon the use of money and power to separate waged labour and the state from childrearing and the household. In the shift from this phase to welfare state mass democracy, patriarchy is shifted from the home to the state, so that bureaucratization and monetarization become instruments of women's subordination.

Among feminist public sphere theorists, Fraser (1997) has been the most insistent that economic injustices must be addressed along with cultural and political injustices. She has strongly criticized several other theorists (particularly Benhabib, 1992 and Young, 1990) for advancing a cultural politics of difference that overrides political economic considerations and for valorizing agency within communicative practice while failing to provide adequate attention to communicative constraints (Fraser, 1995: 161, 1997). For Fraser, these

tendencies are symptomatic of a 'postsocialist condition' manifested in scholars' attempts to fill the void left in the wake of the repudiation of socialism with
new social visions of 'radical democracy' and 'multiculturalism' (1997: 2). She
suggests that a socialist imaginary based on redistribution has been eclipsed by
claims for the recognition of group difference:

> The 'struggle for recognition' is fast becoming the paradigmatic form of political con-
> flict in the late twentieth century. Demands for 'recognition of difference' fuel strug-
> gles of groups mobilized under the banners of nationality, ethnicity, 'race', gender,
> and sexuality. In these 'postsocialist' conflicts, group identity supplants class interest
> as the chief medium of political mobilization. Cultural domination supplants
> exploitation as the fundamental injustice. And cultural recognition displaces socioe-
> conomic redistribution as the remedy for injustice and the goal of political struggle
> (Fraser, 1997: 11).

Fraser advises that the appropriate response to this problem is to develop a new
critical theory that brings together recognition and redistribution in a politics
of transformation: 'For both gender and 'race', the scenario that best finesses
the redistribution-recognition dilemma is socialism in the economy plus deconstruction in the culture' (Fraser, 1997: 31).

While holding separate economic redistribution and cultural recognition,
Fraser also understands them to be intertwined and argues for their integration
in feminist thought. As she suggests, in a context of increasing global material
inequality, questions of the cultural valuation and representation of subjects are
necessarily linked to questions of socioeconomic justice. Nevertheless, scholars
whose inquiry is focused on transnational feminism have criticized her analysis
of the 'cultural turn' in feminist discourse as an oversimplification that fails to
discern that claims for recognition may also be claims for fair redistribution and
justice. Mendoza (2002: 303–4), for example, notes that

> We can follow the intricate dynamics of class, gender, race, and sexual power systems
> to the process of surplus production and also in its transnational linkages to global
> capital; something Nancy Fraser attempted to do in her *Justice Interruptus* (1997),
> but could not succeed in because of the parochial nature of her analysis, the lack of
> attention to transnational economic structures or the Euro-American bias of her
> schema of economic redistribution and cultural recognition.

This charge that Fraser's schema contains a Euro-American bias should be
taken quite seriously. In attempting to facilitate the relationship between recognition and redistribution, she does not disguise her disdain toward demands
for cultural recognition as the primary detractor to a socialist feminism. A
'transformative redistribution-recognition approach,' she warns, 'requires that all
people be weaned from their attachment to current cultural constructions of their
interests and identities' (Fraser, 1997: 31). But this reveals a blind spot in Fraser's
approach. While she makes no willful move to exclude the concerns of Third
World feminists, there is, epistemologically-speaking, a politics of representation
at work in which her attachment to a category of scale—that of the nation—and
a specific national context—that of the multiculturalism debate taking place in

the United States—render some problems un-seeable and some questions un-askable (Jones, 1998). Specifically, Fraser fails to understand that capitalism is one of the most powerful transnational mechanisms for 'weaning' people across the globe from their cultural interests and identities. In this context, holding on to collective cultural attachments can be viewed as an act of resistance against the flow of transnational capital and its drive toward cultural imperialism.

The recognition/redistribution heuristic also begins to look less dichotomous when the imperialistic tendencies of global capitalist media are addressed. Not only do the media fail to fit neatly into functionally-differentiated models, such as that represented by the civil society/state/economy configuration, but they also thoroughly contravene the cultural/economic distinction. Information and communication, in the form of products and services, are cultural commodities that work for global capitalism by providing both a network infrastructure for non-media firms' business operations and an informational environment that lays the ideological groundwork for the acceptance of a consumption-oriented and profit-driven social order (Herman and McChesney, 1997: 10). How, then, is one to distinguish between that which is cultural and that which is economic, even for analytical purposes?

The project of linking recognition claims to redistribution claims becomes particularly acute at a time in which the intensification of globalization processes both enables and obstructs the emergence of a transnational feminist movement. In this sense, Mohanty's (2002) notion of transnational feminist praxis offers a nuanced approach that is missing from Fraser's too-rigid categorical opposition.[2] Mohanty (2002) also maintains that questions of the cultural valuation and representation of subjects are necessarily linked to questions of socioeconomic justice. But she wants to attend to both the micropolitics of everyday life and the macropolitics of global political and economic processes, in order to reveal how the cultures and identities of people around the world are (re)colonized by the forces of transnational capitalist domination. It is crucial within this framework, Mohanty writes, that 'we think of the local in/of the global and vice versa without falling into colonizing or cultural relativist platitudes about difference' (2002: 509).

Feminist political theorists' development of the notion of a transnational feminist public sphere is in its initial stages. Among the most recognized public sphere scholars, a committed awareness of the need to 're-scale' the public sphere seems not to have taken hold until the beginning of the twentieth-first century (see, for example, Young, 2000; Fraser, 2002; Lara, 2003). What I want to suggest, however, is that a focus on the concept of the public sphere, as it has been formulated in Western academic circles, has deterred scholars from seeing that Mohanty and others have been offering important contributions to a theory of a transnational public sphere since the 1980s, contemporaneously with the more visible flurry of critical interventions into Habermas' nation-based concept of the public sphere.

The neglect of transnational feminism's contribution to public sphere theory may be a consequence of its having become associated with Mohanty's (1991:

4) much-quoted appeal for a transnational feminist movement constituted by 'imagined communities of women with divergent histories and social locations, woven together by the threads of opposition to forms of domination that are not only pervasive but also systemic.' As Hansen (1993: xxxvi) observes, 'the language of community provides a powerful matrix of identification and thus may function as a mobilizing force for transformative politics', and yet it also suggests a bounded entity in which consciousness and identity are constituted through political and cultural forms of inclusion and exclusion. The notion of a counterpublic merges with that of a community in offering 'forms of solidarity and reciprocity that are grounded in the collective experience of marginalization and expropriation', but the two categories diverge in that a counterpublic's experience of these forms is 'mediated, no longer rooted in face-to-face relations, and subject to discursive conflict and negotiation' (Hansen, 1993: xxxvi). Overall, within feminist public sphere theory, the concept of community has taken on a debased status in relation to the concept of the public. Young (1990: 312), for example, suggests that it is the ideal of community that lays the groundwork for sexism, racism, ethnic chauvinism, and class devaluation because too strong a desire for unity leads to the repression of differences within groups, even if these groups exist in opposition to a racist, sexist, homophobic society.

The use of the language of community does seem peculiar in a transnational feminist approach that wishes to denaturalize the boundaries instituted by Western modernism, and it appears to contradict Mohanty's concern with women's abilities to forge allegiances across differences. But perhaps we might look at the problem from another perspective. Conceivably, much of Western feminist public sphere theory has been so remiss in paying attention to transnational feminist approaches that Mohanty's famous reference to an 'imagined community of women' has come to stand in for 'a transnational feminist approach' in and of itself. It is possible then that many Western feminists have not been able to see that the aspirations of Mohanty and other transnational feminists are less bounded than 'community' would suggest and, thus, that they are more oriented to the creation of a transnational feminist counterpublic sphere.

Transnational approaches to feminism and the feminist concept of a counterpublic sphere share a great deal in principle: both are oriented to remaining relatively unbounded and open to both the accommodation of differences and the expression of needs and interests in dialogue with other publics. But in its tenacious adversity to West-and-the-rest thinking, transnational feminism maintains an inclusive and expansive attitude toward feminist theory and praxis that is missing from the majority of feminist approaches to the public sphere. As such, transnational feminism has begun to forge a concept that would allow for a better understanding of how women's lives are shaped in a context in which global spaces and places are increasingly integrated and deterritorialized, even as they remain stratified (Kaplan, Alarcón, and Moallem, 1999; Alexander and Mohanty, 1997; Grewal and Kaplan, 1994). Moreover, transnational feminism offers an approach with the potential to mitigate feminist parochialism; as Alexander and Mohanty (1997: xxxvi) advise, in order to think ourselves out of the limitations of the Western liberal formulations of Democracy, feminists must 'imagine political mobilization as the practice of active decolonization'. Thinking through transnational feminism goes beyond locating Anglo-American feminists' complicity in colonial and neocolonial discursive formations, instead offering an opening into collective feminist praxis within global contexts and revealing new possibilities for feminist alliances across geographical and social locations.

The idea of a transnational feminist movement is based on hope, and occasionally on evidence, the fleeting but empirically-observable moments when shared counterhegemonic political consciousness crystallizes into collective political praxis at the global level. The growth in feminist networking that has arisen in conjunction with the United Nations conferences on women is often described as the most visible form of this evidence. To my knowledge, Lara (2003) is the only feminist scholar closely associated with public sphere theory to have addressed this specific development, something that is not entirely surprising given her earlier emphasis on the ways in which social movements frame their demands in the form of cultural narratives (Lara, 1998). New social movement theorists have been tracking the expansion of so-called transnational social movement organizations (TSMOs) at least since the early 1990s, as have theorists of cosmopolitan democracy. While Habermas has shown a keen interest in new social movements since the 1980s, he has just recently associated with scholarship on cosmopolitan democracy and, in doing so, he has been somewhat ahead of the feminist curve within public sphere theory.

The question of how to achieve cosmopolitan democracy is the centerpiece of Habermas' recent book titled *The Postnational Constellation* (2001). Here, where his objective is to explore ways in which global politics might catch up with globalized markets, he joins theorists of cosmopolitan democracy in offering prescriptions for new forms of global governance that are capable of addressing the problems that exist in 'a world of overlapping of communities of fate' (Held, 1998: 24). As with other cosmopolitan democrats, Habermas is concerned with threats to the nation from within, but also with the unsettling of the Westphalian international political order as territorial boundaries are overridden by complex political, economic, and social factors related to war, peace, security, poverty, disease, resource depletion, environmental degradation, trade agreements, technologies, (de)regulation, human rights, social inequalities, regional fundamentalisms, and migrant and displaced populations. Confronting transnational issues, according to cosmopolitan democrats, requires a renewed commitment to international law and policy made under the auspices of existing regional and global intergovernmental institutions, along with the creation of new permanent political institutions with responsibility for correcting problems that have transnational consequences (Held, 1998: 24; Archibugi, 1998).

Cosmopolitan democrats suggest that, because the regulatory state is no longer capable of mitigating the costs and risks of economic globalization, governments must redirect their efforts toward strengthening institutionalized procedures at the supranational level in an effort to redress the social inequalities created and exacerbated by neoliberalism. In a specific sense, this would mean increasing the powers of the United Nations so that it is capable of taking on regulatory functions that would shield the world population from the negative social and political consequences of a transnational economy (Habermas, 2001; Archibugi, Held, and Köhler, 1998; Beetham, 1998: 63–64). The UN must be empowered by member-states that are willing to shift their perspectives from 'international relations' to a world domestic policy where global and regional forms of governance interact with political processes at the national level. In order to take this step, states must be pressured and rewarded by citizens who have developed a transnational consciousness oriented to cosmopolitan solidarity (Habermas, 2001: 111).

For Habermas and other theorists of cosmopolitan democracy, the participation of nongovernmental organizations (NGOs) in UN-sponsored meetings has become the hallmark for an emerging transnational civil society presaging the development of 'world citizenship.' In *The Postnational Constellation*, where his primary concern is with the development of transnational forms of solidarity through the creation of collective identity, he does not spell out the precise procedural mechanisms by which 'world citizens' are to pressure the state to adopt redistributive social policies. Yet, the overall uniformity of Habermas' approach to procedural democracy suggests that it is possible to extrapolate from his earlier work, particularly from *Between Facts and Norms* (1998), in order to gain a sense of how a global civil society is expected to exert influence over both the state and the quasi-state represented by the UN. In Habermas' conception, the state's legitimacy is dependent upon the degree to which it remains open to influence arising from a mobilized public sphere. He suggests that the constitutional state maintains its accessibility through the institutionalization of 'the public use of communicative freedom' even as it 'regulates the conversion of communicative into administrative power' (Habermas, 1998: 176). For its part, civil society makes use of the public sphere as a way of detecting, identifying, thematizing, and dramatizing problems and offering solutions. The 'public influence' arising from discursive interaction within the public sphere 'is transformed into communicative power only after it passes through the filters of the institutionalized *procedures* of democratic opinion- and will-formation and enters through parliamentary debates into legitimate lawmaking' (Habermas, 1998: 371; italics in original).

At a time when a transnational feminist approach to the public sphere has become so imperative, I want to suggest that feminists may wish to think twice before accepting Habermas as our guide in understanding the forms of inclusion and exclusion that exist within transnational public spaces. Thus far, both Young (2000) and Fraser (2002) appear to have found some appeal in Habermas' ideas regarding cosmopolitan democracy and 'the postnational constellation'. But feminists who in the past have found reason to be critical of his strict differentiation between civil society, the state, and the market economy, should be no less concerned when this configuration is appropriated for inquiry at the global level. One problem is that Habermas offers an extremely benign formulation of the state's relationship to civil society, one that Dryzek (2000: 26) has described as 'a naïve, civics-textbook version of democracy' that too easily affords legitimacy to the state. Based as it is on the notion that the constitutional state is capable of securing its legitimacy through interventions on behalf of the social welfare of its citizenry, Habermas' argument does not appear especially relevant in a context in which, as Keane (1998: 34) observes, nation-states are 'redirecting their priorities in the field of economic governance toward the interests of large corporations and the wealthier social classes'. Another problem is that Habermas operates on a highly functionalist model in which there is a harmonious co-existence between money and power and a democratic civil society (Schecter, 1999). Habermas accepts a combination of liberal democracy with a capitalist economy as the largely immutable condition of a well-ordered society, leading Dryzek (2000: 26) to conclude that his theory of democracy can no longer be considered a contribution to critical theory because 'there is no sense that the administrative state, or economy, should be democratized any further'. In a direct rebuke to a Marxist notion of social revolution, Habermas (1998: 372) maintains that 'Civil society can directly transform only itself, and it can have at most an indirect effect on the self-transformation of the political system.' The public sphere is limited in its capacity to act on its own, and, as a result, public opinion is converted into political power ('a potential for rendering binding decisions') only when it affects the beliefs and decisions of authorized members of the political system (legislators, officials, administrators, etc.) (Habermas, 1998: 359). In devising a theory that understands the lifeworld as a sphere for discussion but not decision-making, Habermas tacitly accepts the domination of communicative action by systemic imperatives (Schecter, 1999).

In addressing 'the postnational constellation', Habermas has not made a significant departure from his state-centric model—he has merely elevated it to a global level. This should pose a problem for any transnational feminist approach that embraces a socialist agenda. Cosmopolitan democracy focuses on 'globalization from below' as a development in response to the market-driven policies and practices that sustain corporate capitalism as the central figure for 'globalization from above'. Yet the role of a transnational civil society, as the vehicle for 'globalization from below', is merely to strengthen the state, along with the UN, so that they are able to maintain social integration in a functionally-differentiated society that is overburdened with social inequalities visited upon it by a global economy that has escaped the state's control (Habermas, 2001: 52). This model eliminates from consideration any groups that are unwilling to accept that their social needs can be satisfied by the combination of liberal democracy and capitalism that Habermas imagines to be the foundation of a well-ordered society. As Stolze (2000: 155) has observed, Habermas' conception of weak public spheres allows citizens 'to *discuss* anything they like— presumably even the large-scale overthrow of capitalist social relations', but it undermines their ability to act in order to make structural changes in society (italics in original).

Moreover, it is not at all clear how a transnational civil society is to compete against the neoliberal agenda that has come to be embraced at both the national and the supranational level of politics. The UN is a weak organizational locus, not only because the international political order is a statist one but also because it represents a constellation of member-states that 'have been instrumentalized, or at least intimidated by, global market forces' (Falk, 1998: 326). Neoliberal market orthodoxies have also deepened the quagmire for NGOs that do not wish to lose their connections to transformation-oriented movements. Habermas and other cosmopolitan democrats have tended to try to fit feminist and other progressive struggles into a fixed model in which, as a feature of the 'third sector' known as global civil society, it is isolated as 'an alternative to both the state-centric international order and the networks of global markets' and treated as though it were 'uncontaminated by either the power of states or of markets' (Chandhoke, 2002: 35). But as soon as one begins to look at how the emergence of a new transnational civil society through UN encounters has been produced through actions, interactions, and struggles, the creation of institutional structures through actors' practices, and the limitations that actors face within institutional structures, it becomes clear that civil society, the market, and the state (or the state-centric international order) not only influence, affect, and constitute one another but do so in a way that reinforces an increasingly common vision, in which the notion of human progress through democratic cooperation is linked to a distinct solution: a model of a world order based in a neoliberal set of policies offering to generate levels of economic prosperity that will lift any nation or person out of poverty so long as they remain faithful to the principles of the beneficent market (Mittelman, 2000: 74).

In shoring up the distinction between 'globalization from above' and 'globalization from below', cosmopolitan democrats fail to recognize that, whereas the status of outsider is central to the anticorporate protest movement's efficacy as a social force, the opposite is true for NGOs that have become critical insiders, formally included at the table where decisions are being made under the auspices of the UN. As such, it is not clear that NGOs represent an unambiguous example of 'globalization from below'. If a transnational feminist approach to the public sphere were to address this, it would be far better served by the insights of transnational feminists than by those of cosmopolitan democrats. Many transnational feminists have come to understand that, as 'occasional counterpublic spheres' formed around an event, the world conferences on women present only a partial, and generally more exhilarating, view of how the institutionalization of women's rights issues within the structures of the UN affects the prospects for a nascent transnational social movement. As several feminists have observed, to work within the existing structures of the UN system is to contribute to and maintain an institutional home in which 'women's issues' are mainstreamed into deeply gendered bureaucracies that co-opt the language of progressive social movements, while structurally excluding feminist discourses and actions oriented to transformation, particularly those opposed to the notion that deregulation, liberalization, and privatization are the best routes to democracy.

A more panoramic view reveals that the price of access to the UN as supranational site for advancing women's equality has been a bureaucratization of feminism that distances insiders from their outsider feminist constituencies (Alvarez, 1998). Questions of who and what NGOs represent have been high on the agenda of feminism for several years, especially since the Fourth World Conference on Women in Beijing, which left in its wake the phenomenon of 'NGOization' featuring a new, globetrotting set of professional feminist NGO representatives making contacts at international conferences, and working on lobbying and funding, while the local level disappears as insubstantial in comparison to global political interactions. As Mendoza (2002) has written:

> The global or transnational . . . becomes a privileged space to inflect political meanings and strategies. . . . In this form, politics becomes evanescent, dense and often a virtual activity. It appears to occur through flows, linkages, scapes and circuits and less through vertical lines. UN world conferences can be seen as prototypes of these global political interactions as well as the political networks on the Internet. Only when indigenous peoples or Third World women and feminists take their struggles to the Internet or the UN do they become politically significant, but not in their local political manifestations of resistance (Mendoza, 2002: 299).

Rather than to renounce or to celebrate global political interactions that take place under the auspices of the UN or throughout the virtual spaces of the Internet—and today, these are inextricably linked—it is important to come to a better understanding of their mechanisms of inclusion and exclusion. This is not possible from the perspective of theories of cosmopolitan democracy that invoke images of 'self-conscious constructions of networks of knowledge and action, by decentred, local actors, that cross the reified boundaries of space as though they were not there' (Lipschutz, 1992: 390). Nor is this possible from the point of view of conceptions of cosmopolitan democracy in which there seems no more is at stake than amorphous networks of communication that lend themselves to the creation of forms of solidarity among 'world citizens.'

Approaches to cosmopolitan democracy, if they focus on media at all, tend to concentrate on those groups that are already included in the public sphere—transnational actors with access to the use of new information and communication technologies, particularly the Internet, for forming networks, organizing protests, circulating information, documenting the practices of transnational corporations and multilateral organizations, and magnifying NGO influence at UN-sponsored meetings. From this perspective, the public sphere appears to be in a perpetual state of progress. As Jameson (1993: 357) has observed, today's media developments *do* seem to have mobilized a public sphere that is filled with 'new people, other people, who were somehow not even there before'. The expansion and splintering of the public sphere are occurring in tandem, with a hyper-plurality of groups forming both new connections and new enclaves as they cross boundaries through cyberspace.

If, within this purportedly global public sphere, the diversity of human existence is now registered at the interstices of new media and the globalizing market, the associated forms of invisibility are more than an auxiliary development, as global disparities in access to communication are growing rather than diminishing (Hamelink, 2000: 33).[3] When gender is factored into the equation, the gap between 'information-haves' and 'information have-nots' is an especially wide one, with poverty, illiteracy, and lack of access to basic infrastructure such as electricity and telephone lines blocking the majority of the world's women from having any opportunity to represent themselves and their concerns (WomenAction, 2000). The answer to closing this gap is not a simple matter of making women more visible in the public sphere by more thoroughly mainstreaming them into processes of globalization. The increased concentration of media and information industries under neoliberal globalization is one of the central factors limiting women's communicative access along with their potential to influence the structure and practices of the media.

Today, public sphere theory is at yet another crossroads involving communication. Since the United Nations Beijing Conference on Women, remarkable progress has been made by a growing number of local, national, and international women's networks whose efforts are focused on global information dissemination, monitoring of governmental and intergovernmental organizations, and the creation of educational programmes to promote women's social, political, and economic empowerment. Feminist activists accentuate the importance of networks as places for creating solidarity, exchanging experiences, and sharing strategies. This is a partial snapshot of what transnational public space looks like today. But, there is more. The so-called information society serves the needs of its creator—a global capitalist environment in which forms of communication and information have become products and services whose status as 'intangible goods' is best finessed by treating them as though they have the power to set us free. People are a part of the equation, but the New Economy does not wish to suffer the slings and arrows of citizen-activists; rather, it needs consumers, users, and information technology workers who possess competences and capabilities called 'knowledge assets'—the workers are themselves considered the 'knowledge assets' of a 'knowledge economy'. Since the Beijing Conference, where communication was recognized as vital for women's empowerment, it has become apparent that, within a neoliberal framework, this is to be achieved by more thoroughly mainstreaming women into globalization processes as a new industrial proletariat working at low-skilled and semi-skilled jobs in the information processing sector. It will be incumbent upon a transnational feminist approach to the public sphere to find a way to address this simultaneous inclusion and exclusion of women rather than to walk away from it as though it were a lamentable ending to an otherwise appealing narrative.

Notes

1 See, for example, Smythe, 1957; Schiller, 1969, 1976; Dorfman and Mattelart, 1975.
2 Hereafter, I refer to the approach associated with Mohanty and other 'Third World feminists' as 'transnational feminism,' although, in comparing this to the definitions of 'transnational feminism' arising from new social movement approaches within the fields of political science and sociology, it is clear that there is no overarching definition that is capable of encompassing all political commitments. My use of the term 'transnational feminism' is, in part, meant to distinguish approaches that are oriented to de-colonization from those of the more postmodern, postcolonial variety.
3 Drawing from ITU and OECD statistics, Hamelink offers data that underscores this disparity: 'In 1996 there were 743.66 million main telephone lines in the world. Europe (274.23 million), the United States (170.57 million) and Japan (61.53 million) represent 68% of this total, compared with 1.8% in Africa. . . . In early 1997, some 62% of the world's main telephone lines were installed in 23 affluent countries, which account for only 15% of the world's population. The estimated number of PCs in the world in 1996 stood at 234,200,000. The share for Europe (72,864,000), the United States (96,600,000) and Japan (16,100,000) was 79%, while for Africa it was only 1.3%, representing 0.64 computers per 100 inhabitants. . . . Of the total number of television sets in the world in 1996, Europe, the United States and Japan possessed 47% while Africa possessed only 3%. . . . Internet host computers are distributed throughout the world in such a way that the United States (51.5%), the EU countries (23%), Canada (6.1%) and Japan (5.2%) represented 85.8% of the world's total in 1997. . . .'

References

Alexander, M. J. and Mohanty, C. (1997) *Feminist Genealogies, Colonial Legacies, Democratic Futures.* New York: Routledge.
Alvarez, S. (1998) 'Latin American Feminisms 'Go Global': Trends of the 1990s and Challenges for the New Millenium' in S. E. Alvarez, E. Dagnino and A. Escobar (eds), *Cultures of Politics, Politics of Cultures.* Boulder, CO: Westview Press.
Archibugi, D. (1998) 'Principles of Cosmopolitan Democracy' in D. Archibugi, D. Held and M. Köhler (eds), *Re-imagining Political Community: Studies in Cosmopolitan Democracy.* Stanford, CA: Stanford University Press.
Beetham, D. (1998) 'Human Rights as a Model for Cosmopolitan Democracy' in D. Archibugi, D. Held and M. Köhler (eds), *Re-imagining Political Community: Studies in Cosmopolitan Democracy.* Stanford, CA: Stanford University Press.
Benhabib, S. (1992) *Situating the Self: Gender, Community and Postmodernism in Contemporary Ethics.* New York: Routledge.
Calhoun, C. (1992) *Habermas and the Public Sphere.* Cambridge, MA: MIT Press.
Chandhoke, N. (2002) 'The Limits of Global Civil Society' in M. Glasius, M. Kaldor and H. Anheier (eds), *Global Civil Society 2002.* London: London School of Economics.
Dahlgren, P. (2001) 'The Public Sphere and the Net: Structure, Space, and Communication' in W. L. Bennett and R. M. Entman (eds), *Mediated Politics: Communication in the Future of Democracy.* Cambridge: Cambridge University Press.
Dean, J. (2003) 'Why the Net is not a Public Sphere', *Constellations* 10(1): 95–112.
Dorfman, A. and Mattelart, A. (1975) *How to Read Donald Duck.* London: International General.
Dryzek, J. S. (2000) *Deliberative Democracy and Beyond: Liberals, Critics, Contestations.* Oxford: Oxford University Press.
Falk, R. (1998) 'The United Nations and Cosmopolitan Democracy: Bad Dream, Utopian Fantasy, Political Project' in D. Archibugi, D. Held and M. Köhler (eds), Re-imagining Political Community: Studies in Cosmopolitan Democracy. Stanford, CA: Stanford University Press.

Felski, R. (1989) *Beyond Feminist Aesthetics: Feminist Literature and Social Change*. Cambridge, MA: Harvard University Press.

Fraser, N. (1989) *Unruly Practices: Power, Discourse and Gender in Contemporary Social Theory*. Minneapolis, MN: University of Minnesota Press.

Fraser, N. (1992) 'Rethinking the Public Sphere: A Contribution to the Critique of Actually Existing Democracy' in C. Calhoun (ed.), *Habermas and the Public Sphere*. Cambridge, MA: MIT Press.

Fraser, N. (1995) 'The Uses and Abuses of French Discourse Theories for Feminist Politics' in N. Fraser and S. L. Bartky (eds), *Revaluing French Feminism: Critical Essays on Difference, Agency, and Culture*. Bloomington, IN: Indiana University Press.

Fraser, N. (1997) *Justice Interruptus: Critical Reflections on the 'Postsocialist Condition'*. New York: Routledge.

Fraser, N. (2002) 'Transnationalizing the Public Sphere', keynote lecture presented at Graduate Center, City University of New York, conference on 'Public Space' (February 2002), http://www.yale.edu/polisci/conferences/fraser1.doc, last accessed: December 23, 2003.

Garnham, N. (1992) 'The Media and the Public Sphere' in C. Calhoun (ed.), *Habermas and the Public Sphere*. Cambridge, MA: MIT Press.

Grewal, I. and Kaplan, C. (eds) (1994) *Scattered Hegemonies: Postmodernity and Transnational Feminist Practices*. Minneapolis, MN: University of Minnesota Press.

Habermas, J. (1987) *The Theory of Communicative Action, Vol. 2, Lifeworld and System*, T. McCarthy (trans.). Boston, MA: Beacon Press.

Habermas, J. (1989/1962) *The Structural Transformation of the Public Sphere: An Inquiry into a Category of Bourgeois Society*, T. Burger (trans.). Cambridge, MA: MIT Press.

Habermas, J. (1992) 'Further Reflections on the Public Sphere' in C. Calhoun (ed.), *Habermas and the Public Sphere*. Cambridge, MA: MIT Press.

Habermas, J. (1998) *Between Fact and Norms: Contributions to a Discourse Theory of Law and Democracy*, W. Rehg (trans.). Cambridge, MA: MIT Press.

Habermas, J. (2001) *The Postnational Constellation: Political Essays*, M. Pensky, (ed. and trans.). Cambridge, MA: MIT Press.

Hamelink, C. (2000) 'Human Development' in *World Communication and Information Report*, United Nations: United Nations Education, Scientific, and Cultural Organization.

Hansen, M. (1993) 'Forward', in Negt, Oskar and Kluge, Alexander, *Public Sphere and Experience: Toward an Analysis of the Bourgeois and Proletarian Public Sphere*, P. Labanyi, J. O. Daniel and A. Oksiloff (trans.). Minneapolis, MN: University of Minnesota Press.

Held, D. (1998) 'Democracy and Globalization' in D. Archibugi, D. Held and M. Köhler (eds.), *Re-imagining Political Community: Studies in Cosmopolitan Democracy*. Stanford, CA: Stanford University Press.

Herman, E. S. and McChesney, R. W. (1997) *The Global Media: The New Missionaries of Global Capitalism*. London: Cassell.

Hohendahl, P. U. (1979) 'Critical Theory, Public Sphere and Culture, Jürgen Habermas and his Critics', *New German Critique* 16: 89–118.

Jameson, F. (1991) *Postmodernism: Or, the Cultural Logic of Late Capitalism*. Durham, NC: Duke University Press.

Jones, K. T. (1998) 'Scale as Epistemology', *Political Geography* 17(1): 959–988.

Kaplan, C., Alarcón, N. and Moallem, M. (eds) (1999) *Between Woman and Nation: Nationalisms, Transnational Feminisms, and the State*. Durham, NC: Duke University Press.

Keane, J. (1998) *Civil Society: Old Images, New Visions*. Stanford, CA: Stanford University Press.

Kellner, D. (2000) 'Habermas, the Public Sphere, and Democracy: A Critical Intervention' in L. E. Hahn (ed.), *Perspectives on Habermas*. Chicago: Open Court Press.

Landes, J. (1988) *Women and the Public Sphere in the Age of the French Revolution*. Ithaca, NY: Cornell University Press.

Lara, M. P. (1998) *Moral Textures: Feminist Narratives in the Public Sphere*. Berkeley, CA: University of California Press.

Lara, M. P. (2003) 'Globalizing Women's Rights: Building a Global Public Sphere' in R. N. Fiore. and H. L. Nelson (eds), *Recognition. Responsibility and Rights: Feminist Ethics and Social Theory.* Lanham, MA: Rowman and Littlefield.

Lipschutz, R. (1992) 'Reconstructing World, Politics: The Emergence of Global Civil Society,' Millennium: Journal of International Studies 21: 389–420.

McChesney, R. W. and Schiller, D. (2002) 'The Political Economy of International Communications: Foundations for the Emerging Debate About Media Ownership and Regulation', United Nations: United Nations Research Institute for Social Development.

Mendoza, B. (2002) 'Transnational Feminisms in Question', *Feminist Theory* 3(3): 295–314.

Mittelman, J. H. (2000) *The Globalization Syndrome: Transformation and Resistance.* Princeton, NJ: Princeton University Press.

Mohanty, C. T. (1991) 'Under Western Eyes: Feminist Scholarship and Colonial Discourses' in C. T. Mohanty (ed.), *Third World Women and the Politic of Feminism.* Bloomington: Indiana University Press.

Mohanty, C. T. (2002) ' "Under Western Eyes" Revisited: Feminist Solidarity Through Anticapitalist Struggles', *Signs: Journal of Women in Culture and Society* 28(2): 499–535.

Murdock, G. (1995) 'Across the Great Divide: Cultural Analysis and the Condition of Democracy', *Critical Studies in Mass Communication* 12(1): 89–95.

Negt, O. and Kluge, A. (1993) *Public Sphere and Experience: Toward an Analysis of the Bourgeois and Proletariat Public Sphere*, P. Labanyi, J. O. Daniel and A. Oksiloff (trans.). Minneapolis, MN: University of Minnesota Press.

Pateman, C. (1988) 'The Fraternal Social Contract' in J. Keane (ed.), *Civil Society and the State: New European Perspectives.* London: Verso.

Poster, M. (1995) 'The Net as a Public Sphere', *Wired* 3(11).

Postone, M. (1992) 'Political Theory and Historical Analysis' in America' in Calhoun, Craig (ed.), *Habermas and the Public Sphere.* Cambridge, MA: MIT Press.

Schecter, D. (1999) 'The Functional Transformation of the Political World: Reflections on Habermas', *Studies in Social and Political Thought* 1 (June): 33–49.

Schiller, H. (1969) *Mass Communication and American Empire.* Boston: Beacon Press.

Schiller, H. (1976) *Communication and Cultural Domination.* White Plains, NY: International Arts and Sciences Press.

Smythe, D. (1957) *The Structure and Policy of Electronic Communication.* Urbana, IL: University of Illinois Press.

Stolze, T. (2000) 'A Displaced Transition: Habermas on the Public Sphere' in M. Hill and W. Montag (eds), *Masses, Classes, and the Public Sphere.* London: Verso.

Ryan, M. P. (1992) 'Gender and Public Access: Women's Politics in Nineteenth-Century America' in C. Calhoun (ed.), *Habermas and the Public Sphere.* Cambridge, MA: MIT Press.

WomenAction (1995) 'Alternative Assessment of Women and Media Based in NGO Reviews of Section J, Beijing Platform for Action', United Nations: Commission on the Status of Women.

Young, I. M. (1990) *Justice and the Politics of Difference.* Princeton, NJ: Princeton University Press.

Young, I. M. (2000) *Inclusion and Democracy.* Oxford: Oxford University Press.

Notes on contributors

James Bohman is Danforth Professor of Philosophy at Saint Louis University. He is author of *Public Deliberation: Pluralism, Complexity and Democracy* (MIT Press, 1996) and *New Philosophy of Social Science: Problems of Indeterminacy* (MIT Press, 1991). He has also recently edited books on *Deliberative Democracy* (with William Rehg) and *Perpetual Peace: Essays on Kant's Cosmopolitan Ideal* (with Matthias Lutz-Bachmann), both with MIT Press. He is currently writing a book on cosmopolitan democracy.

Nick Crossley is a senior lecturer in Sociology at the University of Manchester UK. His interest in the public sphere stems both from his earlier work, *Intersubjectivity* (Sage 1996), and from his more recent work, *Making Sense of Social Movements* (Open University 2002). His chapter in this volume rejoins a paper published in the *Theory, Culture and Society* journal in 2003 (20(6)), which explores the potential of the work of Pierre Bourdieu for the sociology of social movements.

Gemma Edwards is an ESRC-funded research student at the University of Manchester, Department of Sociology. She is currently completing her thesis on white-collar trade union activism from a Habermasian perspective. Her research interests include feminist critical theory, social movements, and the analysis of industrial protest.

Michael E. Gardiner is an Associate Professor in Sociology at the University of Western Ontario, Canada. His books include the edited four-volume collection *Mikhail Bakhtin: Masters of Modern Social Thought* (Sage, 2003), *Critiques of Everyday Life* (Routledge, 2000), *Bakhtin and the Human Sciences: No Last Words* (Sage, 1998, co-edited with Michael M.Bell), and *The Dialogics of Critique: M. M. Bakhtin and the Theory of Ideology* (Routledge, 1992), as well as numerous articles dedicated to dialogical social theory, ethics, everyday life and utopianism. Most recently he has co-edited (with Gregory J. Seigworth) a special double issue of the journal *Cultural Studies*, with the title 'Rethinking Everyday Life: And Nothing Turned Itself Inside Out' (Routledge, 2004).

Ken Hirschkop is Senior Lecturer in English Literature at the University of Manchester. He is author of *Mikhail Bakhtin: An Aesthetic for Democracy* (Oxford

University Press, 1999), co-editor with David Shepherd of *Bakhtin and Cultural Theory* (Manchester University Press, 2001) and has written on the politics of the new technologies, popular music, and issues in cultural theory and the philosophy of language. He is currently working on a study of the social meaning of linguistic turns in the twentieth century.

Lisa McLaughlin is an Associate Professor in Women's Studies and Mass Communication at Miami University-Ohio. Her research centres on feminism, political economy, and the public sphere in a transnational context. Most recently, she has been exploring the ways in which feminist civil society organizations are attempting to use the forum of the United Nations in order to influence the development of a global communication policy framework.

John Michael Roberts is a lecturer in the Department of Sociology and Social Policy. Publications include *The Aesthetics of Free Speech: Rethinking the Public Sphere* (Palgrave, Macmillan, 2003), *Critical Realism and Marxism* (co-editor; Routledge, 2002) and *Realism, Discourse and Deconstruction* (co-editor, Routledge, 2003).

Index